CW01024062

PAPER

PAPER

Material, Medium and Magic

Edited by Neil Holt, Nicola von Velsen and Stephanie Jacobs

With photographs by Thorsten Kern

PRESTEL

Munich · London · New York

Paper as Material

Paper as Medium

Paper as Symbol

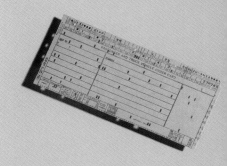

Paper Surfaces

Paper Spaces

Paper and Book

Preface

Until just a few years ago, the ubiquitousness and ready availability of paper could have been described in a typical daily routine unfolding from, say, the bread bag and the coffee filter to the newspaper and the mail, to the pocket calendar and the notebook. The rapid increase of digital media fundamentally changes how we interact with paper in ways each person experiences differently once they take a moment to contemplate the issue.

Yet paper will always remain an artistic medium, a recording medium, an archive, and much more: it is a quintessentially sensual and emotional material and – it helps with focusing. At least this is what the American linguist Naomi S. Baron was able to establish in surveys she did in 2015 among students in Japan, Germany, the U.S., and Slovakia. Offered a choice between paper, smartphone, laptop, or e-reader, 92 percent of respondents stated they could concentrate best with paper.

It could be said that paper itself essentially means 'concentration.' The mechanically opened fibers are soaked in water and then pressed – the pulp is concentrated. The sheet of paper is a surface; it ends at its edges and doesn't have any interactive links or cookies roaming unsolicited across its surface. On the contrary, paper allows one to concentrate as it protects one's space of perception and sharpens one's senses.

Such a history of paper has not, to our knowledge, yet been told. That's why this volume combines emotional stories, practical knowledge, surprising aspects, and fantastic images of paper. It is precisely this diversity of approach and access that allows us to unfold the various aspects of paper in a new way, through word and image, typography and book layout. Because our collaborative work on the subject made us realize that one's individual experiences with paper make for different perspectives on the subject, we start out with the personal stories.

Neil Holt: Paper has always been a working material of sorts for me, a material with which, and on which, I could create. As a child I made lots of things out of paper and cardboard; with scissors and glue, ideas quickly turned into things. At design school there was a paper workshop with a trained bookbinder. He gave us students an understanding of how, with nothing but paper, creative ideas can

"Paper enthusiasts are spread all over the world, but they live in scattered isolation, and one does not know of the other's quiet love. Only rarely does chance reveal the same, but when it does, a harmony may arise."
Armin Renker,
Die Kulturgeschichte des Papiers (The Book of Paper),
1934

be realized as three-dimensional sketches or concepts without great effort or tools. There we also learned how products with considerable stability, strength, and statics can be created through folding and unfolding. I learned, for instance, that Egon Eiermann developed the shape of the façade tiles for his Horten department store through experiments with paper and the folding of a sheet of paper.

Then, as I became increasingly interested in typography and book design, I became more involved with paper as a one-dimensional carrier. And I soon realized what crucial influence quality, paper tint, and haptics have on the effect of the finished product. As a teacher I notice that knowledge and terminology about paper are often lacking, while at the same time interest in the material and in printed matter is very strong. In creative practice and in teaching, it has become an important concern for me to draw attention to and address the properties, the possibilities, and the effect of a material that, on the face of it, is inconspicuous and subservient.

Nicola von Velsen: As long as I can remember, paper has been my close companion; it was a practical utensil and a precious treasure, working tool, and medium. Many memories are brought back through paper: various envelopes, beautiful tickets, sugar packets, orange wrappers, particular fruit bags, and the tissue paper in exquisite shops. I remember schoolmates who found happiness in autograph books, stamps, or picture cards. Then exercise books, index cards, and calendars structured time, provided stability, facilitated learning. Later art, especially the works of draftswomen and draftsmen, interested me; no matter how incidental the material, they transformed it into the greatest treasures by infusing it with their sense of form and sensibility or developing the latter in resistance to the material. And always books. Ever since I learned to read, books and their texts and images offered me the sheltered space through which the great wide world became accessible. The paper between the book covers was the most astonishing of all: it smelled, had different surfaces, different formats, different shades of white, and the type on it varied greatly. And, lastly, I want to mention the handwritten letters and postcards: they were a medium of no small importance for all the longing and trepidation, all the contacts and friendships. Much time was spent writing them; appropriate papers and envelopes were used, replies were expected, beautiful lines surprised. And reading them took time; you turned the sheets of paper around, inspected the envelope. You had a paper deposit of remembrance you could pick up from time to time. Notebooks or calendars, not to mention the diary, stand for similar states of mind.

Conversations about paper often take on a personal tone. This is, perhaps, not surprising, for paper is not just a magical **material** that appeals to all our senses. Ever since it was developed paper has been a **medium** for all arts and a repository of knowledge, a witness of emotions. For a long time it was a **symbol** of socially central values, such as contracts or stocks or paper money. Paper as **surface** is of central importance, because format and surfaces are just as important as the object being designed, as are small paper surfaces such as playing cards or functional ones such as maps. The **space** made by paper provides an endless supply of possible areas of application and design: here paper is folded, because one of the fascinating properties of this material is that it can have direction and movement without the need of hinges. **Paper and book**, finally, cannot be conceived one without the other; in the book paper takes on three-dimensionality and is identified as object.

The **material** underscores that paper does not just appeal to all the senses: its rustling flatters the ear, its color tone pleases the eye, the nose catches its smell, the hand recognizes its strength as well as the textures of its surfaces. But as material, paper also reveals entirely different aspects: its production and the evolution of paper technology, its raw materials as well as the development of application areas or trade are fascinating topics. Paper is a resource-conscious material that is based on an easy-to-understand production idea.

As a **medium** paper is, perhaps, primarily associated with literature – for centuries, text was created on paper, the writing-hand goes through the writing instrument, and the voice of the author articulates itself. Only then it is translated into print. Letters, diaries, memos, index card boxes: all kinds of paper become a medium or a specific material impulse for those who write – and for all those who read invariably also a touching trace of the person writing. Paper is central to music, too, and not just as carrier of notation: it can even become a sound-emitting body itself, as in a work by Ben Patterson. In the visual arts paper plays a key role as medium and ground, both as a surface to be configured and as active space. For drawing and graphic printing, paper has been important from the beginning, and then in the silhouette and its evolution. With 'Paper Art,' we look at works that explicitly address paper as working material.

Paper as Symbol focuses on symbolic functions of paper. For centuries, paper mills or other important entities embedded their own marks into paper to make it identifiable or forgery-proof, as in the case of money or contracts. This chapter also describes how paper itself basically develops the medium from which, in a totally different sense, digital storage evolved. In the early twentieth century, the punch cards that had been previously developed in weaving mills to control weaving patterns were adapted via the Hollerith cards for use in the U.S. census.

Paper Surfaces addresses two topic areas: on the one hand, it examines to what extent the actual format of the paper, the two-dimensional sheet or 'leaf' of paper provides information in everyday life. On the other, it discusses the key issue of design, of surface and ground, foreground and background. In this sense, surface is also about how characters, and images, are arranged on paper in the most appealing and understandable way.

Paper Spaces surveys the myriad forms of folded paper and manipulated paper. This chapter covers everything from origami, design, and architecture to everyday folding boxes and bags. Here it becomes evident once again that this volume can open up and introduce topics, yet by no means is able to present all of them in their full complexity.

The final chapter, **Paper and Book**, brings history back to itself. Just as the subject of paper is discussed self-reflexively on paper, the book combines the sequence of chapters into one context and one object. This is why it was important to us to realize many of the themes addressed here also in, and through, the book itself.

All chapters develop their themes in a rather cursory manner, discussing them by reference to the individual examples or stories we selected, because we consider them particularly descriptive. Making that selection was often difficult, because there are so many other fascinating paper-related topics. The sequence is interrupted by two insertions offering practical information: *Paper A–Z* and *Paper: A Practical Guide* encapsulate useful basic knowledge about paper. With this the book aims at a broad public that read, and look, and understands with hand, eye, and mind how knowledge about paper can facilitate work and add to the fascination of a magical material.

We would like to express our sincere gratitude to all authors and all those who kindly provided advice. This book could not have been realized without the friendly cooperation of the German Museum of Books and Writing (DBSM)* at the German National Library, Leipzig, the enthusiastic support of paper lovers of all sorts, and the Prestel publishing house. — *Neil Holt and Nicola von Velsen*

"The museum as guardian of a paper treasure of incredible variety, entrancing beauty, and the demure power of seduction of an angel, which nimbly skates over the useless and constantly invoked contrast between 'paper' and 'digital'" Stephanie Jacobs

Paper
as
Material

Paper
Soup

Paper production in a Japanese illustration showing the following steps: cooking, washing, beating, dipping, pressing, and drying.

"What is paper ultimately? A soup. A fiber soup that is evenly spread in a thin layer and then dewatered." This is how Érik Orsenna (b. 1947) puts it in his declaration of love to paper. So paper is an evenly distributed and dewatered fiber soup. From the late Middle Ages onwards, paper developed into the indispensable substratum of our literacy-, calculation- and accounting-based culture.

Coming from Asia, the art of papermaking was decisively improved in thirteenth-century Italy. In paper mills, scarce and laboriously gathered rags were processed by waterwheel-powered stamping mills to create a liquid suspension from which the flax or hemp fibers could be skimmed with the aid of a dip mold (basically a rectangular wire mesh bounded by a wooden frame or deckle), thus producing flat, watermarked sheets of paper.

In 1390, papermakers from Italy helped establish the first paper mill in Germany in Nuremberg, which was soon followed by others. The first paper mill in England was established in 1490 by John Tate, in Stevenage, Hertfordshire. The late-medieval technique continued, with some technical improvements, until the early industrial period in the second quarter of the nineteenth century.

This wooden model of a sixteenth-century paper mill was created in 1956 to illustrate the processes of papermaking. In eight rooms of a house with eleven figures and related equipment, it depicts the sorting and shredding of rags, the digester and the stamping mill, the vat room, the sizing area, the drying loft, and the smoothing and grading of the paper.

This model is based on copperplate engravings from various books that were originally published in France and subsequently also appeared in German translations, including in particular Nicolas Desmarest's (1725–1815) *Art of Papermaking*, as translated by Christian Ludwig Seebass (1754–1806), and the *Encyclopédie* of Denis Diderot (1713–1784).

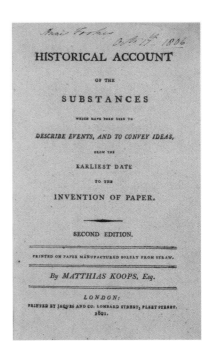

Matthias Koop's historical account of the invention of paper. Published in London, this second edition was partly printed on paper and straw.

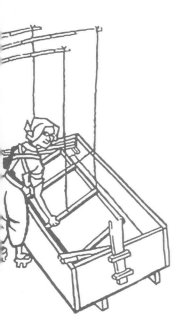

Room 1 The material brought to the paper mill by the rag picker (the rags) is sorted by type of fiber, coloring, and quality, and then shredded.

Room 2 Adding water, the rags are digested. This macerating process lasts several weeks. After this treatment, the rags are cut into small pieces by a vertically mounted scythe blade.

Room 3 The shaft of the water wheel consists of a tree trunk. Cams set into this main shaft raise the wooden hammers of the rag-stamping mill at precisely coordinated intervals. When the hammerheads fall back into the stamping trough filled with water and rags, the iron nails set into the hammer 'defiber' the rags.

Room 4 The fibrous material processed in the rag-stamping mill is then suspended in a large amount of water in the pulping vat. Three papermakers with two dip molds and one deckle alternate to produce about 3500 sheets of paper in one working day. The 'dipper' or 'vatman' is the first of the papermakers: he uses the dip mold to skim a layer of fibrous material which, spread out on the mold's mesh, forms a paper sheet within just a few seconds. The dip mold is then taken over by the 'coucher' and turned face down. The still-wet paper sheet is squeezed (couched) onto a piece of wool felt and covered by another piece of felt. In the meantime the dipper forms the next sheet of paper with a second dip mold. Eventually, this results in a pile of 181 sheets of paper between 182 pieces of felt, called the 'post'. This pile is dewatered in the wooden wet press. The third papermaker, the 'layer', has the job of separating the paper sheets and

Wooden model of a historical paper mill made in 1956 by the Herbert Bunzel Company. It shows the various steps of papermaking in the sixteenth century.

the felt pieces. The felt pieces are stacked for the next post, while the paper is pressed one more time in the 'white post' and then taken to dry.

Room 5 In the drying loft of the paper mill the dipped and pressed sheets of paper are hung to dry on ropes usually made of horse-hair.

Room 6 The dipped and pressed paper acts like blotting paper if inscribed with watery ink: the ink runs and the writing is no longer decipherable. To prevent this, the paper-makers boil a glue or 'sizing agent' from animal waste such as scrap leather or sheep's hooves. The paper is dipped in this protein-based glue and then the superfluous sizing liquid is squeezed out in the sizing press. Immediately after this the individual sheets must be separated again.

Room 7 In a second area of the drying loft the sized sheets are then hung to dry.

Room 8 When the sized paper has dried, the individual sheets are carefully checked. Irregularities or impurities can be removed with a small knife. Next the individual sheets are smoothed and counted and packaged depending on quality (prime quality or rejects). Twenty-five sheets of printing paper or twenty-four sheets of writing paper make a quire and twenty quires make a ream. A label indicating the quality and place of manufacture is printed on top of the ream.

The late eighteenth century saw the beginning of the industrialization of paper-making, which would gradually change the individual steps of the production process.

Milestones in this development include the invention and introduction of the Hollander beater in the seventeenth century, which facilitated the mechanical separation of the fibrous parts of the rags.

In the mid-nineteenth century, Friedrich Gottlob Keller (1816–1895) in Saxony, found a way to cut wood with a grindstone to create pulp that could be used for papermaking. This laid the foundation for the low-cost industrial production of paper.

In 1798, the Frenchman Louis-Nicolas Robert (1761–1828) built the first paper machine and took out a patent for his long screen machine in 1799. A mechanically jiggled screen or mesh made it possible for the first time to produce a continuous paper web rather than the previously dipped individual sheet. The Englishmen Bryan Donkin (1768–1855) and Henry Fourdrinier (1766–1854) improved the paper machine by adding a drying section. This marked the beginning of industrial paper production. The long screen or Fourdrinier machine, as it came to be known in the English-speaking world, included a horizontal forming section, drainage rollers, suction boxes, and couch rollers as well as the drying section. Since which time paper production has included the following stages: pulp preparation, paper machine, and finishing.

The paper mill at Zerkall, Renker & Söhne, *c.* 1950.

Schematic representation of the principal steps in industrial paper production.

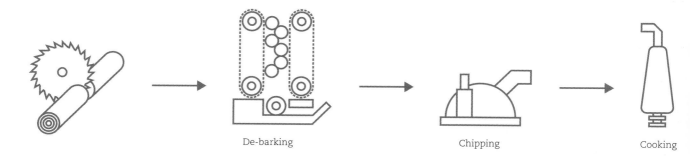

De-barking　　　Chipping　　　Cooking

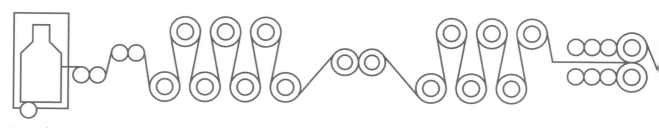

Super calender　　Wire section　　Press section　　　Dryers　　　Coaters

Pulp preparation

The fibrous material for paper production consists of primary fibers – the pulp from macerated wood or rags. The fibers used for recycled paper are called secondary. The pulp, whose composition differs depending on the paper quality, is ground and dissolved through added water. Besides the fibrous raw material, additional substances affecting the paper quality are added to the suspension. These include auxiliary substances, fillers, and coloring agents, which may be mineral substances or particular chemicals. These additives affect the coloring of the paper as well as functional qualities such as grease resistance.

Industrial paper factory in Wisconsin Rapids, c. 2005.

The paper machine

In the forming section of the paper machine the fiber-water suspension is spread evenly across the entire width of the mesh. Because the fibers settle next to and on top of another on the mesh, this creates the best possible fiber orientation. At the same time the water drains or is sucked up. A gallon of the fiber-water suspension captured on the mesh merely contains about 20 grams of fibrous and solid material. At the end of the forming section the paper web still contains roughly 80 percent water, but the paper sheets have already formed.

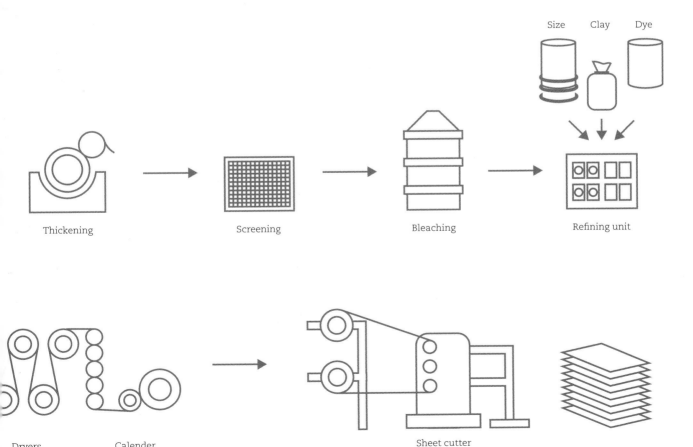

Thickening

Screening

Bleaching

Size   Clay   Dye

Refining unit

Dryers   Calender

Sheet cutter

Further drainage is achieved through mechanical pressure in the press section. There the paper web passes together with an absorbent, endless felt cloth between steel, granite, or hard rubber rolls. As a result of the pressing process the paper structure is compacted and its strength increased. The remaining residual water is vaporized from the paper in the drying section. There the paper web passes through multiple steam-heated drying cylinders, which allow the raw paper to dry evenly to a residual moisture content of just a few percent. In some paper machines the drying section is followed by a smoothing or 'calender' section which consists of multiple vertically arranged rolls that lend the paper web a smooth surface and even sheet-density.

The finished paper web is wound onto a steel roll or 'tambour.' Its residual moisture content is now down to 5 to 8 percent. Depending on the type of paper, a tambour can take a paper web with a length of up to 60 km (approx. 37 miles) and a weight of up to 25 tons.

Paper storage in the Gmund
Paper Mill, 2011.

Finishing

Today, coating is the most important finishing process. In this process a coating substance consisting of pigments and binding agents is applied to the raw paper to create a solid or printable surface. The surface of the paper web is smoothed through a process called 'calendering' where the paper passes under pressure through multiple heated rolls. When treated this way, the paper surfaces can become smooth, glossy, satin-glossy, or matte depending on the pressure applied to the web.

The final step in industrial paper production is cutting the paper web to particular sheet or roll sizes, which is achieved through machine cutting. In this process the paper web is cut into sheets in the sheeter or into smaller rolls for web printing by means of roll cutting machines. — *Frieder Schmidt*

Paper being packaged at the Sihl paper factory in Zurich, *c.* 1939.

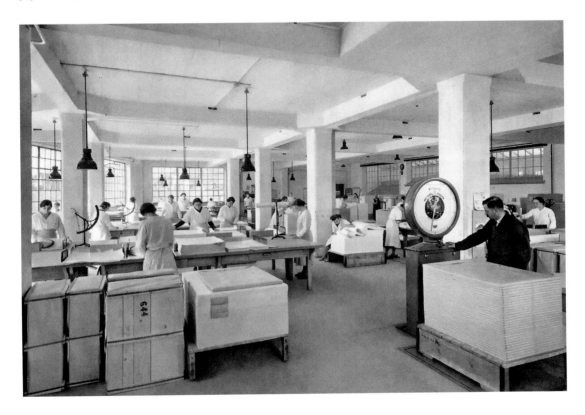

What is Paper Made of?

Take some mashed and boiled plant fibers, soak them with pure mineral water, and you have paper pulp. This simple recipe was developed over two thousand years ago in China, reaching Europe via Arabia. It might, however, have gone unnoticed, had another discovery not been made: when a sieve is used to drain water away from the pulpy mass, a consistent 'fleece' takes shape – paper.

The supporting structure of paper is essentially a grid of individual fibers. The more the pulp is watered and beaten, the larger the surface area in which the fibers come into contact with each other during the drying process. The cutting, pounding and grinding of the pulp, its boiling and watering, as well as the addition of chemical additives, determine the quality of the paper. There are various names for paper pulp, such as mash, blend and paste. Either way, they all produce an unpleasant odor.

The long-fibered bast from the inner bark of plants such as jute, hemp, linen and nettle, as well as agave leaves and cottonseed are particularly suitable for paper production. The rags once used to make paper were replaced by wood as demand increased. Since the mid-nineteenth century, wood has been processed into mechanical pulp using grindstones or by adding soda or sulfites to attain higher quality. Ninety percent of today's global paper production is based on these two materials.

In order to satisfy the different requirements of modern-day paper, chemicals, fillers, minerals and dyes are added. Thanks to technical processes allowing for short-fiber materials to be included, one can also experiment with special finishes By adding stone powders or silicones, for example, specific looks to the paper can be created, such as stone, cement or leather. On the other hand, wood, a valuable natural resource, can also be replaced by waste paper, bamboo, straw, and sugar cane. The use of bio-waste from food production has even given rise to the creation of new types of paper, such as apple paper. The paper industry has always been at the forefront when it comes to recycling waste.

Opposite: Water and pulp, the basic ingredients of papermaking.

Raw Materials for Making Paper

Paper essentially consists of fibers and fillers and, to a lesser extent, chemicals additives.

Waste Paper

With a share of over 50 percent, waste from paper, card and cardboard play a significant role as a raw material in the production of new paper. It is primarily recycled into cardboard or newsprint. As the quality of the fiber and the tear-strength diminishes with each use, fresh fibers are often added to the waste paper pulp. Both bleached and unbleached recycled papers have a 100 percent waste paper content.

Rags

Linen, hemp, or cotton textiles were for a long time the only raw material used to make paper. Rag paper made from textile scraps represents only a small proportion of paper produced today.

Wood

Depending upon the tree, wood fibers have different qualities, which determine whether they are suitable for wood-pulp or cellulose-pulp paper production. As a rule, the longer fibers of soft woods make firmer papers, whilst the shorter fibers of deciduous trees, due to their transparency, are suitable for graphic paper.

Wood Pulp

This is the general description for the fibrous pulp that is acquired following the different grinding processes of debarked tree trunks. Wood pulp produced by this method also contains lignin and resins, meaning that ground wood paper is low strength, yellows quickly and is less resistant to aging. These papers tend to be used for short-term applications, such as newspapers, magazines and certain types of packaging.

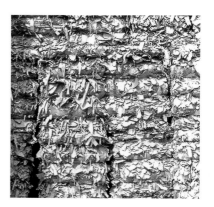

Cellulose

Next to waste paper, cellulose is the most important base product in paper production. Pulp is produced by shredding, various boiling processes, and by adding chemical solutions made from vegetable cellulose. Ninety percent of the pulp is wood. During the process, as much lignin as possible is removed from the cellulose, making it suitable for higher-end paper production.

Fillers

Making up to a maximum of 30 percent of the base paper, fillers include calcium carbonate (lime), gypsum, china clay and talcum powder. They affect the shine, smoothness, opacity, porosity, rigidity and whiteness of paper. When it comes to the paper's coating, pigments will determine its color, and binders, such as casein or starch, determine its resilience and water-resistance. The fillers also increase the paper weight.

Chemical Additives

Binders, dyes and optical brighteners, sizing agents, as well as dry and wet strength agents are all chemical additives that can influence the properties of paper when it is produced. — *Anita Brockmann*

Opposite: Raw materials for papermaking: rags (here from the rag-sorting room of a paper mill in Heilbronn, c. 1905), wood, recycled paper, and alternative raw materials such as apples.

This page, bottom, left to right: Lignin, cellulose, and kaolin.

Fig. 1.

Fig. 3.

Fig. 4.

The Art of Paper Making

Papermaking is a manual process, in which hands, the body, and the flow of water are brought together. A form of choreography occurs at the papermaker's vat: dipping the scoop sieve in, lifting it out and gently wobbling it until the water runs free and then pressing the sheet on to the felt. These steps are important in that they guarantee evenly thick sheets with a smooth surface.

All crafts are based on human ratios. So if you were to create your own paper, your own dimensions need to be aligned to the format. At a height of about 1.70 m, I should therefore format sizes of up to 60 cm × 80 cm, but no larger.

Using water as a tool for the production of paper sheets is of fundamental importance to the papermaker. Understanding the flow and speed of water affords an even distribution of fibers and teaches the maker to sense and respect, patience and humility, as well as his or her own limitations.

There are wonderful moments when creating paper, such as the moment of raising the sieve scoop and strain-hardening the fibers by gently shaking the pulp, as well as the sounds coming from the water. These are moments of great meditative calm. The creator feels as if they are a part of a river. For me, the magic of handmade paper lies in perceiving its subtle details, which, with all my senses, I can co-determine through many changes. The aesthetic appeal and properties of various papers can be shaped at microscopic level. I have noticed that the sound of paper changes depending on the degree to

which the fiber has been milled. The drying method also influences the paper surface. And the inner balance of the paper is reflected in its bend. Recently, I designed a nearly transparent white paper with opaque white lines. The sheets were dried on wooden boards. This resulted in a wood grain on the paper surface – a beautiful detail that is only visible at a second glance. This surprising element, like every other detail, helps to us understand the entire universe of hand-made paper. Making paper has been my passion for nearly forty years. — *John Gerard*

The paper artist and creator John Gerard at work: Removal of the scoop sieve (*left*); working on the pulp; peeling the paper sheet from the felt.

Handmade Paper

The Zerkall paper mill is located on the northern edge of the Eifel in the valley of the Kall River, which flows into the Ruhr in the village of Zerkall. The water-powered mill, first mentioned in 1512, served successively as a grinding mill, a fulling or walk mill, and oil mill until 1887, when a small cardboard mill was set up in the building. In 1903, the Düren paper manufacturer, Gustav Renker, acquired the mill to set up a modern production facility for the manufacture of traditional laid paper on a rotary cylinder mold. The high quality of the water in the Kall River meant the location offered the best conditions. Since which time, the Zerkall paper factory has been producing genuine laid papers in a cylinder mold and processing them into writing, advertising, printing and artist's papers in various formats, surfaces and colors. The resulting papers are acid-free, neutral glued, alkaline buffered, and manufactured without optical

Cylinder molds for making mold-made papers.
Cotton fibers and cellulose are the paper raw materials.

View of the paper mill in Zerkall.
Artificial pond holding the water
for the production of paper.

brighteners and so meet the strict international requirements for maximum aging resistance. The paper is scooped with a sieve-like cylinder, which slowly rotates in the vat around its axis, working almost like a human hand movement. With regard to structure and volume, cylinder-mold paper is therefore largely like true handmade paper. Watermarks and ripples are especially clear and rich in contour compared to machine-made paper, as they are on the rotating scoop and reach the screen side of the paper. In order to preserve the all-round deckle edge while scooping, the round screen must be subdivided into the format with a fixed division before production. Due to the large variety of formats and the different screen structures, Zerkall uses a different cylinder mold for each batch. Further processing and converting is then mainly done by hand in order to preserve the genuine deckle edges. Today, traditional manufacturers of handmade paper can be counted on one hand: in addition to Zerkall, there are Hahnemühle in Germany, Fabriano in Italy, St. Cuthberts in England and Arches in France. — *Felix Renker*

Washi: Japanese Paper

Paper is a natural product that can be experienced visually, haptically or acoustically. Lightweight paper produces different sounds from those produced by heavy paper. Rough paper arouses different feelings than those from smooth paper. Translucent paper opens up new perspectives for its application.

The oldest surviving paper fragments in Japan date back to the year 701. Said to be the first paper made in Japan, they are company registers that are archived at the *Shōsō-in* the Imperial Treasure House in Nara. Until then, paper had been imported from Korea. The copying of Buddhist sutras led to the growth of paper production in the seventh and eighth centuries. To this day, there is a high degree of continuity in the development, quality-improvement and use of paper in Japan. The name Washi derives from *Wa* for old Japan; handmade/traditional and *shi* for paper, this is why *Washi* became the term for all Japanese handmade papers.

Nagashizuki

The traditional Japanese process of hand-papermaking is fascinating, because it involves laying several layers of fiber on top of one another. As a result, the usually fine paper becomes very strong and difficult to tear. The smallest constituent parts of the paper are plant-fibers, which determine its particular character, materiality, volume, weight, stability, gloss, and overall design. The length and width of the vascular cells, the raw fibers, are decisive for the fiber-composite structure in surfaces and solids. In Japanese papermaking this differs from that in Western culture due to the raw material and the process used, as well as to the additive *neri*.

Raw Materials

The three raw materials most commonly used in Japan are characterized by relatively long fibers with specific features:

Workers debarking *kozo* at the Awagami paper manufacture in Japan.

Kozo (*Broussonetia papyrifera*), length: 3–25 mm, diameter: 0.025 mm; very long, strong, and soft.

Mitsumata (*Edgeworthia papyrifera*) length: 1–5 mm, diameter: 0.02 mm; glossy, elastic, dense.

Gampi (*Wikstroemia sikokiana*), length: 2–4.5 mm, diameter: 0.018 mm; transparent, silk-like, durable.

The papers produced are used for different purposes according to their fiber-specific properties: *Kozo* for calligraphy and for the traditional paper sliding doors found in Japanese architecture; *Mitsumata* for restoration purposes; *Gampi* for the application of gold leaf.

In the past, silk cocoons, animal-produced silkworm fibers, were also used to make precious papers.

Unlike in Japan, high-quality papers in Europe are made of cotton; in the past, they were made of linen or flax. Linter from the ripe cotton bole is made into fiber sheets, which are then used in papermaking. Depending on cultivation, the band-like fibers are usually shorter than the Japanese fibers. Such papers have a higher grammage as well, which is also partly attributable to the filler materials.

Various cultures to this day still use local raw materials: in Nepal, for instance, the inner bark of *Lokta* (*Daphne cannabina*), a plant of the *Daphne* genus; in China, whole stalks and stems of bamboo; and in Tibet the inner root fibers of *Stellera chamaejasme*, a plant of the *Stellera* genus.

Preparing the Fibers

The branches are debarked and the white inner bark is then separated from the outer bark. This inner bark is boiled, cleaned, rinsed, beaten with a wooden hammer or masher, or mechanically made into paper pulp in the *naginata* (the Asian version of the Hollander beater used to defiber the raw material, which is crushed rather than

Kigami, handmade paper from Japan.

ground). The technical processes used in fiber production affect the quality of the paper.

The root extract *neri* serves to perfect Japanese papermaking. This starchy substance slows down the draining of the water, thereby improving sheet formation. *Neri* is derived from the roots of the Japanese *tororo-aoi* plant (*Abelmoschus manihot*) a plant of the genus *Albelmoschus*, until recently classified as genus *Hibiscus*.

The Papermaking Mold

Dip molds are the papermakers' 'gems', because making them requires a lot of time and elaborate work.

In the Western technique, the sieve, the ribbed mold (with copper or bronze wires), or the fine wire mesh (for woven paper) is invariably attached to the wooden frame or deckle. In the Japanese tradition, by contrast, the *su* (sieve) of the *suketa* is laid on top of the *keta* (wooden frame) and held in place only by the cover (the

The paper scooped with the su is couched on the stack of paper without an intermediate layer. After each sheet a narrow ribbon is inserted to make it easier to separate the sheets after pressing.

The *nagashizuki* papermaking technique. The dip mold is repeatedly dipped into the pulp vat. Excess pulp is poured out over the back edge of the *suketa*.

The paper is dried by applying pressed, damp sheets of paper onto a firm surface with a roller. The paper stays smooth and retains its shape.

covering frame). A holding device used in the dipping process allows for the production of very large formats. Very thin bamboo splints or interconnected blades of grass are used for the ribs or wires of the sieve. They are tied together in parallel sequence with yarn to form a surface. Depending on the paper thickness, the ribs form a kind of 'watermark' in the paper due to the greater or smaller amount of superimposed pulp in the dipping process.

The Dipping Process

The dipping process is unique and requires great skill: dipping the mold, catching the paper pulp, lifting out the dip mold and gently moving the mold horizontally to give direction to the fibers, which will also cause them to interlace. The remaining pulp mass is quickly poured off again over the back edge of the mold. Depending on the quality and thickness of the paper, this process is repeated several times. As a result, multiple, thin pulp layers are superimposed on one another, thus creating a very strong, tear-resistant yet thin sheet of paper.

Thanks to the fiber consistency and the addition of the root extract *neri*, no layer pads are needed in the process of couching the papers. Each sheet has to be couched precisely onto the stack to ensure that the papers can be properly separated after pressing. The sheets are dried on heated metal plates; in the past they were dried on wooden planks, which would cause wood textures to show in the paper. Fine brushes or rollers are used to apply the damp papers onto the metal plate. As a result, the paper has a slightly shiny, smooth surface on one side and a rougher one on the other.

A Digression on the History and Use in Art, of Washi

In her 2013 performance *Washi Tales*, the artist Kyoko Ibe (b. 1941) makes extensive use of paper. Openings resulting from cuts in the paper allow viewers to look through them and make the installation lighter. The paper's grain direction is already influenced by the movement of the dip mold during the production process and must run parallel to the openings. Otherwise the space-filling, hanging surfaces would tear.

The making of paper yarn from *shifu* (paper cloth) also requires a particular grain direction. In Japan this tradition traces back to the early seventeenth century. — *Therese Weber*

Kyoko Ibe, *Washi Tales*,
performance, 2013.

Color by Design

James Cropper has been producing paper and cardboard in England's Lake District since 1845. The paper mill has made an international name for itself with dyed papers that are custom-made for use as packaging of fine textiles or other luxury items, as well as catalog and book covers.

In most cases, color development begins as soon as the customer has registered his interest or order. The commissioned color designers will usually come to Cropper to work with the papermakers and paint lab to realize a color concept. There are around 4000 colors in the laboratory and around 200,000 digitally stored color mixes in the database.

In order to develop a new color shade, the specialist expertise of the papermakers is needed. Colors are often an abstract idea in the designer's imagination. To actually achieve the designer's objective, the paper professionals need to know exactly what it is going to be used for, what influences the paper will be exposed to and how it is to be further processed or used. In short, every factor will have an effect on the color. The actual use and the exact application of a product must always be perfectly understood so that further dynamics such as light and refraction can be analyzed. In practical testing, for example, color fastness is important, as is the effect of wear and tear on the colors. It would be annoying if the dye used to make carrier bags happened to rub off on to textiles.

After measuring the sample colors, these values are then used as a basis. Software plus a good deal of knowledge and experience will then be used to find different ingredients for the color recipe. Up to five colors or pigments can be mixed to create a specific color. After this 'recipe development,' handmade samples of the paper are produced (color patterns made from paper). Many attempts may be needed to hit the precise tone in the paper mix. The entire process is initially run through manually. The result is then tested in different light backgrounds and shades, after which final machine production will only go ahead once all has been approved.

— *James Cropper Paper*

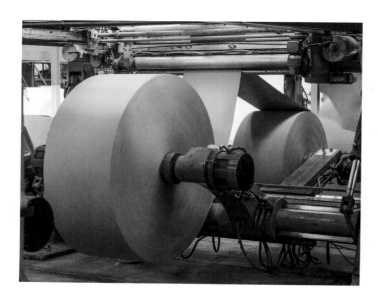

A view of the production floor of the James Cropper Colored Paper Mill in the Lake District, Great Britain.

Paper as a Building Material

We think of paper as a thin, unstable material, certainly not one that might be suitable in the construction of houses or any permanent built structure. And why should we? After all, for anyone looking for a non-mineral or non-metallic building material, there is always wood.

Wood is a sympathetic, renewable material. It is pleasing to the touch, warm, and it is easy to work with, both with modern digital processing systems and on site should something have to be modified. Wood, however, does not have an even texture, but perhaps therein lies its charm. This inconsistency can cause practical difficulties in construction because we always build with safety in mind as an absolute first priority. New processing methods have been developed to change the inconsistent nature of wood, such as crushing it into small chips, which are then glued back together, or peeling wood into thin veneer layers, glued together to form boards. This method can be used to create boards larger than the original trees, and by superimposing individual layers the inconsistency is eliminated. This achieves a wood-based material of almost industrial quality and its potential is fully borne out by today's modern timber engineering projects.

So what has all this got to do with paper? From a construction perspective, paper is merely a further development of this industrially processed wood. Fibers are split down even further and then reassembled until paper is formed. When paper is stacked, glued together and geometrically structured to size, it becomes a much stronger material than veneered or wood-fiber boards.

Paper is just the right product for bio-based applications in the building sector: it can be produced cheaply, it consists primarily of renewable or recyclable raw materials, and it is extremely robust given its weight. It can even be produced in sheets with high absorbency, and as foam with comparatively simple chemical properties.

These new uses and applications for paper have given rise to a question to whose answer a new research project at the Technical University of Darmstadt is dedicated. Although only a handful of experimental structures on which to base research exist, the question remains: what can paper really do in the building industry? The interdisciplinary research team (from the fields of paper chemistry, mechanical engineering, statics, building engineering and environmental sciences) brings these expert departments together to explore how this fascinatingly simple, traditional material can be employed in completely different applications. The research and development is concerned with very practical aspects, such as environmental compatibility, the material-appropriate construction, costs, and fire and water resistance. And what about related materials? As paper is two-dimensional perhaps textile-engineering approaches could be applied? As a material, paper has huge potential for the construction industry and we should be eager to see the results in the future. — *Ulrich Knaack*

Paper Types and Paper Industry

The paper industry produces a wide variety of paper types. The four most popular are packaging paper, graphic paper, tissue paper and specialty paper.

Packaging paper takes up most of the overall paper production. Corrugated cardboard boxes for the cosmetic industry and the fashion industry also belong to this group and are typically used for shipping.

Graphic papers are the second largest group and include all papers that can be written or printed on. They include paper for newspapers, magazines, stationery or printing paper as well as papers for notebooks and writing pads.

Hygiene papers make up a small part of production. These include toilet paper, tissues, kitchen towels and facial wipes.

In most cases, this type of paper will only be used once before getting lost in the paper chain, as they are disposed of via the sewer or with household waste.

The smallest group of **specialty papers** comprises a variety of paper types, each with very special characteristics. The range goes from banknote paper all the way to electrical insulation paper, which is among one of the most expensive papers around, and others such as roofing cardboard, photo papers and decor papers.

The production of paper and cardboard amounted to around 411 million metric tons worldwide in 2016.

The four world's biggest manufacturing countries are China, USA, Japan and Germany. The ten largest international paper manufacturers are: International Paper (USA), Nine Dragon Paper Holding (China), West Rock (USA), UPM (Finland), Stora Enso (Finland), Oji Paper Company (Japan), Sappi (South Africa), Smurfit Kappa Group (Ireland), DS Smith (UK), Nippon Paper (Japan).

The European paper industry's proportion in the total world production was at around 106 million tons in 2014. Although the number of individual companies and paper mills in Europe has significantly decreased in recent years, the production capacity of the remaining locations has gone up. Therefore, the turnover has remained relatively consistent.

Opposite: Annual production of the paper industry in tons: worldwide in 2015.

Packaging paper
paper and cardboard

231,022,000 t

Graphic papers

101,391,000 t

Sanitary papers

  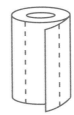

34,778,000 t

Specialty papers
paper and cardboard

16,294,000 t

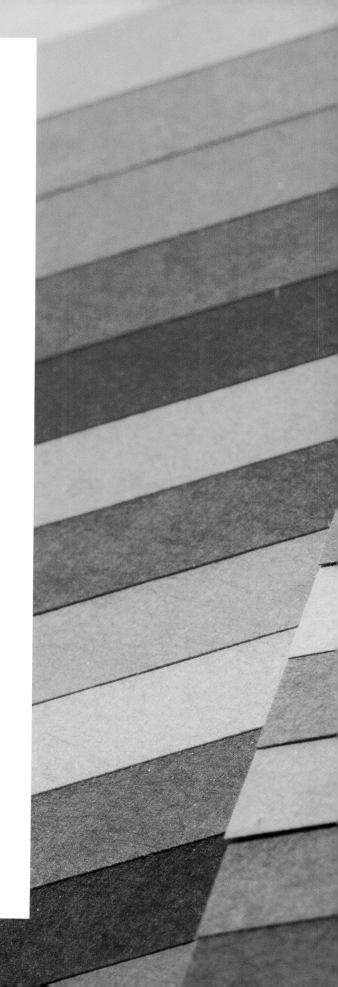

Paper A—Z

There are about 3000 different kinds of
paper. This Paper A-Z describes the most
important types of paper and gives an
overview of the raw materials and the
production techniques used in making
them.

Paper < 170 g/m²
Cardboard > 170 – 600 g/m²
Paperboard > 600 g/m²

Area-density/Grammage

This is the term used to denote paper, cardboard in grams per square meter (gsm or g/m²). Paper products of up to 200 grams per square meter are classified as paper, those between 200 and 600 grams as cardboard and those above as paperboard. In countries that use U.S. paper sizes, a measure called *basis weight* is used.

Art paper

High-quality and relatively heavy paper that is coated on both sides and has a smooth surface. High-resolution single or multicolored images require paper that is smooth and evenly absorbs printing ink. For this reason the irregular fiber structure of the base paper > **Natural paper** is covered with a coating > **Coated paper.**

Banknote paper

Long-lasting, durable, and age-resistant paper suitable for multicolored printing. Equipped with watermark and other anti-counterfeiting agents, such as metal threads.

Bank paper

Bank or bond paper is high-quality wood-free writing paper, with even transparency and often tagged with a watermark.

Bible paper

Woodfree specialty printing paper, sometimes with rag content and mostly containing filler with very low grammage or basis weight. Bible paper must have very good mechanical and age-resistant qualities.

Blotting paper

Voluminous, highly absorbent paper that has high filler content. It is mostly made of pure cotton in the form of bleached linters and pulp. Plain varieties, such as notebook inlays, contain mechanical pulp. Good absorption is obtained by a rough grinding of the raw materials. White blotting paper often has an additive of dyed fiber.

Book paper

Paper for the manufacture of books. It is either woodfree or wood-containing. Depending on its volume, i. e. the ratio of thickness to its mass, the paper may contain more or less filler. Sometimes the volume is important as it dictates whether the paper is sealed. The descriptive terms are 1.5x 1.75x 2.0x 2.2x 2.5x volume. Spruce, Eucalyptus, Esparto (a coarse grass type) and sulphate pulp is used for its production.

Book printing paper

Either woodfree or wood-containing. It tends to be volumnious, thick and has a high area-density.

Cable filling paper
> Electric insulating paper

Car panel board
Voluminous, bituminous board made of recovered paper. It is used as interior lining and padding material for motor vehicles, as acoustic insulation, for covering and as fiberboard for various building uses.

Carbonless copy paper
This NCR (No Carbon Required) or auto-copying paper enables copying without the use of a carbon copy paper sheet in between the original and the copy. The paper is prepared in such a way that when pressure is applied, a color reaction or ink transfer takes place. NCR Paper is mainly used as continuous feed forms, wage and salary invoices, sales slips and as pre-printed forms for monetary transactions.

Cardboard
One layer card is simply thick paper. For the manufacture of multi-layered types of card (these often comprise of layers made of different raw materials), a number of sheets of wet paper web are pressed together so that they stick together without adhesive. With multi-layered card > **Folding cardboard** the front side may be coated or uncoated. In addition there is also multi-layered cardboard where the layers are pasted onto each other with adhesive (pasted cardboard).

In terms of area-density (150–600 g/m^2) then card spans the area of paper and cardboard. In addition to folding boxes, it is also used for high-quality packaging, fancy boxes, book covers, displays, paper cups, as well as for milk and juice cartons.

Cast-coated paper
Coated paper that gets its shine by molding the wet or wetted surface on a dry, highly polished chromed cylinder, as opposed to simply glazing it.

Chemical pulp
Fiber matter that is chemically separated from vegetable raw materials whereby the non-fibrous components are substantially removed. Depending on the method used, sulphite or sulphate pulp is produced. Apart from recovered paper, these make up the most important ingredients of paper manufacturing.

Chromo cardboard
Multi-layered with a coated top layer made of chemical pulp or recovered paper. Chromo paper is used for folded boxes, shoeboxes, decoration or book and brochure binders.

Chromo imitation cardboard
Multi-layered board that is covered on either one or both sides with a woodfree layer and is smooth on one side. Sandwiched between these two layers are interleaving layers of mechanical or recovered paper pulp. At least one of the layers is made of bleached pulp.

Chromo paper

> **Label paper**

Cigarette paper

Light unsized paper (18–24 g/m^2) made of linen and hemp fiber that is today increasingly being replaced by special pulp varieties. The paper is specially equipped in order to increase its ability to burn. It has a filler quota of 30 percent.

Coated paper

By coating the paper evenly, a smooth and sealed surface is achieved. This is very well suited for reproducing high-resolution images. The coating solution is applied in coating machines. Multiple pre-coating takes place in the paper machine. The market differentiates between wood-containing and woodfree quality in single and double-sided coated types. > **Label paper** > **Rotogravure paper** > **Illustration printing paper** > **Art paper** > **Offset paper**

Colored paper

Collective term for paper that is colored, printed, super-calendered, or patterned (e. g. marbled) on one side.

Copying paper

Uncoated paper that comes in wood-free or wood-containing varieties. It can be white or multicolored and has the format of DIN A4 and DIN A3.

Corrosion preventive paper

> **Packaging paper** impregnated or coated with anti-corrosive agents that either prevent or impede the rusting of iron and silverware. The effect of 'Vapour Phase Inhibitor' (VPI) paper is based on the gaseous compounds that are emitted.

Corrugated paper

Collective term for corrugated paper that is produced as corrugated web and used primarily for > **Corrugated paperboard**.

Corrugated paperboard

Corrugated paperboard is a paper-processing product. It was invented in 1871 in the USA. Due to its excellent packaging qualities, the new material quickly established itself. It is manufactured by passing the paper web between two crimped or corrugated rollers, which press the wave effect into the paper by means of heat and pressure. The crimped paper is then pasted on one or both sides with a layer of smooth paper. In many countries corrugated paper is predominantly manufactured out of recycled paper > **Testliner** > **Corrugated paper**.

Crêpe Paper

Also known as crinkle paper. The paper web is shortened when crêped. This raises the level of stretchability in the machine direction and the paper then becomes more pliant and resistant to mechanical impact. The pleats or crinkles in wet crêped paper are created on a cylinder with the use of a crêpe scraper that crushes the wet paper web. The paper is then removed and dried. Crêpe paper is used for decorative packaging (crêpe tissue paper, garden crêpe paper) and for filtering purposes (coffee filters). It can also be used for masking during painting and glazing as well as for hygiene purposes > **Crêpe sanitary paper**.

Crêpe sanitary paper

One layered paper, wood-containing and/or manufactured from recovered fiber. As opposed to > **Tissue sanitary paper**, it is crinkled in its wet state. The crinkle factor is about 20 percent. This way the fiber compound can be reshaped without losing its strength. The drying process that follows fixes the crinkling. It is commonly used as toilet paper and for paper towels.

Decor paper

Woodfree paper that is processed in a series of steps. Before it is impregnated with artificial resin, it is often printed with various decorations (e.g. a woodgrain pattern). The final products are laminated boards and chipboards that are in turn used for manufacturing furniture and interior fittings.

Document paper

Paper with high age resistance, it is woodfree with rag additives or solely made from rag. It is used for written documents that have to be stored over a long period.

Drawing paper

The range of drawing paper comprises of woodfree and wood-containing varieties whose characteristics are specially adapted to the requirements of drawing and painting techniques. Drawing paper is sized in its composition as well as on the surface. It is only slightly translucent (opaque) and more often it is washable.

Duplex board

Duplex board consists of two layers of material made from recovered paper.

Electric insulating paper

Strong pore-free paper that is impregnated with synthetic resin and made from pulp. It is sometimes produced with rag additive. Electric insulating paper must not contain filler or electrical conductive contamination (metal, carbon etc.), salts or acids. The pore-free state is achieved by finely grinding the pulp.

Electric insulating paper that possesses a high strength is produced for the use of so called 'cable filling paper' that is spirally wrapped around conductor wire. 'Electrolyte paper' is an example of an electric insulating paper that possesses high absorbency and purity factors. The wafer-thin condenser paper must be uniformly thick and pore-free. It is one of the most expensive papers.

Endpaper
Paper that is white or dyed to various colors, ribbed or embossed, and that is pasted into the front or back inner-cover of a book. This automatically masks the folded edges of the material that covers the book.

Envelope paper
Envelope paper is produced in many variations for envelopes. These may include woodfree or wood-containing, smooth or super-calendered on one side, white or colored. It is imperative however that the paper is non-transparent, capable of being written and printed on and crease-resistant.

Filtering paper
Made of soft pulp or occasionally with unsized waterproof paper that has rag additive. Filtration speed and release capability (separation factor) are both dependent on the amount and size of the pores. They are additionally influenced by various degrees of pulp refining and by crêping.

Fine paper
Quality description for a large amount of high-quality, woodfree paper that has rag additive or is sometimes completely manufactured from rag. The highest demands are placed on fine paper in regard to its even transparency, surface properties, and light resistance.

Fine paperboard
Fine paperboard, or hardboard, is characterized by high resistance to bending, tearing, and by its surface hardness. It is used for the manufacture of hand paperboard and wrapping paper and is made up of higher quality recovered paper, pulp, textile by-products and occasionally ground wood pulp. It has either no or a minimum amount of filler. In order to increase its strength and water resistance, synthetic emulsions are added. Very often the board is post-treated by glazing, lacquering and embossing. Bookbinding board, fireboard, jacquard board, gasket board, trunk board, shoeboard, pressboard, and punching board are among the various fine boards.

Flame-resistant paper
Flame-resistant paper may ignite but must extinguish immediately and then carbonize. This is achieved by impregnating the paper with substances that produce a protective gas that displaces the air when the paper is heated. Other chemicals such as soluble glass (sodium silicate) increase the ignition temperature.

Folding cardboard

Single or multi-layered board made of primary or secondary fiber, sometimes coated on one side and capable of being chanelled and scored. It must have the necessary rigidity for packing.

Glassine

Greaseproof paper made out of finely ground pulp. Its high transparency factor is obtained by strong glazing (polishing between rollers). As it is used as chocolate wrapping paper, it must be able to be embossed. Additionally, it is used for interwoven pages in photo albums, wrapping paper, canned fish, protective covers for books, envelope windows etc.

Glossy paper

> **Colored paper** > **Illustration printing paper** > **Cast coated paper**

Graphic paper

Printing and writing paper that includes > **Fine paper**. After the raw material a difference is made between wood-containing and wood-free paper. Amongst the former are > **Newsprint** and > **Rotogravure paper**, which make up the majority of the wood-containing paper manufactured.

Greaseproof paper

The level of grease resistance is achieved either by grinding the pulp extremely finely over a long period of time and pore-free sheet formation on the paper machine > **Imitation parchment** > **Glassine** or by parchmentization of the pulp > **Vegetable parchment**. In addition, the level of grease resistance is increased with various auxiliary additives.

Grey cardboard

Cardboard made from recovered paper that is rough or smooth on just one side. It is also lined on one or both sides. Grey cardboard is used for pre-cut forms like cardboard boxes and as bases for note pads, drawing pads and calendars.

Handmade paper

Up until the paper machine was invented in the nineteenth century, paper was made by hand, manually scooped out of the vat, sheet by sheet. Today, that process is only used in the production of a few special types of paper. For this manual process of paper production, the mold (i. e. a frame covered with a taught stretched sieve) is dipped into a fiber suspension. When it is lifted out, it is shaken lightly in order to distribute the fibres evenly. At the

same time the water seeps through the mesh of the sieve, back into the vat. The removable folded frame ('lid') prevents the suspension from dripping down the side. The wet sheets that have been deposited between felt layers, are then stacked into the press, drained of water and dried. Handmade paper always has a typical frayed edge that is formed on the inside of the deckle frame (sieve). Today, paper that is called 'handmade paper' is normally mechanically scooped with a cylinder sieve.

llustration printing paper

Woodfree or > **Wood-containing paper** and double-sided > **Coated paper**. Standard illustration printing paper normally has glossy, matt and granulated surfaces. It is used for multi-colored printing for periodicals with smaller circulations e.g. trade journals and magazines, manuals and reference books, schoolbooks, and advertising brochures, as well as company reports and brochures.

Imitation parchment paper

Woodfree paper produced by fine-grinding certain types of pulp and additives over a long period of time. Imitation parchment is very similar to vegetable parchment in terms of its appearance and qualities (especially its greaseproof qualities), however, it is neither water- nor boil-proof. It is used as wrapping paper for meat and sausage and fluted paper for cookies and biscuits.

Impregnated paper

Water-resistant paper with sealing, anti-corrosion or heavy anti-inflammable qualities. This is achieved by dipping the paper in an impregnating solution.

Kraftliner

Kraftliner is a paper with a basis weight of 120 g/m² upwards. It consists mainly of bleached or unbleached sulphate pulp and is used for the top layer of corrugated paperboard.

Kraft paper

Packaging paper made from bleached or unbleached softwood sulphate pulp (kraft pulp) or equivalent fiber with mechanical solidity and pliancy. Kraft paper is suitable for the production of paper bags because it can withstand the varying demands placed upon filled bags. Crêped kraft paper is characterized by its stretchability. The term 'kraft tissue paper' is used for thin, multi-ribbed kraft paper that is smooth on one side and is under 30 g/m². It is used for wrapping silver cutlery, metal objects, and above all glass. Depending on its intended use, kraft paper may be coated with bitumen or synthetic substances in subsequent manufacturing processes.

Kitchen paper towels

Made from crêped paper that has been manufactured using pulp or recovered paper. They are used in the home and as wiping towels in industry.

Label paper

A paper that is mostly coated on one side and suitable for offset and multicolored gravure. The paper is generally capable of being varnished, bronzed and punched. Sometimes also resistant to moisture and alcohol in order to ensure that the labels are removable e.g. during the bottle wash process in breweries.

LWC paper

LWC (Light Weight Coated) paper is coated on both sides and contains mechanical pulp. It comes on reels and has a grammage or basis weight of less than 72 g/m². It is used for magazines, mail order catalogs etc. Rotogravure or web offset printing is used. > **Coated paper**

Machine-coated paper

> **Illustration printing paper**
> **Label paper**

Machine-made cardboard

Various types of board mainly used for the manufacture of cardboard boxes.

Machine-made paperboard

Manufactured from recovered paper as a continuous web on a cardboard machine. In contrast > **Winding paper** is manufactured on specialized machines.

Magazine paper

Choosing appropriate magazine paper depends upon the number of copies to be printed and other requirements such as the reproduction of images, outer appearance, and impact of advertising. Magazines in mass circulation are normally printed on a rotary printing machine.

Marble paper

Effect-paper in various colors that has an irregularly dyed and patterned surface. Colored paper of this type is used as > **Endpaper**.

Mechanical pulp

Generic term used for pulp that is completely or almost completely produced by mechanical means.

Metal paper

Refined paper covered on one or both sides with a thin film of metal foil.

Millboard

Collective term for all solid paper-board.

Moisture-resistant paper

By adding alkali water-resistant agents to the fiber suspension, a paper is created that will still remain strong even when wet.

Natural paper

> **Uncoated paper**

NCR paper

NCR standing for 'No Carbon Required' > **Carbonless copy paper**.

Newsprint

A strong and wood-containing rotary printing paper that has been machine-finished or super-calendered, 40–56 g/m^2 raw material is used, for this is predominantly recovered paper. Due to the short-lived nature of the product, the demands placed on the paper regarding visual quality and printability are lower than those placed on other paper (e.g. coated paper). Generally, it is assumed that only low-resolution images can be printed. The impact of light and oxygen causes the paper to yellow.

Newsprint must possess qualities that allow it to run through the machine well. Today's modern printing techniques require paper with high tear resistance so that the flow of the rapid-production machines is not interrupted. Newsprint is used for daily, weekly and advertising newspapers. It is mainly processed in offset printing and increasingly for colored editions.

Offset paper

Collective term for printing paper that has properties suitable for offset printing. The paper should not give off dust when being processed and should maintain stable dimensions. Offset paper that is woodfree or wood-containing can be coated (glossy, matt, embossed) or uncoated. It is processed from reels or sheets.

Oiled paper

Term used for paper that has been impregnated with wax or paraffin > **Wax paper**. In the past, the base paper was soaked in dry oils such as linseed or poppy seed oil. Oiled paper is waterproof and water-resistant.

Packaging paper

Collective name for papers of the most varied pulp composition and whose common feature is only its intended use. The selection and mixing of the fibers depend upon the requirements of the paper. Most importantly it should be tear-, burst- crease- and abrasion-resistant in addition to possessing elasticity and strength. Very often the paper needs to possess good printing qualities (packaging can be an advertising medium). For special purposes the paper may also need to be made waterproof and water-resistant, smell or steam proof. For this, either special additives are added to the pulp, or the paper is coated or impregnated with synthetic materi- als and/or combined with metal foils. Thin packaging paper weighing less than 30 g/m² is called wrapping tissue paper > **Tissue paper**.

Paper

A product made out of mechanically or chemically produced plant fiber, which is meshed together in a watery suspension. Together with additives, fillers, dye or glue it is then formed into sheets.

Papier mâché

Kneadable handicraft pulp created by rubbing paper into water. Glue or adhesive paste is often added in order to obtain cohesiveness. Formed by hand and often used as a basis for molds and for producing plastic (3D) objects that harden when dry.

Paper in sheets

Formatted paper mostly used for graphic purposes, for example in printing offices. Contrary to paper in reels, it is already cut to ordered size.

Paperboard

The most important difference between paperboard and > **Cardboard** is that paperboard has a higher weight or density (usually greater than 600 g/m²). Being thicker it has higher physical properties. Because it is technically difficult and uneconomical for a machine to pro- duce a sufficiently thick single layer fleece in one operation, paperboard is made by pressing together several wet layers.
For the production of > **Winding board**, Fourdrinier paper machines are used to wind one or more wet pulp fleece onto a formatting roller until the desired thickness is reached. > **Machine-made board** is usually made of layers of different composi- tion, the upper layers are usually made of the higher quality material. The term then allocated to the product can depend on the raw material used such as wood paper- board (manufactured from wood pulp) and grey paperboard (manu- factured from recovered paper) or can derive from its use, such as box paperboard, > **Roofing board**, grey bookbinding paperboard, > **Car panel board** and decoration board. The term > **Millboard** is used to differentiate between sturdy paper- board and > **Corrugated paperboard**. This is multi-layered paperboard consisting of various layers of smooth and corrugated paper.

Parchment paper
> **Vegetable parchment**

Photographic paper
Base paper used for photographic paper that must be moisture-resistant, keep stable dimesions and obtained from chemically neutral pulp that is free of impurities (such as traces of iron or copper). Such impurities would bring about an undesired separation of the metallic silver. These days, paper with a thin doublesided coating of polyethylene has replaced barite paper. The coating prevents the chemicals and water from soaking into the base paper when the photos are developed. This also means that the rinse and dry phases are shortened.

Postcard cardboard
Either wood-containing or woodfree and supercalendered. The prescribed minimum basis weight is 170 g/m². Official Post Office postcards have a basis weight of 190 g/m².

Poster paper
Contains a high amount of filler and is often colored. It is also weather-resistant. The poster formats are based on a 1/1 sheet that is equivalent to DIN A1.

Primary fiber
Also known as fresh fiber. It is the basic raw material for the paper industry. Cellulose and mechanical pulp are manufactured from the renewable primary product; wood.

Printing paper
Term that embraces all wood-containing and woodfree printable paper that serve as a medium for printed information. In addition to swift and even color absorption and drying (printability), dimensional stability, sufficient opacity (reverse printing must not show through), and smoothness, it is essential that the paper is strong and stiff so that it can pass rapidly and efficiently through the machine and not cause any malfunctioning (pressroom runnability).

Rag paper
Pure rag paper is manufactured solely from rag. In the past these would have been linen scraps, but these days are more generally cotton by-products from the textile industry, mainly plant fiber cellulose from cotton, linen, hemp and ramie. Papermakers consider rag as the finest raw material. Paper manufactured in this way is often stronger and more age-resistant than any other paper type made from bleached pulp. Rag paper, as well as paper with rag content and pulp additives, is used for bank notes, certificates, documents, financial record books, maps and copper etchings. It is also used for expensive writing and watercolor paper and additionally, for special technical processes.

Recovered paper

In terms of quantity, recovered paper is the most important raw material in the paper industry. The major recipients are the producers of newsprint, packaging paper and sanitary paper. Due to the fact that the fibres are shortened during every procedure, the life cycle of recovered paper fiber is limited. A constant supply of virgin fiber is therefore one of the basic prerequisites needed to maintain the recycling loop.

Recycled paper

Term for paper made of 100 percent recovered paper. It is used for graphic paper, boxes and sanitary paper.

Roofing board

Paperboard that has been dipped in tar, bitumen and/or asphalt. Roofing board is manufactured by soaking the 'naked roofing board' in the dip mixture and then covering it with sand. Roofing board is the only paper product that contains reprocessed wool.

Rotogravure paper

Mostly wood-containing, strongly super-calendered (smoothed) paper with a high percentage of ash **> Coated or uncoated paper**. The paper must enable ink to be absorbed evenly at high printing speeds from the ink cells of the rotogravure rollers. In order to do so, it is essential that the paper has a certain amount of softness and suppleness. It is used for magazines, mail order and travel catalogs, prospectuses and newspaper or magazine supplements with high print runs.

SC paper

SC stands for super-calendered. This is a super-calendered uncoated wood-containing paper that contains filler additive. **> Magazine paper**

Sack paper

> Kraft paper

Sanitary paper

Sanitary paper consists of cellulose wadding, tissue and crêpe paper that is manufactured from recovered paper and/or pulp with the addition of wood pulp. Due to high levels of everyday use, the term 'tissue paper' has been adopted as a collective term for sanitary paper internationally. It is used for producing toilet paper and numerous other hygiene products such as paper handkerchiefs, kitchen paper towels, paper towels and cosmetic towels.

Sanitary tissue paper

A sanitary tissue paper made from pulp or recovered paper pulp, sometimes using mechanical pulp additive. It has a closed structure and is crêped slightly. It is so thin that it is hardly ever used in single layer form. Depending on the requirements, the number of layers is increased. Crêping takes place with a dry content of over 90 percent. The high level of softness is achieved by dry crêping and a low basis weight. It is normally used as a two- or more layered article.

This pliant and highly absorbent product is predominantly made of chemical pulp and/or de-inked recovered paper – partly with the addition of mechanical pulp. Depending on its use it may be made moisture proof. It is used for face tissues, paper handkerchiefs, serviettes, kitchen towels, paper towels, and toilet paper.

Secondary fiber
Obtained from recovered paper and used for manufacturing paper, card and paperboard.

Security paper
High-quality woodfree paper, sometimes containing rag and watermarked in order to prevent forgery. Paper that is secure against misuse and counterfeit. The partially chemical security measures used during the paper manufacture are kept confidential.

Shoe paperboard
Shoe paperboard is strong and flexible hardboard made of recovered paper and is free of mechanical pulp and filler. It is used as insoles, hoods and joints for shoeware.

Silicone paper
Used to prevent glue as well as adhesive pastes and substances from sticking. By coating the paper with silicone, an adhesive paper with a surface that is repellent against most substances is created. It is primarily used for self-adhesive papers and foils e.g. for the manufacture of labels.

Sized paper
The ability of paper to absorb fluids is reduced by sizing, thereby creating the precondition for writing properties needed for ink. Sized paper is used for many other purposes (printing, coating, sticking) whereby the sizing fulfils many tasks. It regulates the water intake and increases the water and ink resistance (picking resistance).

Soft paperboard
Soft, voluminous paperboard that possesses felt-like characteristics. Used as masking board, packaging board, or stencils.

Specialty paper
All types of paper that have special properties as characteristic features. In order to attain these properties, particular raw materials are often necessary.

Suitcase paperboard
Sized, dense, elastic, flexible, and strong fine-paperboard. The surface is normally treated in order to make it water repellent. The board can be pressed, folded, bent, riveted and sewn.

Super-calendered paper
Paper that is smoothed and compressed between calender rollers and thereby achieving a shine that can be highly glossed or matt. Used as e.g. > **Magazine paper**. The glazing effect obtained in the calender roller machines is based on friction, temperature and pressure.

Surface sized paper

Page-surface sized paper that is generally obtained with the help of a size press within the paper machine.

Synthetic fiber paper

Paper that is manufactured with synthetic fiber such as polyester and polyamide, spun rayon and partially with the addition of fillers. The fibers cohere by means of a binding agent. The hardy and heavy-duty synthetic fiber paper is used for the production of maps and important documents such as driver's licences and vehicle registration documents.

Tea bag paper

According to the type of processing, there is a distinction between heat-sealing and non-heat-sealing tea bag paper. The paper is made of e.g. Abaca (Manila) pulp with the addition of of high alpha pulp. It must be highly porous, water-resistant, tasteless and have an area-density of 12–15 g/m^2.

Testliner

Strong paper or paperboard with undetermined pulp composition and is primarily made of recovered paper. It is often formed to make > **Duplex paper**. The area-density is less than 125 g/m2.

Thermo paper

Thermo active paper is coated on one side. It is used for printing text and graphics in thermo-plotters (e.g. for technical drawings) and thermo-printers (e.g. labels, tickets, cash register slips and other sales slips).

Thin paper

Thin printing paper or > **Bible paper** was used for the first time over 100 years ago for printing bibles. It is paper with a low weight made from rag and bleached kraft pulp. It is used in advertising printing (catalogs, prospectuses, mailings etc.) and job printing (periodicals, brochures, instruction leaflets and forms etc.).

Tissue paper

Collective term for thin paper with a basis weight of less than 30 g/m^2, which may vary according to its use and composition. It is mainly used for packing sensitive and delicate objects, such as bottles and fruit (especially for oranges), wrapping tissue paper and, in a waterproof form, for wrapping flowers. In addition it is used as base paper for manufacturing carbon paper, as lining paper in envelopes and, together with aluminium foil, in cigarette packaging. The extremely fine Japanese silk paper is produced with a basis weight of 6–8 g/m^2.

Toilet paper
> **Sanitary tissue paper**
> **Crêpe sanitary paper**

Transparent paper
By grinding high-quality fiber (hard chemical pulp types, rag) gently over a long period of time, a raw material is obtained and used to manufacture transparent paper. The transparent drawing paper is rendered suitable for writing, fingerprint-resistant, erasure proof and of stable shape by sizing the surface. Transparent paper can be subsequently impregnated or 'parchmentized.'
> **Vegetable parchment**

Triplex cardboard
Cardboard, smooth on one side and comprising the following three layers: surface layer made of chemical pulp and/or wastepaper; an interfacing middle layer made of wastepaper; and a bottom layer made of mechanical and/or chemical pulp and/or recovered paper.

Vegetable parchment
Also known as parchment paper, vegetable parchment is a packaging material of high purity with grease-proof qualities. It is particularly strong in both dry and wet states. Manufactured from bleached pulp it is sometimes combined with aluminum foil and used for packaging butter, margarine and other fats as well as cheese and other products in the foodstuff industry.

Wall base paper
Collective term for paper that is suitable for the production of wallpaper. This paper can be single or multilayered (Simplex/Duplex), woodfree or wood-containing, coated or uncoated and may also be laminated and pre-glued.

Watercolor paper
> **Woodfree paper** drawing paper with either high rag content or manufactured solely from rag. It has a rough or structured surface. The paper should take well to watercolors but the colors should not bleed through the paper. The paper needs to be erasure proof.

Watermark paper
> **Bank paper** > **Handmade paper**

Wax paper
Mostly woodfree paper impregnated with paraffin, wax or a wax/paraffin/synthetic mixture. Depending on the temperature applied for the impregnation and cooling processes, the paper can either have just a surface coating or be completely saturated by the impregnating solution. The former is water repellent (water can permeate the paper to a certain degree) whereas the latter only has a small amount of wax on the surface and is watertight. Depending on the impregnating solution and method, the product can be manufactured according to its field of application: e.g. packaging for bread and sweets and razor blades.

Winding paper

This is millboard and is manufactured by winding one or more wet pulp webs onto a formatting roller.

Wood cardboard

A cardboard with light or grey lining layers manufactured mainly from mechanical pulp.

Wood-containing paper

Wood-containing paper contains more than 5 percent mechanical wood fiber. In addition to unbleached pulp, it mostly contains mechanical pulp > **Primary fiber** and/or > **recovered paper** pulp > **Secondary fiber**. The proportion of pulp, mechanical pulp and recovered paper pulp is varied according to use. Due to the fact that under the influence of light and oxygen, paper with a high wood content, such as newsprint, turns yellow quicker than woodfree paper, it is therefore mostly used for shortlived products. The wood content favourably influences the opacity of the paper. This reduces print from shining through when printing both sides of the paper.

Woodfree paper

Paper made of chemical pulp fiber. It can contain up to 5 percent mechanical pulp fiber.

Writing paper

Uncoated paper that is suitable for writing with ink on both sides. The written characters may not run or seep through. Writing paper, which is always sized and suitable for printing, may either be wood-containing or woodfree. Filler additives make the paper less transparent. In order not to impede the nib from gliding over the paper, the paper surface is often super-calendered (smoothed). Woodfree writing paper is especially diverse in its usage: formula paper for PC printers and copying paper, document reader paper, and woodfree writing paper > **Fine paper**.

Foto-Molerus
A 121
Wangen i.A.

Agfa Lupex

Agfa Lupex

Agfa Lupex

Agfa Lupex

8255

Agfa Lupex

Agfa Lupex

Agfa Lupex

Lith. Deutsch-Vorsatz

Lagerformat Tamaño en almacén } 60×78 cm Stock-Size 23¹/₂×30³/₄ ins.	LITHO GERMAN BOOKEND PAPER	PAPEL DE GUARDAS LITOGRAFIADO ALEMÁN

Gewicht — peso — weight
45 Kilo 1000 Bogen
45 „ 1000 hojas
100 lbs 1000 sheets

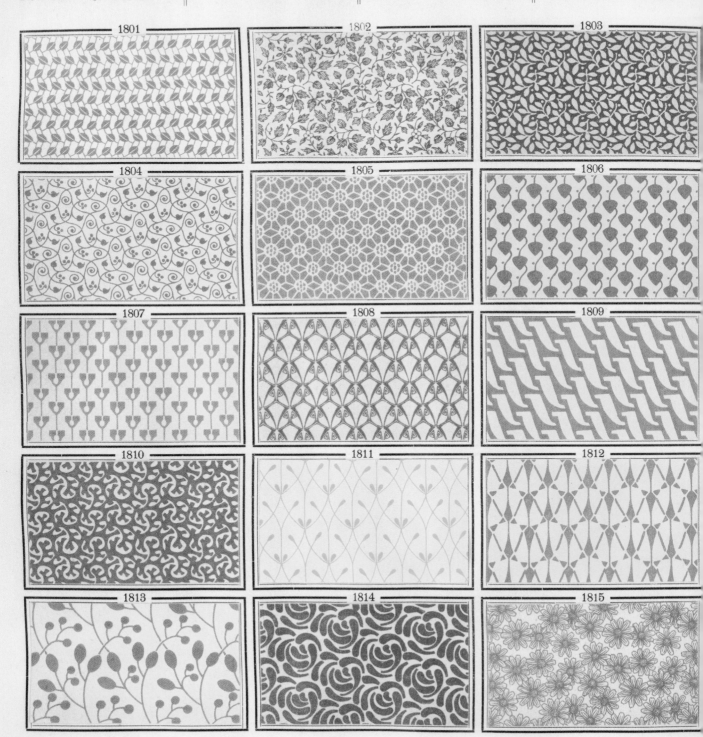

Colored Paper

For many of us the words 'colored paper' summon up all kinds of, usually positive, associations, often bringing back childhood memories of doing handicrafts with plain-colored glossy papers, sometimes ones that were already gummed on the back. Others may think of the many beautifully designed volumes of the *Insel-Bücherei* book series, which over the decades since its inception in 1912 featured ever-new variations of cover design. The dedicated book-lover will enjoy the descriptions in Arno Schmidt's novel *The Stone Heart* (*Das steinerne Herz*, 1956) in which Herr Eggers, a bibliomaniac who pursues all books with passion, finds in the attic of Frieda Thumann an old *Statistical Manual of the Kingdom of Hanover* (*Statistisches Handbuch des Königreichs Hannover*) with its gorgeous endpapers: "coffee-colored with blackish-reddish streaks around hundredfold-magnified starch granules."

Colored paper is a semi-finished product: it is designed and refined in separate, often multi-stage, processes. It is of great importance to the work of bookbinders: as cover papers they lend aesthetic and haptic qualities to cardboard covers; with a waxed or otherwise treated surface they can protect the interior of the book against moisture and dirt; as endpapers they are placed between the insides of the covers and the actual body of the book. Cover papers, carefully matched in terms of color, pattern and texture, may also be used to create accompanying slip cases, boxes or folders for maps and other supplements.

Beyond bookbinding proper, colored paper may also be used as cardboard packaging of all kinds for high-end consumer goods and luxury articles. Jewelry and toys, soaps and other perfumery products, Christmas tree decorations and cigars, playing cards and musical works all sell much better in accordingly embellished packaging. In the manufacturing of albums, an industry that burgeoned from 1860 on, there was a similarly great need for interestingly designed fancy papers, since there was a strong demand for the kind of individually customized and accessorized books in which one could keep photographs, postcards, devotional pictures, picture cards or stamps.

Brocade paper, negative printing plate, gold-colored embossing on light green ground. Pattern: floriated scrollwork with grapes. Published by Johann Michael Munck, Augsburg, c. 1730

Martin Engelbrecht, *Eine Gold und allerley gefärbtes und geprägtes Papiermacherin*, c. 1730.

In all these uses, glued-on colored papers served visually and haptically to enhance plain and often cheap support materials. The same was done for furniture, musical instruments and telescopes. Paste paper lining the drawers of a precious-wood veneered secretary or marbled paper covering a telescope tube, show the wide range of applications of various kinds of colored paper.

Craft, workshops, and industrial plants can be identified as different points of production for colored paper and each lend a distinct character to the paper they produce. Handcrafted paper produced with individual artistic ambition is often held up as a counterexample to lovelessly mass-produced industrial goods, but there is a second distinction to be made. Some types of colored paper require the creative process to start afresh with each new sheet of paper (think of paste or marbled papers), while for other types there are artists who create designs, engravers who create the printing plates for brocade papers, and printing blocks for calico or chintz paper, and finally factory workers, who produce print after print and color them with the aid of stencils. The colored-paper industry invested as much creativity as possible into the design stage and achieved impressive color variations. Through the use of a wide range of finishing technologies – coating, spraying, embossing, pressing, bronzing, varnishing, calendering, etc. – the big companies in the colored-paper industry were able to offer tens of thousands of different varieties in extensively structured assortments. Aschaffenburg was the center of this industry, which emerged around 1810; and it was there it found its demise in the 1960s.

It is possible to identify several reasons for the decline of the industrial manufacture of colored paper. Originally, it was the colored-paper industry that produced coated white glossy paper from white machine paper; now however, the paper-manufacturing industry itself has learned to build up an assortment of coated papers that can be sold as chromo and art paper. Over time, these paper varieties have been produced with such high-quality surface finishes that offset printers these days are able to apply completely uniform colored areas to them, and if need be varnish them. Further, by watching the colored-paper industry, modern packaging production has learned the many techniques that appeal to customers – embossing, metallic effects and so on. Enameled tin cans, for example, which used to compete fiercely with cardboard packaging, now often have to make way in turn for plastic packaging. And whenever interest in the tactile qualities of paper and cardboard increases, the paper-manufacturing industry meets the demand with carefully tailored products. Under these circumstances it is therefore not surprising that since around 1980 there has been a strong renewed interest in the traditional craft techniques of manufacturing colored papers.

Leather box from the mid-nineteenth century. The inside compartments are lined with various colored papers.

Block printed paper (calico paper), floriated scrollwork, black pre-printed on white ground, light green, red, yellow, and blue painted. Buntpapierfabrik Gottfried Philipp Wilhelm Leipzig, no date.

Block printed paper (calico paper), large floriated scrolls in negative print blue on white ground, Germany, c. 1800.

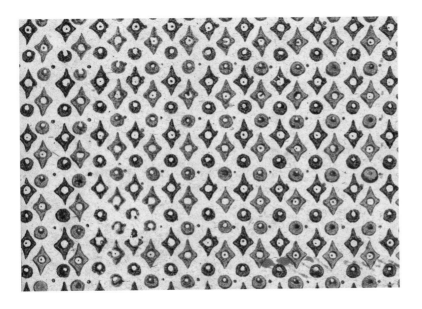

Block printed paper (calico paper), stars and dots red and blue on white ground, c. 1790.

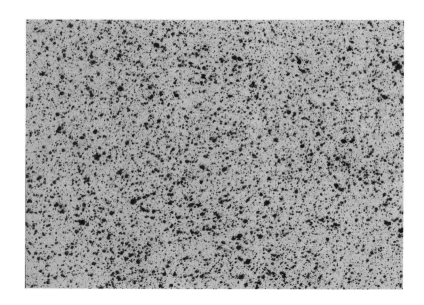

Speckled paper (plover marbled
papers), black on yellow ground,
France, c. 1800.

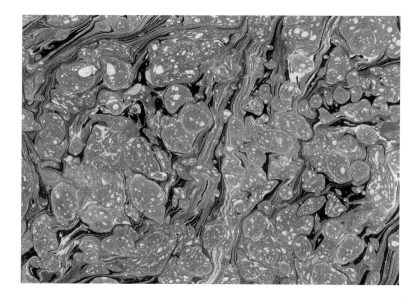

Multi-colored stone
marbled paper, c. 1840.

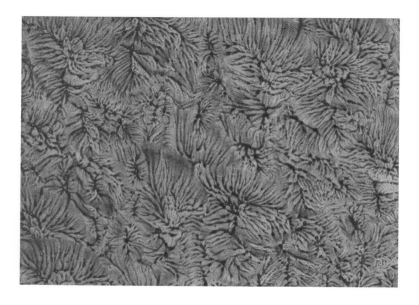

Veined paste paper,
monochrome, France, c. 1800.

At the same time, ambitious artistic and creative people are breaking new ground through the use of new coloring agents, modern tools and workshop equipment. Yet it is easier to keep alive techniques that require renewed creativity and a fresh start for each additional sheet. Plain-colored coated paste papers may serve as the starting point. While still wet, it is possible to displace the paint layer and introduce ornamentation with the appropriate tools. For example, through sprinkling with a screen and bristle brush one can create colored papers that are called plover marbled papers due to their resemblance to birds' eggs. In paste papers the paint may be applied with putty knives; this is one of the modern craft techniques that is completely without historical precedent. Stencils were already used in the manufacture of multi-colored brocade papers and in the coloring of 'dominotier' papers. Combining this with spraying

Left: Snail marbled paper, multi-colored, c. 1730.

Below: Fancy marbled paper (drawn using little sticks) in the colors carmine, light blue, grayish-green, yellow, and white, 1768.

techniques (or airbrushing) resulted in stencil-sprayed papers. Silk-screen printing as a modern porous printing process adds further enhancement to serial (including multi-color) printing and has yielded connections to old textile printing processes. Just as *indienne* printing used to require the manufacture of special printing blocks for each individual color, one can now print using multiple screens consecutively.

Still, marbled papers, whose dipping process allows for the manufacture of individual sheets, remain the starting point as well as the point of culmination. In the sixteenth century patterns were introduced to Europe from the Ottoman Empire and found their way into family albums. While the complicated manufacturing technique gained currency only slowly, the products came to be known as 'Turkish paper'. Today the original Turkish forms are internationally

Paste paper with brown-red-pink striped pattern by Franz Dathe, bookbinder in Leipzig, c. 1930.

known as 'ebru' and are just as prized as 'suminagashi,' the special Japanese form of paper marbling. Publications by experts such as Phoebe Jane Easton (*Marbling, a history and a bibliography*, 1983), Einen Miura (*The art of marbled paper*, 1989), and Richard J. Wolfe (*Marbled paper, its history, techniques and patterns*, 1990) have introduced a wider public to the great variety of different marbling techniques. And in the meantime a new generation of creatives has emerged who inspire people across national borders and oceans.

— *Frieder Schmidt*

Opposite: Paste paper with displacement décor on blue-painted ground, c. 1750.

Below: Paste paper with displacement décor by Hugo Ochmann, bookbinder in Leipzig, 1906.

Robakidse:
Kaukasische Novellen

83

Büchner: Dantons Tod

88

Holbein: Bildnisse

95

Carus: Über große Kunst

96

Vögel und Nester

100

DANTES NEUES LEBEN

101

Walther v. d. Vogelweide:
Gedichte und Sprüche

105

Rembrandt: Zeichnungen

108

Gunnarsson:
Der Königssohn

109

le Fort: Zwei Legenden

111

vollmoeller: Parcival

Poe: Erzählungen

129

Hofmannsthal: Alkestis

134

Droste-Hülshoff: Gedichte

139

Der Bamberger Dom

140

Charles Sealsfield: Die Prärie am Jacinto

141

Gide: Der verlorene Sohn

143

Meereswunder

158

Sibyllen und Propheten

165

Die Tempel von Paestum

170

Huch: Der letzte Sommer

172

Hebel: Schatzkästlein

177

Dumpfe Trommel

183

Cover Papers of the *Insel-Bücherei*

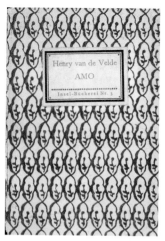

When the publisher Anton Kippenberg (1874–1950) sent out the first dozen volumes of the *Insel-Bücherei* book series in the summer of 1912 to find buyers and readers, he was well aware of the effect of the outer appearance of his books. This is evidenced by the bookmarks with publisher's advertising that were enclosed within the small volumes: written in capital letters under the image of a ship (Insel's publisher's mark) is the title of the series, '*Insel-Bücherei*'; then, separated by two lines, a line in italics informs us that "Each volume is ribbon-bound in a colored-paper cover 50 pfennigs."

The Insel publishing house was looking for a more sophisticated cover design than that usually found in hardcovers for its new series of books which, while reasonably priced, were nonetheless carefully typeset in selected fonts and printed on woodfree paper. To that end, Kippenberg drew on block-printed papers that were produced by Giuseppe Rizzi in Varese, in Lombardy, Northern Italy. Modeled on older Italian papers and distributed throughout Europe from around 1904, Rizzi's colored papers, which measured 40 × 50 cm and featured single-, two-, three- or multicolored patterns, were printed on cream-colored paper and smoothed.

On the basis of monochrome prototypes, Kippenberg developed a design concept for his book series. Since the original papers were too expensive for him to use and, moreover, would have produced too much waste per print sheet, Insel-Verlag reprinted the patterns with variations of its own. While the Italian patterns were produced with special glue paints and acquired their characteristic effect due to the viscosity of the aqueous block printing inks, the prototypes in Leipzig were reproduced with a process camera and then printed as duotone lithographs. As a result, the colors of the early *Insel-Bücherei* book covers were quite similar to the Italian models.

Accommodating four or eight copies, one print sheet allowed the respective number of cover papers to be produced in a single print cycle. In most cases the dimensions of the original were retained. Initially, the volumes of the *Insel-Bücherei* featured only a single title label, but soon spine labels were added. This allowed the use of different cover papers for the same title or of identical cover papers for different books.

With his concept of colored paper covers Kippenberg had adopted a course that allowed for rapid expansion of the book series: in 1912 it comprised twenty-seven titles; sixty-five additional titles were added in 1913 and again in 1914, and the series quickly became a mainstay of the publishing business.

Cover papers were increasingly produced with individual designs geared to the particular book. From a bibliophilic perspective this is quite understandable: text, typography, illustration, paper and cover should add up to a harmonized whole.

By the time of its 100th anniversary in 2012, the *Insel-Bücherei* series had reached the number 1365. Yet due to double and multiple allocations, the number of published titles is much higher. Numbers of poorly selling titles were first re-assigned in 1919.

Until 1945, all books were published in Leipzig; from 1945 until September 1960 some were also published in Wiesbaden and, from October 1960 on, in Frankfurt am Main. Between 1991 and 2009, the publisher's imprint read 'Insel Verlag Frankfurt am Main and Leipzig' and from 2010 on 'Insel Verlag Berlin'.

In 2001, the manufacturing documents related to the cover design at the Leipzig publishing location were donated to the German National Library. In the period from 1993 until 2002, Insel-Verlag drew on more than fifty colored paper samples from the Collection of Historical Papers at the National Library in Leipzig for its cover designs. It also uses colored papers designed by individual contemporary artists, notably the Hamburg-based artist Gisela Reschke. — *Frieder Schmidt*

Opposite: A selection of Insel book covers. The first Insel volumes with colored contents were printed in 1933 and, soon after, the first papers featuring imagery related to a book's contents were designed for book covers.

Right: Two book covers with papers created by Gisela Reschke.

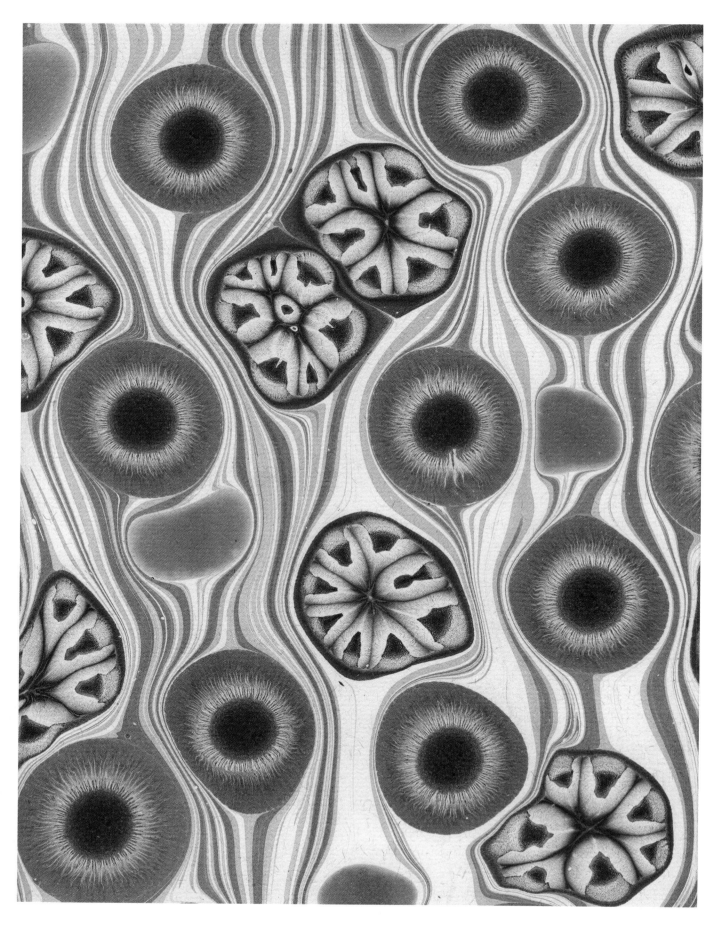

Marbled Paper

The art of marbling came from Japan, through the trade routes of the Silk Road to Iran and Turkey. In the sixteenth century, travelers from the East brought the first marbled papers to Europe, where the unusual style and forms of the graceful patterns gave rise to great interest. Scholars, such as Athanasius Kircher (1602–1680), described the processing of marbling, whose technique differed so much from anything previously known, as follows: "Ink is not applied directly on to the paper, rather is it dropped onto a viscous liquid. A floating layer of pigment is created, which is finally transferred on to a sheet of paper."

Unlike other paper-based trades in Europe, marbling was not considered a proper tradecraft, with its techniques very rarely being handed down from generation to generation. Time and time again, practice of the skills required would fall into obscurity, which in turn meant they needed to be rediscovered – usually through self-teaching. Standing in this tradition, Dirk Lange (b.1973), is one of the few, globally active professional marbled-paper makers. Fascinated by antiquarian book covers with marbled bindings and marbled endpapers, he began in 2008 to study this technique intensively. He learned his skills through contemporary and historical sources, but above all, through the constant search for the ideal composition of the marble base, dye and binding agents and, of course, the paper.

Dirk Lange is an artist, deeply rooted in his craft. He has not only mastered traditional marbling patterns, an area in which he is expert, but also goes beyond the conventional boundaries of marbled paper with his experimental works and free-hand, graphic designs. In 2013, a collaboration between Lange and the, artist Kerstin Brätsch (b. 1969) in their New York studio, resulted in the creation of large-formatted, marbled pictures, which were jointly exhibited at London's Serpentine Sackler Gallery and at Art Basel. Some of them were also acquired "with gratitude to the master marbler Dirk Lange" by MOMA, the Museum of Modern Art in New York. — *Julia Rinck*

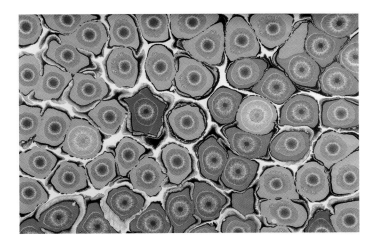

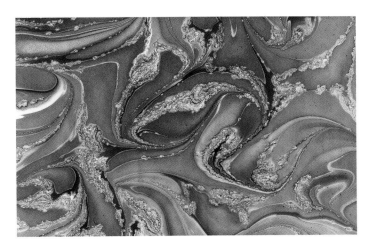

The handmade marbled papers Dirk Lange designs for bookbinderies and restoration workshops are created in a traditional manner using self-produced paints based on lightfast pigments on a gelatinous ground of Carrageen moss, gum tragacanth, or Pysillium seeds with paints.

A Collection of Painters' Books

Painters' books are limited-edition, numbered, signed, and exquisite bound books or loose portfolios by pre-eminent artists. They constitute a separate genre of artistic design, in contrast to which, for example, there are also 'artists' books' or 'book objects' whose outer forms no longer have to have anything in common with the familiar book and so play all the more creatively with alienated use.

Of the four thousand painters' books in the collection of the Herzog August Library in Wolfenbüttel, Germany, none is painted; they are all printed. But in what quality! By the best printers in the world, on paper from the most famous mills and bound by the imaginative cover designers to whom the artists have entrusted themselves.

The variety of creatively sophisticated and, indeed, even absurdly complex printing techniques – with original reproductions, etchings, lithographs, collages, ingenious folds and bindings for poems, stories, fairy tales, songs and epics – is astounding. And even more so is their presentation, conducive to silent contemplation,

in a spacious gallery with raised display cases, which ideally showcases the singular preciousness and sanctity of the painters' books.

The artists of the painters' books used the best quality specifications to create consummate masterpieces of aesthetic pleasure, down to every last detail. They have made the most wonderful books possible, created for viewers who are open to sensual experience: books that have become total works of art.

In the mid-1950s, stimulated by his friendly encounter with Jean Arp (1886–1966) in France, the then director of the library, Erhart Kästner (1904–1974), became acquainted with – and came to love – the so-called '*livres de peintres*' that were created in the context of the avant-garde art movement. With them he established a new collection at the baroque library in Lower Saxony, a sister institution of the Duchess Anna Amalia Library in Weimar, Thuringia.

Inspired by Anita Vogel (1924–2011), who was a pioneer in the field of paper conservation and would later become his wife, Kästner devised a unique mode of presentation for these painters' books in the conservation workshop that was equipped for this purpose. He was so enthusiastic about the sublime French printing and the quality of the book covers that, with

View of the collection of painters' books of the Herzog August Library in Wolfenbüttel, Germany, which comprises about four thousand volumes.

conservational aspects as well as the full enjoyment of users in mind, he had special luxurious cassettes designed for each painter's book. Due to the widely differing formats and volumes as well as the major conservational challenges the originals pose, none of these painters' books are standing on shelves; instead, they are all lying flat as they are stacked horizontally. To make this possible, the conservation workshop manufactured tailor-made cassettes of acid-free cardboard, which were covered with imaginatively designed colored paper. Stored inside these cassettes, the valuable painters' books were protected from light and shock and, most of all, were dust-free: ideal conditions in conservational terms. On the white spines of the cassettes the titles are printed uniformly in a noble Latina font, and in

this atmospheric and unusually inspiring hall, with its numerous temporary exhibitions they evoke a promised land of painters, sculptors, draftsmen, engravers, type founders, paper millers, book cover designers – an intimate book museum for emancipated voyeurs. Here it is all about the perfect form of all details in the collaboration of the hands involved – from the artist's conception to individual paper production to aesthetically sophisticated layout, to perfect printing technique to elegant binding: everything is meticulously coordinated and harmonious.
— *Thomas Wessel*

CREVEL · MIRÓ · BAGUE D' AURORE · 1957

FRÉMON · TÀPIES · GLEICHUNG / EQUATION · 1986

BRAQUE · LE TIR A L'ARC · 1960

CENDRARS · LÉGER · LA FINE DU MONDE · 1919

CARROLL · ERNST · DIE JAGD NACH DEM SCHNARK · 1968

The Monsterkamer

The *Monsterkamer* (The Sample Room) is an independent physical and digital platform for designers, publishers, and graphic professionals, which I founded in 2013. At our showroom in Amsterdam we display an extensive and regularly updated collection of paper, graphic materials and applications from Dutch and international companies, allowing quick access to the current samples of many paper producers and dealers in one place. We also offer consultations: anyone searching for the right paper, a printer, binder or graphic application for a professional design project in a print edition can make an appointment and will receive advice.

The *Monsterkamer* also organizes a comprehensive activity program to promote knowledge-sharing and collaboration: open-door events with speakers, company presentations, expert meetings, and student visits. Our own magazine on and about paper, *Plain Paper*, is released at the increasingly popular annual 'Plain Paper Party.'

Each issue of *Plain Paper*, edited in cooperation with the graphic designer, Philip Stroomberg, is produced on very different papers. 'The Surface Issue' of 2017, for example, contained the following papers: Circle Gloss, Colorplan, Curious Matter, DuO-Oktav, Elation, JAC Script, Microflute e-golf cardboard, Monnalisa/Natural Evolution Smooth, Multidesign Smooth, Munken Kristall Rough, Superfine and Wibalin Lite.

We work with the support of different paper producers and distributers, gathering professionals together to share and improve knowledge about paper. Thus *Monsterkamer* combines the physical experience of high-end print production with all advantages of a digital platform and networking. — *Esther Krop*

Events at *De Monsterkamer* featuring experts, here Sebastiaan Hanekroot (top) and Astrid Vorstermans (bottom).

Opposite: Colored papers photographed by Justina Nekrašait for *De Monsterkamer*.

The Graphic Paper Trade

In the general paper trade, producers (paper mills or paper factories) supply paper to the wholesaler in sheet form. The supplier then has two tasks to fulfil: to store his stock and to distribute it to paper processors, printers and the retail trade. As a consequence, wholesalers are well placed to guarantee a certain depth and variety of assortment, to provide a wide range of different paper grades and to ensure an organized distribution of products through their own logistics systems.

Paper processing, on the other hand, is about the production of various end products made of paper, such as note pads, booklets or envelopes. These goods are then passed on to retailers, such as traditional stationery shops.

Supplies to printing companies are made according to demand after extensive consultations for certain production requirements, such as paper rolls for large book and magazine print-runs or sheet formats for smaller or specialized books.

In the last hundred years, the market has faced great challenges and changed as a result. This was, of course, due in part to the two world wars, but above all due to transformations in technology, new customer demand, as well as changes in the nature of the product itself. Until recently, paper consumption had increased massively in spite of, or even as a result of, digitization. The introduction of smartphones and tablets together with the intensive use of the internet have changed the behavior of commercial and private consumers. This resulted in a sharp decline in the sale of graphic papers, and its demise is yet likely.

With the proliferation of individual printing devices in print shops, offices and private households, the customer base and paper requirements have changed, too. Today, customers are less likely to visit a print shop because the majority of people own a small-to-medium-sized digital printing device: all they really need is the 'printer' or photocopy paper. Wholesalers continue to offer this kind of paper in ever-shrinking selling units. It is usually cut to size by the paper manufacturers before being packaged and placed on pallets. Wholesalers, nowadays, are distributing such paper goods as and when required directly to the end user, and also to stationery and office supply shops or supermarkets and progressively more and more to online retailers. When looking for a good selection of copying papers, there are specialized retailers and even online shops that offer a wide assortment. Although wholesalers still supply to printing companies, much of the demand is now increasingly being met by the paper manufacturers themselves.

— *Heinrich Spies*

Images of paper and stationery businesses in London, Berlin, Vienna, and Munich.

Paper
as
Medium

Blick ins Rinken
Bezugspunkt des Blicks wurde der
Aufklärung, einem Blickpunkt.

Was ist Aura?

Die Erfahrung der Aura beruht auf der Übertragung einer in der menschlichen Gesellschaft geläufigen Reaktionsform auf das Verhältnis der Natur zum Menschen. Der Angesehene oder angesehen sich Glaubende pflegt den Blick aufzuschlagen, erwidert in seinem Blick. Die Aura einer Erscheinung oder eines Wesens erfahren, heißt, ihn mit dem Vermögen antworten, einem Blick aufzuschlagen, belehnen. Diese Vermögen ist voller Poesie. Wo ein Mensch, ein Tier oder ein Unbelebtes solches seinem Blick seiner erwar aufschlägt, zieht es uns zunächst in die Ferne. Sein Blick träumt, zieht uns seinem Träume nach. Aura ist Erscheinung einer Ferne so nah sie sein mag. Worte selbst haben ihre Aura; Kraus hat sie besonders genau beschrieben: "Je näher man ein Wort ansieht, desto ferner blickt es zurück."

Soweit Aura in der Welt ist noch träumen ist. Aber so erwachte Augen erblickt nicht die durch den Blicken, wenn der Traum sich in ihm erloschen ist. Im Gegenteil: dann ist wird sein Blick wirklich unwidersteh. Es hat auf, dass Blick der Geliebten auch zu sehen, indem Blick des Geliebten ist Erfa

Literature, Writing, and Paper

Paper is not just the most important means of passing down literary texts but also, I contend, its most important consistent inspiration. Paper generally is the first and last thing the writer faces, regardless of whether it is blank or already written on, white or colored, fragrant or malodorous, a single sheet, a notebook, or a stack, a site of creation or a sign of the opposite.

Bill Watterson's cartoon character Calvin shows Hobbes, his stuffed tiger, a blank white cube: "It's a writer's block! You put it on top of your desk and then you can't write there anymore!" The writing block is rendered tangible here.

Paper along with its precursors (such as stone, wood, and wax tablets, palm leaves, and papyri), its digital versions (the formats of a page), and its larger manifestations (canvas, wallpaper, wall, street) is the material equivalent of leisure as an idea: the epitome of freedom, a sign that all possibilities are still open, an instrument of delaying and slowing down, and also therefore, in the case of writer's block, in and of itself too demanding. Paper is a space of downtime but not necessarily a full, fulfilled, and happy time.

Anyone like me, whose job entails reading literature in its ephemeral, aggregate state in archives more often than in books, cannot overlook the significance of paper. Hence I would like to highlight some of paper's inspirational qualities. I have chosen to scratch the surface of many things and examine in-depth only a few. The headings I have used, (white paper, watermarks, scrap paper etc.), serve less the purpose of analysis than the aim of showing: of presenting the object along with the thesis. Namely, that paper is the most important consistent inspiration of literature and the only space of leisure we can describe and study in detail, because we hold it, preserved, in our hands.

Walter Benjamin, "Was ist Aura?" ("What, then, is aura?"), draft for *The Artwork in the Age of Mechanical Reproduction* on a piece of paper advertising San Pellegrino mineral water.

White Paper

According to Lothar Müller in his 2014 book *White Magic: The Age of Paper*, the white sheet of paper "waits to be covered with writing, numbers, drawings, and as a symbolic form it moves into the center of modern authorship. [It is] the metaphor of the concept of the original, the site of writing *in actu*, the symbolic source from which authorship unfolds [...] not just the site of production but an organic component of it."[1]

The same holds true for the visual arts where, since the Renaissance, it is often paper on which the originality of an artist proves itself: just a few lines or dabs and splotches suffice to provoke genius and demonstrate what is behind an idea. The drawing, which needs the space the paper gives it as setting and as productive filling, as blank space, now emancipates itself from the function of the study or sketch and is no longer a template for the translation into larger-scale grand art.

Plato compares our memory to a blank wax tablet. As Socrates explains in *Theaetetus*: "There is in our souls a block of wax, in one case larger, in another smaller, in one case the wax is purer."[2]

The mind is like a white page. John Locke (1632–1704) introduces this metaphor at the very beginning of his 1690 *Essay Concerning Human Understanding*: "All ideas come from sensation or reflection. Let us then suppose the mind to be, as we say, white paper, void of all characters, without any ideas."[3] Locke's metaphor of the mind was quickly developed to encompass more, for it can be taken literally as well: paper itself is a space of experience rather than just imagination.

In 1895, Mallarmé portrayed the night sky as a counterpart to paper: "You noted, one does not write, luminously, on a dark field; the alphabet of stars alone does that, sketched or interrupted; man pursues black upon white."[4]

In August 1917, Rilke, in preparing a transcript as a gift, put asterisks under each of his six selected *Poems to the Night (Gedichte an die Nacht)* – little stars in the squared charting field of the six sheets, because after each poem another one is added and before each poem the last asterisk count is repeated. In the end there are six of them,[5] the same number one tends to see of the Pleiades, the constellation of the poets, in the sky. The poetic image materializes on the paper: the *Poems to the Night* resembles the night.

Ever since Seneca, the sky has been the classic topos of leisure: origin and object as well as defense of leisure. Seneca's definition of leisure laid the philosophical ground for all explorations of paper space, regardless of whether a god dictated the writing on it or a mind pours itself out over it; whether we are bent over a white sheet of paper waiting for the first sentence, or whether we know, with Cicero's smiling augur, that we let our imagination see things in the paper that are not there. Paper is the ideal aesthetic space of

All quotes not otherwise referenced below are transcriptions of the original texts in the holdings of the German Literature Archive in Marbach; all other mentioned objects not specifically referenced also belong to the Marbach holdings.

1 Lothar Müller, *Weisse Magie. Die Epoche des Papiers* (Munich, 2012), p. 127. Published in English as *White Magic: The Age of Paper* (Polity, 2014), trans. Jessica Spengler.
2 Plato, *Theaetetus*, 191c–e; trans. Harold N. Fowler in *Plato in Twelve Volumes*, vol. 12 (Cambridge, MA/London, 1921).
3 John Locke, *An Essay Concerning Human Understanding* (London, 1836), p. 51.
4 Stéphane Mallarmé, quoted in English by Barbara Johnson, "Is Writerliness Conservative?" In *A World of Difference* (Baltimore, 1987), pp. 20–30.
5 Illustrated in Deutsches Literaturarchiv Marbach (ed.), *Ordnung. Eine unendliche Geschichte*, Marbacher Katalog no. 61 (Marbach a. N., 2007), p. 176.

contemplation, on the razor's edge between reality and dream, with a tendency toward the mock-up and the backdrop, toward tinkering and bricolage, and the result of a very mundane, chemical, technical, creative process.

For centuries, marginalia and inserted white pages have been to the book what the traditional left correction column is to the manuscript. The latter sometimes takes up an entire half of the paper and it is more densely written by many authors than the actual text column: port of entry for flights of spontaneity; space for the reader as writer; place of scrutiny and of undermining; room for ideas.[6]

Paper can mark what hasn't even been written yet and as a preliminary architectural design it does something similar. It narrows down, it defines a volume, and it relieves one of questions one doesn't even have an answer to yet. It is an outline and a model, a place giver and place holder. Hölderlin (1770–1843) uses *keimwörter* or germinal words and open spaces to stake out the space of a poem on paper.[7]

In their manuscripts of *Wallenstein* and *Faust*, Schiller (1759–1805) and Goethe (1749–1832) leave open spaces where they still want to add or elaborate; both obliterate these with a squiggle and, in doing so, prevent them from being distorted if they are not needed after all.

Watermarks

Hölderlin who sometimes scratched his verses into window glass and, using a pen without ink, into paper,[8] used a sheet of paper with a watermark most likely produced in France for a double page of his revolution-era novel *Hyperion*: Sallust's words *"pro patria libertate"* (freedom for our country) surround a Phrygian cap.[9]

The paper Walter Benjamin (1892–1940) used to write his memoir *Berlin Childhood around 1900* included thin, translucent sheets of papers bearing the watermark "extra strong" which, when placed on top of one another, amount to a palimpsest. He probably carefully removed the sheets from a copybook bound only in the middle by two stitches and then cut them on the left side and folded them to have a marginal column for changes. Cutting, separating, folding and unfolding, smoothing, cutting off, and discarding: these are the actions that, in this case, preceded the writing and, perhaps, also accompanied it. What the text seeks to call up before the eye again is tested with, and on, paper.

The paper Friedrich Schiller picked for several letters in which he elaborated on his aesthetics is virtually pervaded by watermarks: on the outside bordered by a curved line, and on the inside featuring the image of a musician playing a flute to charm his bear. On this paper he wrote: "The artist, especially the poet, never addresses the real, only the ideal or elements artfully chosen from a real subject." The white page with its watermarks seems to aid with abstraction, help with finding ideas, and facilitate idealization. The paper offers

6 This byway of writing was the subject of a special exhibition in Marbach whose catalog is still available: Deutsches Literaturarchiv Marbach (ed.), *Randzeichnungen. Nebenwege des Schreibens*, Marbacher Magazin no. 129 (Marbach a. N., 2010), pp. 11–63.

7 Friedrich Beissner made the organic metaphor of the germinal word a leitmotif of his edition of Hölderin's complete works (*Grosse Stuttgarter Ausgabe*): the poems unfold from them and the free space they stake out. More than forty years later, Dieter Burdorf introduced the concept of the landscape to describe the spaces that are created on paper in this way: Dieter Burdorf, "Der Text als Landschaft. Eine topographische Lektüre der Seiten 73 bis 76 des Homburger Foliohestes," in Uwe Beyer (ed.), *Neue Wege zu Hölderlin* (Würzburg, 1994), pp. 113–41. A characteristic example of this is Hölderlin's hymn to "Tinian" reproduced here: Deutsches Literaturarchiv Marbach (ed.), Der Wert des Originals, Marbacher Magazin no. 148 (Marbach a. N., 2014), n. p.

8 Wolfram Groddeck, "Friedrich Hölderlin: Unsichtbare Verse," in Martina Stercken and Christian Kiening (eds.), *SchriftRäume. Dimensionen von Schrift zwischen Mittelalter und Moderne* (Zürich, 2008), p. 388.

9 Illustrated in *Ordnung*, p. 146.

resistance to the pen; in Schiller's case the pen probably scratched as the wavy line was not drawn in a casual and free motion but, rather, with effort and haltingly.

Accompanied by all kinds of curved lines of beauty, the first complete edition of Laurence Sterne's *Tristram Shandy* (1763) features three text-free pages: a white page, a black one, and a marbled one that carries its watermark on the outside, as it were, making it the most prominent example of the way in which literary texts of the eighteenth century used open, yet defined, spaces to create a special space of experience for the reader even in the printed book.

Late-eighteenth-century literature and written culture abounds with poetic watermarks, ornaments, and arabesques that are infused with whim, wit, imagination, and reverie as well as with more gushing and encroaching flows of emotion, which invariably means leisure: though no longer necessarily with calm. The paper and the pen help write the manuscript, the text, and help form the thought and the expression.

Epistolary culture – and, after and alongside it, the most successful literary genre of the time, the novel – depends on paper to help give rise to the far-reaching unspeakable emotions and incommensurable thoughts written and almost poured onto it; on its ability to keep the act of creating text visible and thus pass it on to the reader; and, moreover, on being the perfect space to reflect on those processes. Paper as writing and material for the imagination, as a space of experience and contemplation is invariably also meta-paper. Deliberate cut-offs, omitted passages marked by dashes of varying length and width, ellipses indicated by asterisks and squiggles and secret signs, shifting handwriting, colored papers, small or large paper sizes, seals and watermarks – all of it speaks. To the reader it speaks mimicry of the writer and to the writer a partner in dialog, instigator, and reference of the world in his mind.

Paper Formats

Gottfried Benn wrote his poem *Ein Wort* ('A Word,' 1941) on a white card, within the exact dimensions of 5.6 × 3.6 in.[10] He started out in a vertical format, "A word, / A phrase—:", and then turned the card and wrote across its width:

> A word, A phrase—: from cyphers rise
> life recognized, a sudden sense,
> the sun stands still, mute are the skies,
> and all compacts it, stark and dense.
> A word—, A gleam, A flight, a spark,
> A thrust of flames, A stellar trace—,
> and then again – immense – the dark
> 'round world and I in empty space.

10 Illustrated in *Ordnung*, p. 140.

Gottfried Benn began his poem
Ein Wort (1941) on a vertical page
but rotated it to reflect the line of
the poem.

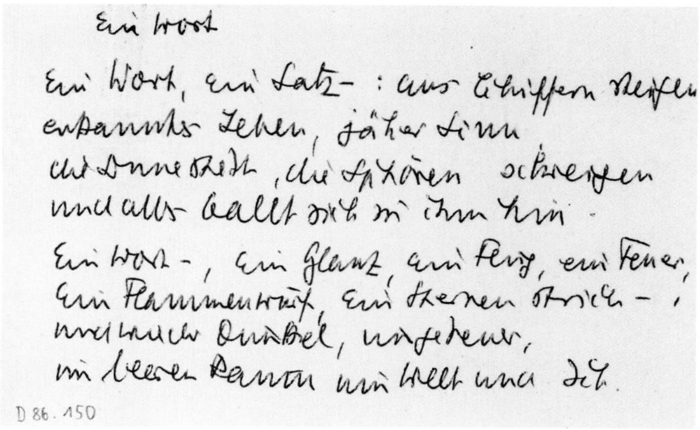

By shifting from the short to the long line, Benn softens the impact of
the opening phrase and writes against its power which becomes literally visible in a writing error: "A word—, A gleam, A flight, a spark."
The spell of its initial character, the upper-case A, is broken only at
the very end of the fifth line when the indefinite article becomes a
lower-case, prosaic 'a.' With this case shift, Benn increases the fric-
tional resistance the verse form offers to everyday language and
widens the free space around the poem. In art and literature, as well
as in the humanities and sciences, the twentieth century develops
paper into a site of open but controlled thinking and cold-stored
material. In the process, the paper as leisure space is increasingly
understood as laboratory space.

Overfilling and underfilling are two sides of the creative approach
to paper, while regularity suggests prose and lack of inspiration. The
only time an even writing on paper stands for the opposite – for
enthusiasm and craziness, rapture and spontaneity, extreme states
of inner or outer distress – is when it occurs on irregular formats:
huge tableaux and construction plans such as those found in the
work of Hubert Fichte (1935–1986);[11] or endless forms such as the

11 Illustrated in *Ordnung*,
p. 118, and in Deutsches
Literaturarchiv Marbach
(ed.), *Schicksal. 7*7 unhinter-*
gehbare Dinge, Marbacher
Magazin no. 135 (Marbach
a. N., 2011), pp. 53 f., 152.

continuous, almost forty-foot-long and just 4.3-inch-wide roll of taped-together individual pieces of paper on which De Sade wrote his *120 Days of Sodom* (1785) in the Bastille;[12] or the 37 meters of thin paper on which Jack Kerouac typed *On the Road* (1957).

Color and Patterned Paper

Not just the sky and other 'primeval forms,' the sun and stars and snow, but the moon, too, becomes, from the eighteenth century on, a natural counterpart of the white page. It has so many faces and colors that Friedrich Kittler (1943–2011), starting in the 1970s, excerpted hundreds of references to moon colors on usually orange index cards. Though lined, Kittler typed on them without adhering to any lines and so they are not always easy to read.[13]

What you write upon is the closest and nearest in the melting pot of the imagination which thereupon seeks to be set in motion. In 1988, Robert Gernhardt (1937–2006) described the Brunnen brand of exercise books in which he wrote for thirty years as, "more authentic than pictures and books, because they are pure movement and no arrival – no matter where or for what the movement is directed."

"Resist the temptation of leaving no trace." In the late 1980s Elfriede Jelinek (b. 1946) sent out provocative pink-colored, lined index cards which each had a die-cut slit reminiscent of a vagina in the middle and the following printed on them: "Caution: nothing comes to mind. Write here in my place that I give you! Please do not press too hard with the tool!" The paper entices one to not just discover metaphors but also to take them seriously and realize them. But even if writing has, on occasion, been compared to the act of penetration – think of the proverbial 'blank' and 'written-on' sheets – paper is merely the writing surface and not the female body.

W. G. Sebald (1944–2001) wrote his stories in large part on lined DIN A4 sheets, by hand, and repeatedly copying out the beginnings of sheets in order to retain – despite changes and variations – the semantic side-view mirror and let first words on the page be first words. When Sebald used unlined sheets, they are usually defined by something. For instance, the sheet on which he practiced the signature of Ambrose Adelwarth had previously been typed on with an almost empty ink ribbon. "*Seufzer*," or "sigh," is the only word that is clearly legible.[14] To Sebald the philologist, paper is the carrier of infinitely many and deep marks that he himself in large part etched into it and invented. It is the surface on which intertextuality can be thought of as three-dimensional space and on which text, sound, and image come together, as if paper were the less-than-idyllic, quite excruciating, yet inspiring counterpart to the *locus amoenus* where Plato (in *Phaedrus*) has the cicadas – the daughters of Mnemosyne – sing.

12 Illustrated in Deutsches Literaturarchiv Marbach (ed.), *Kassiber. Verbotenes Schreiben*, Marbacher Katalog no. 65 (Marbach a. N., 2012), p. 110.
13 Heike Gfrereis and Ellen Strittmatter, "Lemma: *Mondfarben*," in Deutsches Literaturarchiv Marbach (ed.), *Zettelkästen. Maschinen der Phantasie*, Marbacher Katalog no. 66 (Marbach a. N., 2013), n. p.; see also Heike Gfrereis, "Clockwork Orange. Friedrich Kittlers Mondfarbenkartei," in *Zeitschrift für Ideengeschichte* 10 (2016), pp. 97–106.
14 *Der Wert des Originals*, n. p.

Scrap Paper

In 1935, Walter Benjamin wrote down his first thoughts on 'aura' on a scrap of paper that features the red star logo of San Pellegrino mineral water. His famous definition is found right at the end of the first paragraph on this piece of paper: "The unique apparition of a distance, however near it may be. Words themselves have an aura. … What is beheld or believes itself beheld looks up." By incorporating the San Pellegrino logo Benjamin literally gives his text starry eyes.[15]

Hermann Hesse and Ludwig Wittgenstein had already discovered the appeal of using paper as a counterpart, and of writing against the world by having two different texts on a sheet run toward one another. In 1916, when the twenty-seven-year-old Wittgenstein, at the time serving as a forward observer in Galicia, continued writing his first longer philosophical text, the *Tractatus logico-philosophicus,* (which he had started before the war), he wrote the notes for it in the front pages of his notebook, while keeping a diary in the back. On July 29, the two entries came face to face with one another. On the *Tractatus* side we read: "For it is a fact of logic that wanting does not stand in any logical connection with its own fulfilment. And it also clear that the world of the happy man is a *different* world from the world of the unhappy"; and on the diary side: "Yesterday I was shot at. I was scared! I was afraid of death. I now have such a desire to live. And it is difficult to give up life when one enjoys it."[16]

Lots of Paper

The home of Friederike Mayröcker (b. 1924) is the epitome of the poet's apartment built of paper and covered with writing. "In the famous hothouse of her apartment on Zentagasse in Vienna, sheets of paper have overgrown everything; read books pile up, notes stick in the cracks of the furniture, and anyone who has ever set foot in her legendary abode, or is at least familiar with it from pictures, knows that this is not chaos needing hoarder-counseling but, rather, a poetic state."[17]

Paper gives words their place of creation and impact and, even though filled, bestows on them the space that Gottfried Benn, in his 1951 lecture on *Problems of Poetry,* ironically defined as that which, at first glance, gives away the genre: "When you open your newspaper on a Sunday morning, and sometimes also during the week, you will find in a supplement, usually on the top right or bottom left of the page, something that stands out due to the spaced out typeface and special framing: it is a poem."[18]

Set in brevier and indented, quotations in academic articles stand out by the same means and immediately give away that someone else, a more original text, is speaking here and that different rules apply in terms of space and time. Heinz Schlaffer (b. 1939) interprets the way poetry wastes paper – "a large font, antiquated or

15 Sabine Gölz, "Aura di San Pellegrino. Anmerkungen zu Benjamin-Archiv Ms. 931" in Daniel Weidner and Sigrid Weigel (eds.), *Benjamin-Studien 1* (Paderborn, 2008), pp. 209–228. Illustrated in *Der Wert des Originals,* n. p. The document is kept in the Walter Benjamin Archive of the Academy of Arts in Berlin. The exhibition catalog *Walter Benjamins Archive. Bilder, Texte und Zeichen,* ed. by Ursula Marx (Frankfurt a. M., 2006), offers additional examples of the interplay of paper and writing.

16 The *Tractatus* notes are found in *Notebooks 1914–1916,* ed. by G. H. von Wright and G. E. M. Anscombe, with an English translation by G. E. M. Anscombe (Chicago, 1984), p. 77e. Wittgenstein diary is kept at Trinity College in Cambridge: MS 103, July 27, 1916; quoted in English by Ray Monk, *Wittgenstein: The Duty of Genius* (London, 1990), p. 146.

17 Paul Jandl, "Wonne! Euphorie! Ekstase! Mayröcker!," in *Welt Online,* December 20, 2014, http://www.welt.de/kultur/literarischewelt/article135583369/Wonne-Euphorie-Ekstase-Mayroecker.html (accessed January 25, 2018).

18 Gottfried Benn, "Einige Probleme der Lyrik," in *Prosa 4, Sämtliche Werke,* vol. 6, ed. by Gerhard Schuster and Holger Hof (Stuttgart, 2001), pp. 9–44

Friederike Mayröcker in her appartment in Vienna, c. 2010.

self-designed fonts, expensive paper, waste of blank space" – as an "optical equivalent to the traditional acoustic quality of poetry, to rhythm and melody."[19] A reminder of the poem's original functions, prayer, incantation, singing, and dance, ceremony and celebration, discourse with gods and spirits.

Franz Kafka's desk had too much paper lying on it. In the Christmas of 1910, the desk becomes the subject of a huge list: "In this pigeon-hole lie old papers I'd have thrown away long ago if I had a wastepaper basket. Pencils with broken points, an empty match-box, a paperweight from Carlsbad, a ruler with an edge bumpier than a country road, collar studs, blunt razor-blades (the world has no place for them), tie-clips and another heavy iron paperweight."[20]

As if aiming to get this chaos on, and in, his desk under control with an apotropaic format, Kafka used primarily bound sheets for his texts: notebooks of two sizes called *quarthefte* (quarto) and *oktavhefte* (octavo). Yet at the same time he would cross the boundaries of the format by simultaneously writing in multiple notebooks, working on different works, and writing from back to front. Yet he didn't stick to this pure, instantaneous and pneumatic movement for very long, instead taking the notebooks apart to bring the different parts of a project together and thus have an overview again, which then would bring everything to a halt: the 161 surviving pages of *The Trial* came from ten notebooks and, when rearranged, were combined in sixteen bundles of papers on which Kafka then worked

19 Heinz Schlaffer, *Geistersprache. Zweck und Mittel der Lyrik* (Munich, 2012), p. 190.
20 Franz Kafka, *Diaries 1910–1923* (New York, 1988), p. 88.

no longer. "My novel! The night before last I declared myself utterly defeated by it. It is falling apart, and I can no longer contain it," he wrote to Felice Bauer on January 26, 1913. Kafka uses spatial metaphors: "contain" and "falling apart." The removing and arranging of the paper is a substitute action, because what works for paper does not work for the space of the novel. The fictional world is far too large and wide to allow it to be grasped like this.

It needs novelists rather than poets, writers who are able to disregard the paper space and the characters. Accordingly, it is a prose writer, Romain Gary (1914–1980), to whom we owe this gloomy prediction: "For the next Flood God will use paper rather than water."

— *Heike Gfrereis*

The Letter as a Folded Artifact

Letters are media of written exchange between people who – usually due to distance – cannot talk to each other in person and therefore put on paper what they would like to say. Since letters tend to be of a private nature, at least when they are not 'open letters', they are folded and sealed to protect them from prying eyes.

The two letters presented below, however, are neither part of a private correspondence nor public statements. Rather, they are folded works of art in the form of letters. The first such complex and medially structured single-leaf prints were created *c.*1600. They came into their viewers' hands as folded paper, which had to be unfolded in successive stages to gradually reveal their contents. By coordinating a sequence of images they become *folded montages:* picture stories in which the process of unfolding itself is linked to the twists and turns of the content. Occasionally, this results in optical trickery and illusion. The texts incorporated into the pictures elucidate the stories, and at the same time moderate the process of opening which goes hand in hand with the discovery of something hidden: in semantic terms, 'unfolding' is associated with a cognitive process and staged as a play with meaning.

To view the letters one must invariably handle them, straining the fragile material of such sensitive artworks. This is why few specimens survive. The examples from the collection of Werner Nekes (1944–2017) presented here are probably from the Netherlands and date from around 1700. They appear to be woodcuts that were subsequently colored. Measuring only about 6 cm × 7 cm when folded, they can be enlarged to a size of about 19 cm × 15 cm in four folding movements.

1,2] The inscription of the first example explicitly identifies the print as a letter: "A Letter / Written to all the amorous / elderly," (*Een Brief / Geschreven aan al de verliefde / ouden*) (1). It is addressed to the elderly who pursue the temptations of physical love and indulge in lust, thereby making fools of themselves. The reverse shows King David (2) who distinguished himself not only as the poet of psalms and love songs, but also achieved inglorious notoriety for sending

1

2

3

4

the husband of Bathsheba to war and taking advantage of his death, which was thus brought about, to indulge his own desires (2 Samuel 11–12). How "evil lust" could ensnare even an otherwise so honorable man, and what the consequences of indulging in it are is, as the text explains, "illustrated on the next sheet", that is, revealed in the process of unfolding.

3,4] When the reverse is folded down (3), it reveals a view of a castle or palace complex with a park in front of it. As a result of this movement, the figure of King David now appears on a balcony from which he gazes over the entire pictorial space and especially at Bathsheba who is bathing by a fountain below. The view combines the lower half of the image with the upper part that has not yet been unfolded. The image of the balustrade conceals the material break and interconnects not just the two settings of the image, but also the two layers of the folded montage. The next step involves folding up the upper part (4) to develop the scene underneath: King David has descended to a terrace and kneels in front of Nathan who rebukes him as told in the Bible.

5,6] After this, the piece of paper should be turned from the vertical to a horizontal position and again be folded up (5). This offers a first view of the inner part of the letter, i.e. the other side of the print serving as the basis for the folded montage, which shows an elderly couple ardently turning to one another. In reference to the Fall of Man from Paradise, the woman holds an apple as a symbol of seduction. In a final step the lower part needs to be folded down, which causes the idyll of togetherness to be complemented in the lower half of the image by symbols from the iconography of mortality: an open grave, a tombstone, a dead cupid, a scythe, a shovel and a skeleton. The text encapsulates the moral of the story: "This is the despicable end of that deranged love." Anyone squandering his life like this ought to change his ways, turn to God and do penance. Initially buried in the depth of the folds and revealed through unfolding, the meaning lies in the wisdom therein: that ripe old age should not be deceived by the temptations of physical desire, that the thrill of earthly love is subject to the decay of the earthly body, and ultimately only the Christian promise of salvation brings redemption. Thus it is an illustration of the baroque concept of *vanitas*.

6

5

1

2

3

4

Whereas the first letter explicitly addresses a particular group of people, the second one, in opening with the words "A Letter / to You, Oh Man" (*Een Brief / Aan û ô Mens*) appeals to all members of the human race (1). The letter's content is meant to show the way to attain eternal life or, alternatively, end in hell. The reverse shows a view of the city of Sodom with a cut across the middle (2). This folded montage is inspired by the story of Lot who refused to hand over the two angels sent to him by God to the citizens of Sodom, who wanted to molest them shamelessly (Genesis 19). To protect his heavenly visitors, he offered his two virgin daughters to the Sodomites in their place. When the citizens insisted on having the angels delivered up to them, God intervened. He struck the raging mob with blindness, so that Lot might flee with his family and the angels. This is the moment to which the scene represented here refers. While the group of figures – dominated by a blue angel – in front of the entrance to the house on the left-hand side of the image are depicted whole, some of the residents of Sodom in the center of the picture are only hinted at by their lower halves, indicating that this is not a finished picture but one that needs to be modified and transformed through unfolding.

1, 2] If one turns the upper part of the reverse first, the previously bisected figures are completed over the cut, while the angel on the left, who in the first layer had been depicted full-length, now has a grotesquely enlarged head sitting on his legs: another indication that the image is still in transition and the lower part also needs to be turned down(3).

3, 4] When unfolded, the cityscape has turned into a landscape showing Lot and his daughters fleeing with the angels (4). Sodom is in flames due to divine destruction. Between the protagonists and the backdrop of the city in the distance we see Lot's wife as a figure frozen into a pillar of salt. As in the first letter, this narrow vertical view must be turned horizontally and opened upward, causing an abrupt shift from the scene as it had been developed up to this point, and displaying a new image that introduces the moral of the story.

5

6

5, 6] The inner side shows a praying woman, whose garb perhaps suggests the habit of a nun, and a man in a high-spirited, almost dance-like pose, who is holding a drinking vessel. The juxtaposition of the two figures is to be understood as a confrontation of two diverging attitudes: religious devotion versus hedonism. The discrepancy between the two is further reinforced, as the impression is created that the man has just left a gaming table where his cronies are still gathered in play. When in a final step the lower part of the image is folded down, the scene once again goes through a change, concluding thus as a cautionary tale: while the nun ascends to heaven on a cloud surrounded by angels, her antagonist is pulled into the maw of a monster by a devilish figure.

In both letters, the play with folds proves to be highly artificial and calculated with regard to the montage of the imagery they contain. What is fascinating about the folded montages is how effectively the material process of unfolding and the development of content are coordinated. The fact that they involve relatively simple folding of a plain sheet of paper pointedly relates semantically to the clear messages: the realization that earthly life and love is finite, that only a way of life agreeable to God promises salvation, and that he who allows himself to be dazzled by surfaces, rather than looking behind the scenes through unfolding, falls victim to deception. Similar folded montages remained popular until the first decades of the nineteenth century, which while differing in pictorial content, were closely related in their structure and ambition.
— *Christoph Benjamin Schulz*

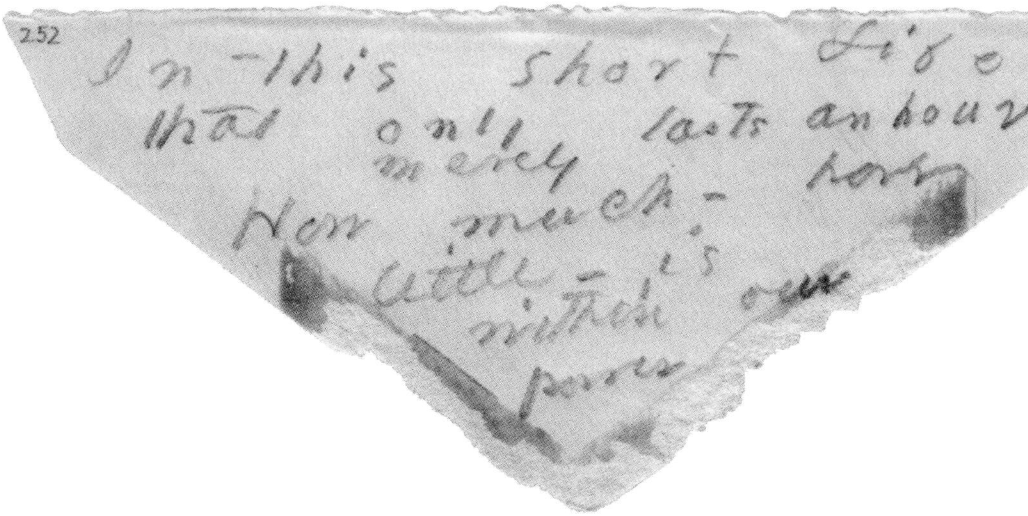

In this short life
that only lasts an hour
merely
How much - how
little - is
within our
power

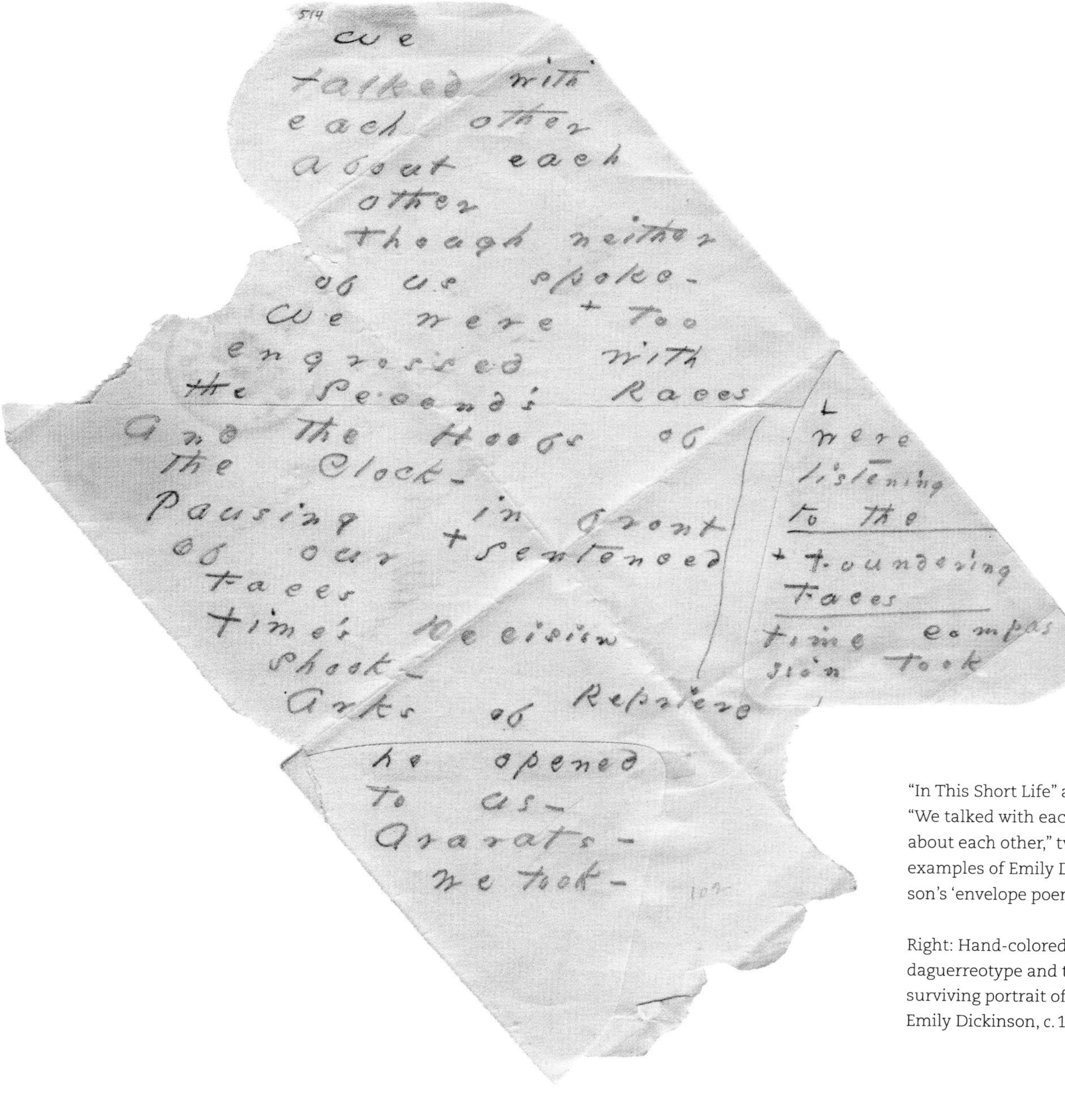

We
talked with
each other
about each
other
though neither
of us spoke -
We were + too
engrossed with
the Second's Races
And the Hoofs of
the Clock -
Pausing in front
of our + sentenced
Faces
Time's Decision
shook -
Arks of Reprieve
he opened
to us -
Ararats -
we took -

+ were
listening
to the
+ foundering
Faces
time compas
sion took

"In This Short Life" and "We talked with each other about each other," two examples of Emily Dickinson's 'envelope poems.'

Right: Hand-colored daguerreotype and the only surviving portrait of Emily Dickinson, c. 1848.

The 'Gorgeous Nothings' of Emily Dickinson

Long after her death, Emily Dickinson (1830–1886) came to be considered one of the most important poets in nineteenth-century American literature. However, it was not an oblivious public that was to blame for her late glory. The poet herself shied away from social intercourse – the bustle of publishing was a horror to her. Indeed she wrote, "reduce no Human Spirit / To Disgrace of Price" and so Dickinson's huge oeuvre of over 1700 poems and countless letters must be considered in the light of such complete seclusion. She left Amherst, Massachusetts, where she was born, only once in her life when she moved for one year from Amherst College, which had been founded by her grandfather, to Mount Holyoke Female Seminary, ten miles away. A life so lonely and withdrawn is barely imaginable. Many of Emily Dickinson's correspondents had never met her in person. Although she loved her siblings and honored her parents (without sharing their strict Puritan beliefs), she was also isolated within her family. In her strongest creative period, at about thirty years of age, she would wear only white cotton dresses, barely left her room and preferred to go into the garden only at night. How eerie! In her neighborhood, she was known as 'The White Lady'. These white dresses always had a large bulging pouch sewn into them in which all sorts of things accumulated: notes, whole poems and tiny fragments or poetry were collected there, to be completed at a later date. Emily Dickinson recorded these poetic elements, snippets and set pieces, on paper that had been used before. She would use things such as envelopes, empty corners and margins of scrap pages or the back of an unimportant document: thoughts, phrases, rhymes, verses – often only the length of a haiku. These fifty-two (known) 'envelope poems' appeared in a facsimile edition some time ago. In some cases, Dickinson seems to have shaped the paper to fit the sense of the words. And so the line "The way hope builds his house" is written on a house-shaped piece of paper. (The poet kept the flap open pointing upwards and pressed the edges down so the upward pointing triangle looked like a roof.) A verse about a bird would typically be written on a wedge- or wing-shaped piece of paper. Heavier subjects such as death, annihilation and danger would be on paper arrows or grenades. In European baroque poetry it was a tradition to arrange the letters, words and verses in such a way that they would form a cross, a heart or an hourglass. This was especially the case with sacred poems, when the text was about the sacrificial death of Christ, spiritual devotion or transience. The manipulation of simple writing paper by Emily Dickinson makes 'The Gorgeous Nothings' an intimate witness to their lyrical power and their enormously modern concept of art. — *Philipp Hontschik*

Arno Schmidt's Card Index

Mathematical, physical, and chemical formulae always mean the same thing. With exact sciences, the meaning of rows of letters never wavers. It is not the same with words. What is the difference between them? In one case, it could be just to do with connected letters, yet with another it could be an explanation of a pattern of thoughts. Anyone who builds with words will know of their ambiguity, their volatility and fragile structure. The writer Arno Schmidt (1914–1979) understood this in the way he went about his work. He created index card boxes, each full of associations between individual words; what the exact references were to, their resonances, equivalents in others languages, their etymological origin, etc. Arno Schmidt even continued this thread in the typeface his novels were printed in. They often appear to be a collection of jotted notes written side-by-side as opposed to a continuous prose text. James Joyce's (1882–1941) *Finnegan's Wake* (1923–1939) is perhaps the only thing more difficult to read. Students of world literature

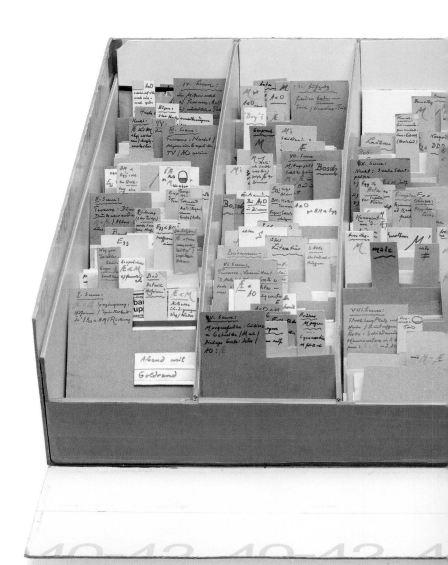

Faced with a shortage of paper in the post-war era, Arno Schmidt wrote down his first stories on a block of telegraph forms. Later he collected cigar boxes and glued together drawers to which he added colored tabs: Arno Schmidt's now famous *zettelkasten* or card index box.

are at one on this point, too. For any reader who prefers it light, sweet and easy, Arno Schmidt's prose is entirely unsuitable. Those independent thinkers, who do not gobble books but take the time to process and get to grips with the original text, however, will find plenty to tackle, and still be entertained. Critics have accused Schmidt's novels of lacking any plot or of being flimsy in their use of linguistic frivolity. This could not be further from the truth: readers of Schmidt's work need to adapt themselves to his way of thinking about language, and the bizarre printed image of his texts, as an obstinate know-it-all doing a rather difficult crossword puzzle. By way of following Schmidt's notes, literary scholars can go on an out-and-out paper chase in search of understanding his genius. Poetry or language, however, which solely appears on a monitor or screen and dismisses all other alternatives, secondary objects and eradications, diminishes any precious understanding. — *Philipp Hontschik*

Letter to Anne Frank

Dear Anne Frank,

If I sent this letter to the post office it would no longer reach you because you have been blotted out from the universe. So I am writing an open letter to those who have read your diary and found a little sister they have never seen who will never entirely disappear from earth as long as we who are living remember her.

You wanted to come to Paris for a year to study the history of art and if you had, perhaps you might have wandered down the Quai Notre-Dame and discovered a little bookstore beside the garden of Saint-Julien-le-Pauvre. You know enough French to read the notice on the door – *Chien aimable, Prière d'entrer*. The dog is not really a dog at all but a poet called Francois Villon who has returned to the city he loved after many years of exile. He is sitting by the fire next to a kitten with a very unusual name. You will be pleased to know she is called Kitty after the imaginary friend to whom you wrote the letters in your journal.

Here in our bookstore it is like a family where your Chinese sisters and your brothers from all lands sit in the reading rooms and meet the Parisians or have tea with the writers from abroad who are invited to live in our guest house.

Remember how you worried about your inconsistencies, about your two selves – the gay, flirtatious superficial Anne that hid the quiet serene Anne, who tried to love and understand the world. We all of us have dual natures. We all wish for peace, yet in the name of self-defense we are working toward self-obliteration. We have built armaments more powerful than the total of all those used in all the wars in history. And if the militarists – who dislike negotiating the minor differences that separate nations – are not under wise civilian authority, they have the power to write man's testament on a dead planet where radioactive cities are surrounded by jungles of dying plants and poisonous weeds.

Anne Frank (1929–1945, murdered at the Bergen-Belsen concentration camp) kept her diary from June 12, 1942 until August 1, 1944. She started it in the family's apartment on Merwedeplein but for the most part wrote it in the rear section of a building on Prinsengracht, the present-day Anne Frank House.

After the Frank family was arrested, Miep Gies took the diary and kept it safe until the end of the war. She returned it to Anne's father, Otto Heinrich Frank, who was the only member of the family to survive the war and the Holocaust. He published the diary which became a huge success as early as the 1950s. To date, the diary has been translated into more than seventy languages, and in 2009 it was placed on the UNESCO List of World Heritage Documents.

Since a nuclear [incident] could destroy half the world's population as well as the material basis of civilization, the Soviet General Nikolai Talensky concludes that war is no longer conceivable for the solution of political differences.

A young girl's dreams recorded in her diary from her thirteenth to her fifteenth birthday means more to us today than the labors of millions of soldiers and thousands of factories striving for a thousand-year Reich that lasted hardly more than ten years. The journal you hid so that no one would read it was left on the floor when the German police took you to the concentration camp and has now been read by millions of people in thirty-two languages.

When most people die they disappear without a trace, their thoughts forgotten, their aspirations unknown, but you have simply left your own family and become part of the family of man.
— *George Whitman*

Einstein's Notes

The Hebrew University in Jerusalem has placed 40,000 original documents from Albert Einstein's (1879–1955) personal records online, as well as a further 30,000 documents that come from either Einstein himself or from his personal circle. These represent the written notes of a mental heavyweight par excellence. If the 40,000 documents from the first batch were to be divided by Einstein's seventy-six years, the figure reached is 526 – far more than just one note a day. If even the slightest jottings preceded the publication of the fair copy, Einstein must have been a tireless note maker. At the age of not-quite twenty-two, he had already published in the 'Journal of Physics', the world's most prestigious peer-reviewed journal, and followed that up with another three articles in the same year. Einstein's brain must have been restless, bubbling away with thoughts and ideas. Sheets of paper, jotted notes and the like came to hold as much as possible of his incessant streams of thought. Even the most gifted researchers need a certain amount of time to return to the requisite levels of abstraction after taking a break or being distracted, thus preventing a continuation of the thought pattern. The world can probably be thankful that Einstein effortlessly slipped back into what he was working on after every lunch break at Princeton University. It is unthinkable, but just imagine what could have been lost, if mundane issues had disturbed Einstein in his work. We will never know. What the papers and documents of the Einstein Archive in Jerusalem do reveal, however, will require a few more decades to decipher completely. Einstein had long promoted the establishment of this university, together with other outstanding Jewish thinkers such as Sigmund Freud (1856–1939) and the theologian, Martin Buber (1878–1965). — *Philipp Hontschik*

Albert Einstein with a note pad
at his home in Princeton in 1940.

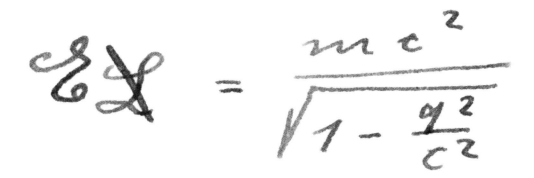

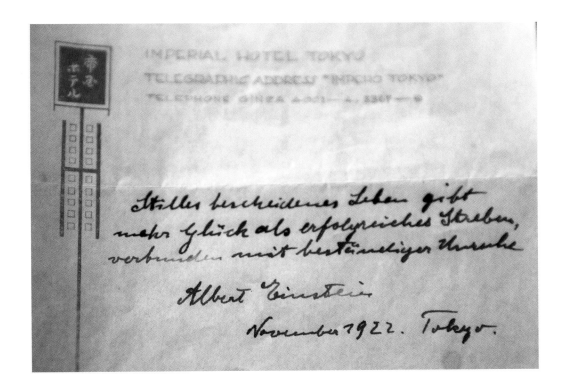

The handwritten version of the equation of relativistic mass, from the manuscript "*Über die Relativitäts-theorie*" (On the Theory of Relativity) by Albert Einstein, written in Zurich and Prague in 1912.

A lecture trip took the world-famous scientist to Tokyo in 1922 where he stayed at the Imperial Hotel. There he gave two notes with short aphorisms to a courier in lieu of a tip. One of the two pieces of writing reads: "A quiet and modest life brings more joy than a pursuit of success bound with constant unrest." In October 2017 it sold at auction in Jerusalem for over 1.5 million dollars.

Revolution:
Music
on Paper

Imagine there was no such thing as paper. Would there be music the way we know it?

Why not? Eric Clapton (b. 1945) to this day can't read music, nor could Joe Cocker (1944–2014); what would they need paper for? Among jazzmen being unable to read music was never seen as a major shortcoming either. A good ear suffices for complex harmonic sequences, and with many good ears the craziest ideas can be readily arranged on a large scale as well. One performer plays something to the others who then repeat it, adding something new to it; they try out some alternatives, agree, and play the whole thing together a few more times – that's usually enough. The memory of professional musicians is a database with almost infinite storage space. Someone like Clapton could probably retrieve one song after another for multiple days before having to repeat any one bar.

Alfred Brendel (b. 1931) and Lang Lang (b. 1982) are also unlikely to be at a loss any time soon. The thirty-two piano sonatas of Beethoven (1770–1827), a few of Mozart's (1756–1791) and Schubert's (1797–1828), half of Bach's (1685–1750) *Well-Tempered Clavier*, the most important works for piano by Schumann (1810–1856), Brahms (1833–1897) and Liszt (1811–1886): they have all of this readily available, many of them since childhood. In general, it appears that in classical concerts the members of the orchestra are the only ones who need to read from music sheets. Soloists, distinguished instrumentalists, as well as many conductors apparently manage without. And even if they learn their pieces by heart at home from sheet music, they could, if they had to, do it by ear as well. Truly.

In other cultures this is actually the norm. Recently, a violinist friend of mine who calls himself a 'gypsy fiddler' was asked by an event organizer to play a Slavic dance by Dvořák (1841–1904). He wasn't familiar with it, though. Eventually, he found it not in printed form at a music store but, rather, on YouTube. He listened to the piece a few times and then played it at night. Probably not exactly the same way as the violinist on the Internet, but it was definitely

Opposite: Autograph of first page of the *Credo* in Johann Sebastian Bach's *Mass in B Minor* (BWV 232) Manuscript from 1748/49.

that Slavic dance by Dvořák. He had learned this from his father who, in turn, had learned it from his father and so on. This is how it works almost everywhere. Almost everywhere, music has always spread like this, changed, adapted itself to the people and thereby survived: passed on from one generation to the other like a language, with all its vocabulary and grammar. In Asia, in Africa, in America, and also in Europe.

At least until paper intervened. Sometime before the turn of the first millennium, musicians – whom we would later call 'composers' – realized what tremendous advantages might result from trying to write down music. "Memory aid and communication" are, according to the musicologist Ian Bent (b. 1938), the motivations behind the first musical works of the Western world that have come down to us in written form – not yet on paper, of course, but on vellum, but the distinction doesn't affect the nature of this prodigious innovation. By notating, a person can outsource his memory and use the freed-up resources to venture into unimagined realms of possibility. He can take a part and add a second one to it and, when he then writes them down as well, even a third and fourth one.

Western polyphony is the upright gait of *Homo musicus*. Notation has unleashed his creativity. And the best thing is that he can let others share in his creativity, no matter where they are and no matter when. A few centuries later, the invention of printing added yet another dimension to this: music broke free from the claims of ownership of church and aristocracy and became a free commodity overcoming social and geographical boundaries. No sooner had

Title page of the Venetian edition of Monteverdi's opera *La Favola d'Orfeo*, which was published in 1609 and includes a dedication to Francesco Gonzaga.

A page from Ludwig van Beethoven's music manuscript of the *Apassionata* sonata of 1806.

opera been invented, than it was printed, and soon half the world knew Monteverdi (1567–1643) and his *Orfeo* (1607); featuring beautiful covers, his madrigals likewise left his home town of Venice and reached Dresden and London in no time.

This did, however, require paper, for animal skin doesn't lend itself well to printing and it is also far too expensive. For a long time, paper was not something that could be taken for granted either. Bach's painstaking handwriting still conveys a sense of how valuable the paper he went through on a daily basis was to him. Don't waste a sheet! When paper finally became cheaper, the scrawling also increased. Beethoven filled sheets and sheets with drafts, which he then tore up, and even when he got down to business – that is, to actually writing down the music at his desk – he didn't worry about the paper. He simply got started, crossed out, started again, wrote in the margin, added bars and deleted others, moved motifs around, and drove his publishers insane. Such was, and still is, the price of notation: when you write something down, you need another who can actually read it. — *Raoul Mörchen*

Bernardo Strozzi, *Claudio Monteverdi*, c. 1640.

Joseph Karl Stieler, Beethoven with the manuscript of the *Missa solemnis*, 1820.

John Cage Finds Music in Paper

Chance takes time. That's the catch. When John Cage (1912–1992) started leaving his decisions as a composer to an oracle rather than to his own taste, he had solved almost all pressing issues at a single stroke. With the exception of just this: which note was to come next? How long was it to be and how loud? What instrument was to play it and in what manner? Before, music flowed readily from his pen; now he needed to consult the *I Ching* for every little thing. And as per the oracle's iron law this meant: cast three coins six times for the pitch, another six times three for the duration, yet another six times three for the tone color, and so on. Even a brief passage could take hours. Later, he would have a computer take over the tedious job, but in 1952?

Now, John Cage was the son of an inventor and rarely at a loss for ideas. If the *I Ching* took too long, what could do it faster? Sitting at his desk, Cage looked at the sheet of paper in front of him and started folding it. Once, twice, three times, four times, without any system. Then he smoothed out the paper again and took another look at it, at the folds and the points in which they intersected. That's it – a template! Cage took a needle, pricked holes into the points of intersection and transferred the pattern made by the holes onto squared paper and from there onto staff paper. The randomly distributed points thus became randomly distributed tones, and

the space between the points became tonal space and space of time. Just a few more simple manipulations and *Music for Carillon*, the first piece of paper music in history that is worthy of the name, was finished.

But a different work and a different paper idea would become even more famous. It was still 1952 and time was still pressing. This time, the dancer and choreographer Joanne Melcher urgently needed music for a new piece. A lot of music. More than Cage could create through folding. Again he looked at his desk for a solution – and indeed found one right in front of him. His idea then turned out to be good for not just one piece, but eventually for eighty-five of them. *Music for Piano* is the name of the legendary series of works that extended into the 1960s and always started out with the same procedure: the close examination of a sheet of paper. For John Cage was surprised to find that none of his papers was really flawless. In each one of them close inspection revealed small marks, stains and bulges. Cage marked these spots, traced the result, and again copied the marks onto staff paper. The *I Ching* was now needed only for fine-tuning: how many marks should I look for? Or: how long should I look? In these matters the slow oracle was still allowed to have a say. The rest was already there: as music in paper.

— *Raoul Mörchen*

The American composer John Cage in front of the handwritten notes for his composition *Concert for Piano and Orchestra, c.* 1958.

COPYRIGHT © 1960 BY HENMAR PRESS INC 373 PARK AVE SO., N.Y. 16, N.Y.

John Cage, *Music
for Piano #1*, 1952.

Ben Patterson Makes Music with Paper

Paper was sacred to Ben Patterson (1934–2016): the notes he wanted to play as a musician were notated on paper, all the smart thoughts that as a librarian he wanted to preserve were written on paper, and as an artist he set down most of his works on paper.

This includes even the piece that is about destroying paper, although the word 'destroy' is perhaps too aggressive. True, in the beginning the paper is whole, then mauled, and in the end lies in tatters on the ground, but there is no destructive frenzy behind it, no will to destroy but, rather, the exact opposite: the intention to create something – a new insight. Paper can be used not only to notate music; it can itself become music, when it is crumpled, torn, rubbed, twisted, inflated like a bag and popped.

The idea for this came to Patterson when he was visiting Cologne. His great dream to be the first black double bass player to play in a symphonic orchestra in the U.S. had failed to materialize. In Canada they were happy to have him, but by then something else was on his mind: electronic music.

The *Westdeutscher Rundfunk*, a public broadcasting institution in Cologne, had the best studio. In June 1960 Patterson set off for Cologne, but his interview with the studio head and composer, Karlheinz Stockhausen (1928–2007), proved disappointing. Patterson found Stockhausen authoritarian and narrow-minded. He decided to leave again the next day. He had just one more evening in Cologne. Someone slipped a note into his hand: an invitation to a small art festival, right around the corner. Why not? He had no other plans. In the studio of the German artist Mary Bauermeister (b. 1934), Patterson then met John Cage. Patterson didn't know of him, but when Cage asked him if he wanted to join in a performance, he said 'yes'– and stayed for two years. He couldn't care less about Mozart and Brahms anymore, he'd much rather help give birth to a new movement. Called 'Fluxus', this movement wanted to break down boundaries and bring into flux what was rigid. How does that work?

Opposite page:
Ben Patterson's *Paper Piece* (1960) during the 1963 'Fluxus Festival' at the Hypokriterion Theater in Amsterdam. In this performance paper is used to make music.

Ben Patterson in Karslruhe, 2014.

You take five players and give each one of them fifteen sheets of paper of varying quality as well as three paper bags. You specify eleven actions to produce sounds with the paper and classify them into four categories. 1. SHAKE. BREAK. TEAR. 2. CRUMPLE. RUMPLE. BUMPLE. 3. RUB. SCRUB. TWIST. 4. POOF. POP! You determine an approximate course of action and define the end: the piece is over when all the paper has been used. This usually takes ten to twelve minutes, as experience indicates. But, hey! It's Fluxus and things could go very differently, too. Sometimes the sheets of paper fell from the tables and stands and landed right in front of a member of the audience. If that person then spontaneously joined in, perhaps even inciting the people sitting next to him to tear up their playbills – that was fine, too. Indeed, all of this has happened.

Ben Patterson wrote his *Paper Piece* in the late summer of 1960, three months after arriving in Cologne. He would go on to organize the world's first Fluxus Festival in Wiesbaden with George Maciunas (1931–1978), tour many times through Germany and Europe with his *Paper Piece* and all the other things that came to his mind, and then he returned to his former home country. Ben Patterson became a music agent, was appointed Professor of Performance and served for two years as Assistant Director of the Department of Cultural Affairs for New York City. And he trained as a librarian. No more tearing paper after that.
— *Raoul Mörchen*

Fine Art
and
Paper

For many centuries, paper was a valuable and expensive commodity used by artists only sparingly and with great care. An early example of this economical use has come down to us in the sketchbook of the French artist Villard de Honnecourt (*c.* 1200–1235). Its thirty-three surviving sheets of parchment are densely filled with some 250 faces, animals, architectural elements, floor plans, and constructions. Villard compiled this book at some point before 1235 as a portfolio to showcase his work, much like artists still do today.

The invention of printmaking techniques – first the woodcut, then the metalcut – in the fifteenth century, triggered a gradual

Opposite: A page form Villard de Honnecourt's sketchbook showing a grasshopper, cat, dragonfly, crab and architectural design for a maze, *c.* 1230

Below left: Hans Holbein the Younger, *Portrait of a Young Woman Wearing a Headscarf*, *c.* 1525.

Below right: Georges Seurat, *Woman Reading*, *c.* 1883.

increase in the number of artworks made on paper. Albrecht Dürer (1471–1528) first published the large woodcuts of his 'Apocalypse' series as a high-quality book in 1498, and his prints then began to circulate throughout Europe. Similar works on paper by other masters not only disseminated their artistic achievements, but also came to serve political purposes as well, notably in Martin Luther's Reformation.

Drawing and printing took on different functions: virtuoso drawings replaced paintings and prints served to distribute them to a wider audience. In this context paper remained only a supporting medium. Its structure, color, and consistency was only rarely visibly incorporated. For example, when the draftsman executed pictorial portraits, such as in the work of Hans Holbein the Younger (c. 1497–1543) in England; or when artists such as Rembrandt (1606–1669), whose biblical scenes used the tone of the paper alongside vigorous strokes of the pen and washes to place his subjects in the light.

From the late nineteenth century on, this way of working changed. Paul Cézanne (1839–1906) allowed the white of the paper to play a part "as paint" and Georges Seurat (1859–1891) used the rough texture of his paper to enhance the *chiaroscuro* effect of his drawings.

A new age in the use of paper in art began with the invention of the collage by Pablo Picasso (1881–1973) and Georges Braque (1882–1963). They used not only standard material but also printed paper, used paper, and inferior paper. Kurt Schwitters (1887–1948) carried the work with found objects to extremes. Nothing was too trivial for him to include in his work. His time, living conditions, and relationships within the art world: all were taken into account and incorporated into his work with pieces or scraps of paper. With great

Left: Georges Braque, *Pipe, Glass, and Newspaper*, 1914.

Right: Pablo Picasso, *Bottle on a Table*, 1912.

Opposite: Kurt Schwitters, *Mz 601*, 1923.

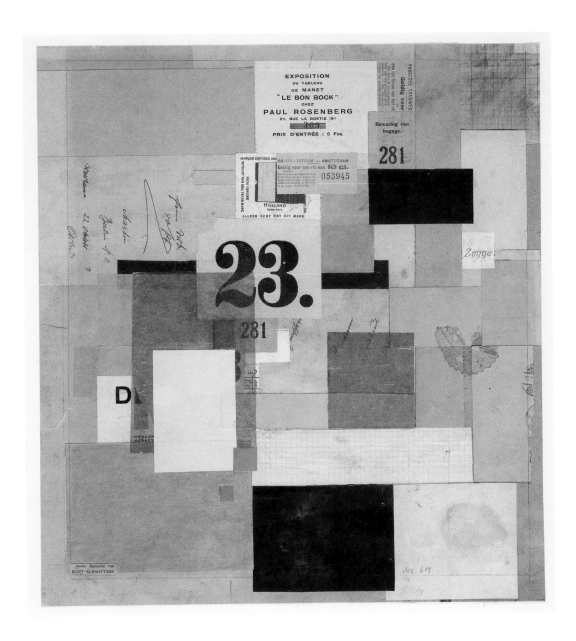

subtlety and wit, he pasted an entire world together in the small format of his collages. Hence his far-reaching influence which intensified in the European and American avant-garde from the 1950s on, as Robert Rauschenberg (1925–2008), Joseph Beuys (1921–1986), and Mimmo Rotella (1918–2006) took up and reinterpreted his impulse. 'Art as contemporaneity,' as called for by Charles Baudelaire (1821–1867) in the 1850s, was put into practice by Schwitters in his 'Merz' and by the Dadaists, especially in view of the violent upheavals caused by the First World War and its aftermath. Despite the historical circumstances, which were anything but peaceful, collage introduced a playful element into the arts. Previously, play had been a subject of art; now, 'homo ludens,' as Johan Huizinga (1872–1945), the Dutch cultural historian, called him, had become a prototype of modernity. Schwitters, and especially Picasso, became the master players with paper and other materials previously overlooked as unworthy of art.

Cutting small-scale, three-dimensional works from paper and folding them – seemingly child's play – describes the way Picasso and a number of other artists worked. Paper led on to cardboard, used or new: Robert Rauschenberg , Joseph Beuys, and Erwin Heerich (1922–2004) also used this packaging material.

Like some other techniques, papercutting found its way from play into art. Examples from Philipp Otto Runge (1777–1810) onward culminated in the late work of Henri Matisse (1869–1954) who used scissor and paper to dissolve painting's boundaries while at the same time cultivating it anew.

At the same time as his collages (the *papiers collés* and *papiers decoupés*), however, reality brutally burst into the aesthetic when the '*décollagists*' or '*affichists*' in Paris began to use the traces of advertising, ephemera and coarse everyday life. They no longer created, but instead chose from the visual coincidences thrown up by the big city.

Compared to drawings, photographs required special, light-sensitive paper, which from the 1970s on became available even in a large pictorial format. Again a new era in the use of paper dawned, which was interpreted in a particularly ambiguous manner by Thomas Demand (b. 1964) who recreated scenes from press and gossip photography in cardboard or paper. Those 'models' were, in turn, photographed using the latest techniques such as digital photography. The uncanny lodged itself within those processes, which resulted in the photograph and the destruction of the model. Photography had returned to 'sculpture,' to paper, only to then hold its own in the universe of controllable media – as a phantom.
— *Siegfried Gohr*

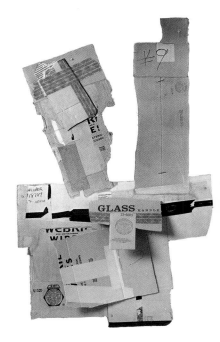

Robert Rauschenberg,
Carbird II, 1971.

Thomas Demand,
Daily #27, 2016.

William Kentridge,
Thinking in Water, 2002.

Paper Art

While the role of paper as a medium in the history of the visual arts has been outlined elsewhere in this volume, the present essay focuses on 'paper art' and, by extension, on an artistic stance that views paper as a material in its own right.

The meaning, the effect, and the 'power' of works made of paper fibers are also expressed in the 'language' of the raw material, the technique, and the construction. If these aspects are taken into consideration in the reception of the work, insight and discourse is enriched and intensified.

The history of paper art is young. The artist and papermaker Douglass Morse Howell (1906–1994) and the master printer Kenneth Tyler (b. 1931), who ran Tyler Graphics in Mount Kisco, New York, each made major contributions to this movement. They were confronted with the demands of visual artists who, eager to experiment, were looking for new forms of expression.

It has taken almost two thousand years, since paper was invented, for an art movement to emerge which, in dealing with color and form, no longer felt beholden to the tradition of painting on a 'ground' such as stone, wood, canvas, or paper. In paper art, paper becomes autonomous and breaks away from its role as support material. It becomes an independent artistic medium that can be shaped in any two- and three-dimensional form. Paper stock or pulp gives rise to an independent language of artistic expression. The challenge of making a work out of the void, with no supporting material, and which itself consists of a substance formed of the finest fibers, necessarily leads to unconventional creative processes and concepts. These are based on the targeted use of pulp from plant-based or recycling materials that are given new functions. The importance of this development lies in the constructive and creative process in which ideas are generated and haptic access is opened up. Paper in this way becomes something more than a carrier of cultural heritage or a means of communication.

Starting in the 1970s or thereabouts, the early forms of Modernist collage, the *papiers collés* of Braque and Picasso, were taken up again by various artists with special regard to the material, paper. This new interest in paper also gave rise to artists making their own paper in order to incorporate the artistic process into the actual production of paper elements. British artist David Hockney (b. 1937), for instance, worked at Tyler Graphics to produce his *Paper Pools* and Robert Rauschenberg worked at the Richard de Bas paper mill in Ambert, France to realize his ideas of 'hand-scooped' paintings. Günther Uecker (b. 1930) became known for his relief-like embossed prints of nails in handmade paper, and Andreas von Weizsäcker (1956–2008) for his large-scale castings of objects in handmade paper.

Around the same time, new tendencies of paper art also emerged in Asia, albeit with different formal aspirations. The artists would commission the production of paper and then use the finished *washi*, or Japanese paper, to realize their concepts. Both in the East and in the West the new visual and object language developed expressive forms.

The International Biennials of Paper Art, which took place from 1986 until 2005 at the Leopold-Hoesch-Museum in Düren, Germany, helped establish paper art in Europe. As a result, biennials and triennials were, and are still being, initiated in various countries. In 1996, the term 'paperism' was introduced during a conference of the International Association of Hand Papermakers and Paper Artists (IAPMA, founded in Düren in 1986). By that time, there were already a number of artists in Europe who had arrived at a distinct artistic mode in paper art.

Paper art differs from the familiar pictorial forms of expression in the use of previously rare constructive and design processes using pulp paper. The development and conception of a work is not based on a prepared ground or prefabricated support material. This also leaves open aspects such as form, size, three-dimensional elements,

Monika Grzymala, *Diptychon #2*
(from the series making paper)
(Detailaufnahme), 2010.

Amar Kanwar,
The Sovereign Forest,
2011–2017.

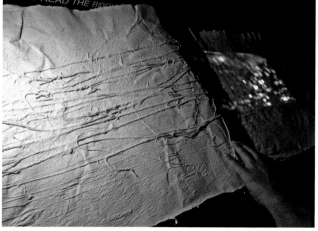

and spatial concepts. The choice of raw material and how it is processed into pulp should also be differentiated for each intended design, as these influence the quality of the work. Thus it is possible to conceive images, objects, sculptures, and installations using fibrillated paper stock or pulp, whose fibers have a higher surface area and branched structure. Paper surfaces and forms are dipped, cast, layered. The fiber composite is created through pressure and/or in the drying process. Formal aspects may be manipulated by means of inclusions in multilayered paper. The expansion of natural fibers and stabilizing elements can serve to provoke and realize creative intentions.

Casting, the layering of pulp over basic forms of various materials, makes it possible to create large-scale works. Shaping, processing, arrangement, the method of joining individual parts, as well as the space between the elements, all become relevant aspects.

The synthesis of construction and form allows new perspectives. Paper takes on volume and can encompass space and be surrounded by space. It is fluffy, light, and hovers in the wind. It is hard and compact, suggesting stone and metal. It is transparent or opaque, fragile and robust, absorbent and water-repellent. It can carry a message on top and within itself, or it can incite transgressions. Paper becomes a material that opens up a complex range of creative and technical possibilities of structuring and reconfiguration in the second and third dimensions: it is moldable and can be modulated. Given these fields of action of artistic expression, paper becomes a creative means in its own right, and this autonomy still offers much potential for further developments.

Artistic approaches

Some artists developed new methods of creating their paintings and objects by collaborating with paper or graphic workshops, as David Hockney (b. 1937) did in creating his *Paper Pools* with Kenneth Tyler in 1978. To make these works he poured runny, colored paper fibers onto handmade and still moist paper sheets. He used cookie-cutter molds and metal strips to create linear demarcations or contours. Because the paper sheets were placed closely together in a mosaic-like manner, there was no limit to the size of the works.

James Rosenquist (1933–2017), working with Tyler, used a spraying device to apply a fine-filament, colored pulp in thin and often translucent layers. In doing so, he overcame the size limits of the dip mold. In combination with collage techniques, his 1992 work *Time Dust* thus reached a size of 218 × 1062 cm.

Chuck Close (b. 1940) also worked with the know-how of workshops such as Pace Prints and the Dieu Donné paper mill in New York. His initial reservations about working with paper disappeared with the discovery of a new technique: he used fibrous material, which in the drying process had agglutinated into small discs of

Chuck Close, *Watermark Selfportrait*, 2007.

Chuck Close, *Georgia*, 1984.

paper fibers, to layer portraits such as his 1984 *Georgia*. Yet another process he developed with his team was the grid technique which involved meticulously filling the colored fibers into the individual compartments of a plastic or metal grid, with the subject invariably being a portrait.

The large-scale works of Monika Grzymala (b. 1970), such as her 2010 *Eclipse*, are based on a very different process. In the cast-Indian-mulberry fibers, structures rise relief-like from the paper surface. Those intersecting lines appear like meshes or networks, which lead to a new kind of spatial thinking.

Spatial referentiality is also a concept in the work of Dorothea Reese-Heim (b. 1943), for instance in the artistic intervention of 'Field project involving the crop flax.' Her installation consists of a marked-out field that serves to show the growing process of the traditional papermaker's plant, flax. It is a continuous process of transformation, a blue sea of flowers at the height of flowering. Once they are harvested, the inner fibers of the flax stalks are turned into pulp. With it figures are painted into the field in a paper-casting process: a transformational process from the germ, to the bud, to the performative.

The wall and floor objects of Alexandra Deutsch (b. 1968) create other references to natural phenomena. Their language of forms and figures leaves open associations and parallels while outlining an artistic microcosm. Molded out of white pulp, the sometimes fragile-seeming objects are given highly contrasting colors in a second work step.

Even the watermark, once developed as the trademark of paper mills, has broken away from its traditional use contexts. In the artist's book *Sheets of Evidence* by William Kentridge (b. 1955), for instance, text and drawings are translated into subtle watermarks of the kind that can only be created in the dipping process of paper-making.

The watermark also plays a dominant role in *Meteorit* (1987–88), an object created by Andreas von Weizsäcker. Its narrative, graphic content is created in the process of dipping paper as well as the casting of objects in a shell-like paper layer.

Crucial for the relief-like structures in the large-size books of Indian artist Amar Kanwar (b. 1964) are material inclusions that are incorporated during the layering of handmade double-ply paper sheets. The materiality of the hand-scooped book combines with documentary footage to document the simultaneity of two modes of existence, as seen in the 2012 installation *The Sovereign Forest* shown at DOCUMENTA (13) in Kassel.

The 2013 installation *Reptiles* of Huang Yong Ping (b. 1954) is about the radical dissolution of communicable information. His material consists of newspapers and books, which are treated in washing machines and turned into papier mâché as a result. The

Therese Weber, *The Absence of the Present*, n.d.

original words survive merely as fragmentary, incoherent signs. His works involve contrasts between Eastern and Western culture.

My own work is about a chronology of time and space, which becomes an object of cognitive interest. At such interfaces new approaches to knowledge as well as imagination are formed. More far-reaching approaches to the construction and reception of the works are created by means of embossings and symmetries, which time and again refer to their origins.

In these various artistic practices paper stock or pulp is not simply material and form. Depending on the viewer's perception and sensitivity, narrative elements, complex stories, and individual contents may be detected. — *Therese Weber*

Huang Yong Ping, *Reptiles*, 2013.

Andreas von Weizsäcker, *Contrade dell' Arte*, 2003.

Silhouette to Lasercut

Hardly any artistic approach achieves such an engaging effect with so little as the paper silhouette. The technique was introduced in the eighteenth century and soon reached a wide audience. Far more than just a society fashion, silhouettes were widely practiced by artisans, members of the aristocracy and the bourgeoisie, as well as by professional artists. This was largely due to the influence of oriental silhouette art encountered by Europeans in the preceding centuries. One of its most renowned representatives was Philipp Otto Runge (1777–1810) who, according to the testimony of his brother Daniel, turned to silhouetting in his early youth. In addition to single forms such as animals, human figures and flower tendrils, whole romantic scenes were created, which then inspired contemporary authors with ideas for fables and stories. The technique of the bare outline devoid of any kind of interior form, shadow, color or perspective, is directly related to the shadow, which according to an anecdote handed down by Pliny the Elder (c. 23–79 CE), established the beginnings of painting. In the second half of the eighteenth century the silhouette was circulated by the French Minister of Finance, Etienne de Silhouette 1709–1767, as a substitute for the elaborate portrait miniature. It was given religious and moral depth by the Swiss theologian, Johann Caspar Lavater (1741–1801), who was of the opinion that the human soul can be seen in its physiognomy, and that facial features recorded in profile could provide information about its nature. The typesetter, Karl Hermann Froehlich (1821–1898), and his friend, the painter and sculptor Paul Konewka (1840–1871), used the silhouette as a basis for book illustrations, the success of which was responsible for the silhouette's continuing popularity into the nineteenth century. Since then, positive and negative space have become familiar as figures of speech; the scalpel and laser-cut have replaced scissors, without totally changing the contour depictions. It can be found in Henri Matisse (1869–1954), who used a silhouette to continue his line of expression, as well as contemporary art figures such as Felix Droese (b. 1950), William Kentridge (b. 1955), and Kara Walker (b. 1969), who have interpreted this art form with expansive installations. Artists such as Max Marek (b. 1957) or Clémentine Sourdais (b. 1980), use silhouettes, scalpels or laser-cut equivalents to penetrate the spatial volume of a book's body and graphically utilize the resulting permeability of the pages as well as narrative. As the cut-out shapes give an open view to the following ones, the successive representations enter an immediate dialogue, in which the narration unfolds from the shape's superimposition and detachment.
— *Viola Hildebrand-Schat*

Philipp Otto Runge,
Dog Barking at the Moon, n.d.

Experiencing Paper

Paper, as a material, is for me the very reason to draw in two respects: firstly, paper is the surface or even the subsurface on which a drawing is created and then becomes visibly alive. The characteristics of the paper in question can also act as the inspiration and purpose for a particular drawing.

My work is the result of the interplay between experimenting with the material, drawing and reflection. The material properties of a sheet of paper, in conjunction with the drawing tool, produce the quality of the line, how it moves and then how thoughts move. The paper being worked with is, therefore, definitive in the creation process of a drawing.

White is not exactly just white. There are countless varieties of white paper: some are close pressed and others open with smooth or rough surfaces that can absorb a lot or a little moisture. There are thin or heavy versions, as well as translucent or opaque ones, and so on. However, I also draw on blank or printed papers that have already been given a purpose, such as maps, pages from books, wrapping paper, circulating folders, sheets of paper patterns, business cards, picture postcards or index cards, etc. We mostly stumble across these items when we are not looking for them. Once I have chosen one of these scraps and brought it to the studio, I mostly forget about it until an idea sparks and I suddenly know just what to do with it. Unlike the white surface of blank paper, which offers all possibilities, the papers with specific characteristics already have hidden features inscribed ready for graphic alteration. It is like a secret coding, directing and determining what the final piece will look like. Such papers each have specific limitations and constrict the possibilities of drawing, thereby challenging and stimulating creative invention. — *Nanne Meyer*

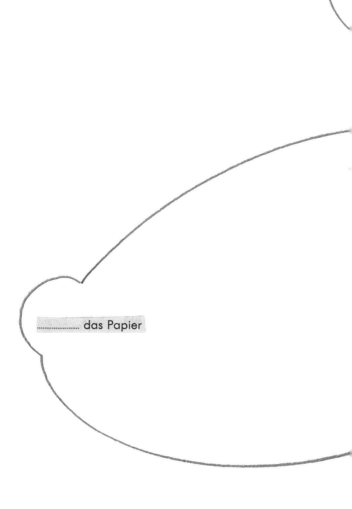

das Papier

linie, mensch

Nanne Meyer, *Das Papier*, 1999.

Trans-Layers

In his wall-covering installation work, Toilet Paper, Turkish artist Şakir Gökçebağ (b. 1965) uses a commonplace, everyday paper object and shows it in a completely different light. He takes an item that typically is seen and used individually and places it in vast quantities in an altered frame of reference. In doing so he lends the familiar object an almost ornamental quality.

The artist uses the transient and almost worthless cellulose paper as an opulent, lavish material for decorating and spatial arrangement. This results in a reevaluation of the raw material itself. These are no longer simple rolls of toilet tissue, they are paper objects, whose worth in this installation opens a new field of meaning. No matter what preconceptions the observer may bring, this works draws him into thinking about cellulose pulp as a material; about white as a surface and as a space; about visual art; about minimalism; about directed lighting; and about the history of personal hygiene. In fact, this piece may lead the observer to wherever he wishes to be lead.

Marcus Graf wrote about this work in 2010: "A collection of toilet paper rolls can become an ornamental symphony, bursting open the formal confines of the circle as well as the conceptual and contextual use of toilet paper. The rigid form of the roll is broken by the unfurled paper web and this in turn establishes new definitions and connotations for toilet roll." — *Nicola von Velsen*

Şakir Gökçebağ,
Trans-Layers 1, 2010.

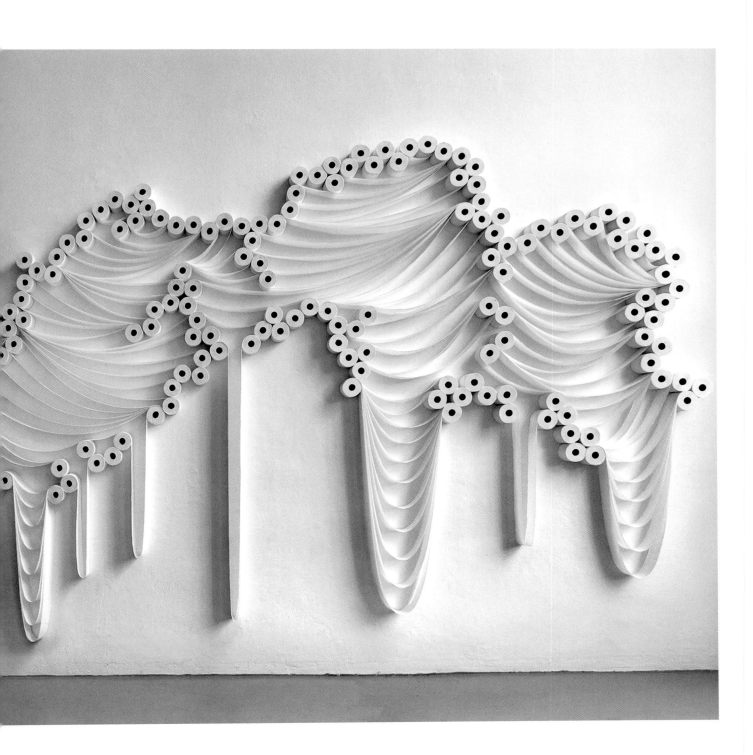

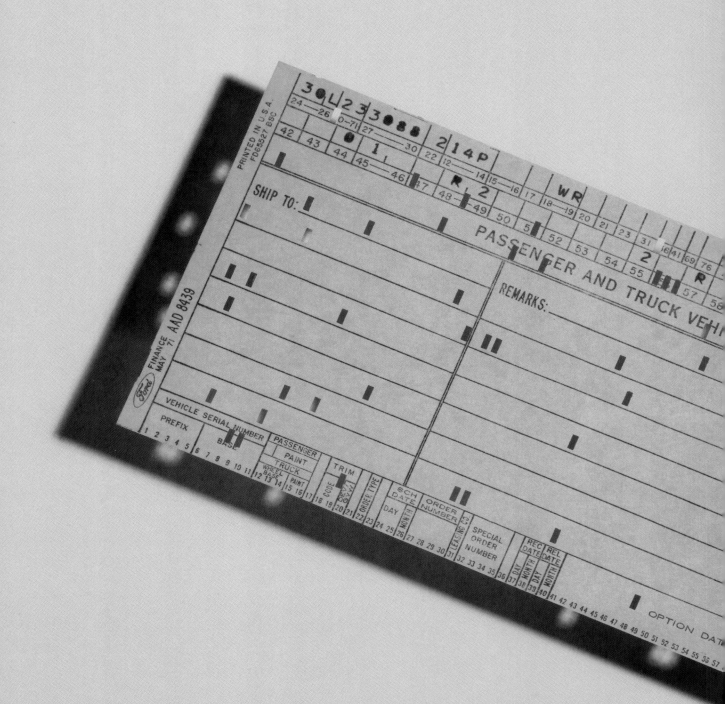

Paper
as
Symbol

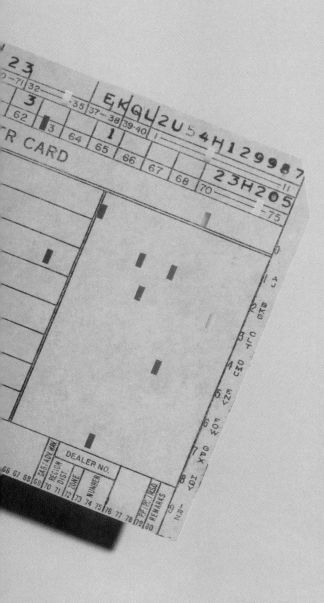

Watermarks

The relationships between paper and water are manifold. While some are obvious, others reveal themselves only when we are aware of their existence and look at the paper objects in a proper way.

Water is at the very beginning of the processes that allow the papermaker to combine natural forces, technical procedures and cultural purpose in his products. Paper is a surface material created by dewatering a watery fibrous suspension with the aid of a sieve or screen. Cellulose fibers with hydrophilic (i.e. water-loving) properties are required as a raw material base. These fibers are created in plants that, with the help of sunlight, form long molecular chains from the elements of carbon, hydrogen and oxygen. Water and carbon dioxide produce carbohydrates or polysaccharides which take on structural functions in the cell walls.

When papermaking took on its distinctive European form in thirteenth-century Italy, the fibrous material used in paper mills already had an entire life cycle behind it by the time it was processed. This material was provided by rags; old textiles that had served their primary purpose. Prior to that, farms had grown the blue flax which had to be harvested and processed in labor-intensive steps. The plants are gently pulled up with the roots; then the seeds are removed through threshing and the fibers are separated from the surrounding matter through a wet process called rotting or retting. Next, the flax stems need to be broken and hackled. Only then is it spun into yarn and linen that can be spread out in meadows and moistened and bleached in the sun.

Linen was valuable and an essential part of the dowries of young marriageable women. It was used to make shirts, bedclothes, tablecloths, diapers, and towels. Only when the linen cloth had been used and washed often, it came to be of particular value for the papermaker. In an entry on ‘*Lumpen*’, or rags, in the *Oekonomisch-technologische Encyklopädie*, which was established by Johann Georg Krünitz in 1801, we read: "All paper used today is made of worn-out linen cloth or rags. The whitest, finest and cleanly washed linen is indisputably the best for this purpose, but the well-worn is always to be preferred over the new."

At the paper mill, the rags supplied by rag pickers were carefully sorted by fiber type, quality and color and then shredded and washed in a stamp mill or hollander. Water was needed in this process both to move the water wheels and as process water for cleaning. The fiber was prepared in a multi-step process. When ready for processing, the fibrous material was finally poured into the pulping vat and evenly distributed through stirring, so that about 2 percent fibers were suspended in 98 percent water.

With the aid of especially constructed sieves, some of these fibers could then be removed from the vat and dewatered in such a way that an even sheet of paper formed on the surface of the sieve. This manufacturing process was an impressive innovation that, starting in the second of half of the thirteenth century, spread from the Italian town of Fabriano in the Province of Ancona. There a process had been developed that made it possible not only to produce paper on an industrial scale, but also to give during the manufacturing process each individual sheet of paper an unchanging mark that served to certify the origin and quality of the product.

What was so special about this process? While the sieves used in older paper manufacturing processes in Asia and North Africa were made of bamboo sticks or reeds and therefore flexible, the Italian papermakers developed dip molds with rigid, well-braced wooden

The figure made of bent wire is attached to the screen with sewing thread. This creates thinner areas in the scooped sheet of paper that become visible as watermarks when held against light.

frames into which bronze wire mesh was placed. Parallel ribbing wires were held in place by perpendicular warp wires and permanently attached to the wooden frame with fine sewing threads. Two similar dip molds combined to form a pair of molds with a shared deckle that could be placed alternately on either mold. The deckle determined the size of the paper and lent the individual sheet its characteristic deckle edge. Three papermakers worked alternately at the pulp vat: the 'dipper' or 'vatman', the 'coucher' and the 'layer'. The dipper removed a certain quantity of suspended fibers from the vat, which then settled on the wire mesh, while the water drained through the screen. The deckle was taken off to be used for the second dip mold. In the meantime the second papermaker 'couched' the dip mold with its screen surface facing down. In the process, the still very delicate and water-laden sheet of paper was transferred to a heavily felted woolen cloth and covered with a second cloth. Once 181 sheets of paper had been placed between 182 felted cloths, the papermakers dewatered this pile, called a post, in the large wet press. After this the layer could, one by one, separate the felts and the wet sheets of paper. When scrutinizing the quality of the new product in grazing light, one could see that the structure of the wire mesh appeared as a relief in the paper pulp. When holding the sheet against the light, the original mesh structure showed in the form of differences of brightness: the paper had ribbing.

A paper described in 1282 was the first to feature a special mark in the paper itself. A cross-like shape can be discerned as a bright form. Many early records of watermarks are displayed in the collections of the *Museo della Carta e della Filigrana* in Fabriano. Papermakers had realized that it was possible to deliberately place figures made of bent wire in the dip mold, so that fewer fibers would settle in those places while the sheet formed. As early as the late nineteenth century, the Italian scholars Aurelio Zonghi (1830–1902) and Augusto

Four screen rolls of bronze wire or brazing solder: these *egoutteurs* or dandy rolls could provide watermarks continuously and uniformly throughout the entire surface of the paper web – for instance, with recurring sequences of words or ornamentation (the examples 1 and 3 from the left). Or they could create so-called localized watermarks which always ended up in the same place in the cut sheet of paper (examples 2 and 4 from the left).

Zonghi (1840–1916) concerned themselves with documenting these watermarked papers; in 1881 the most important watermarks of Fabrianese paper from 1293–1599 were published in a volume titled *Le marche principali delle carte fabrianesi dal 1293 al 1599* (Fabriano, 1881). Among the early examples we already find the names of some papermakers, angel-like figures and bells, everyday tools and weapons, crown and bishop's miter. The further this mode of paper-making spread throughout Europe, the more diverse the imagery of the watermarks became. In 1907, the Geneva-based paper merchant Charles-Moïse Briquet (1839–1918) assembled renditions of watermarks from 1282–1600 in a four-volume work titled *Les filigranes: Dictionnaire historique des marques du papier dès leur apparition vers 1282 jusqu'en 1600* (Geneva, Paris, London et al., 1907). It included 16,112 renditions of individual watermarks in the form of black-and-white line drawings arranged in alphabetic order of the French names for the particular images. The tracings of the bright watermark lines were now more reminiscent of the wire figure on the dip mold. After World War II, the watermark researcher Gerhard Piccard managed to compile records of about 130,000 watermarks up to 1600. Today his comprehensive watermark file is digitized at the *Stuttgart Hauptstaatsarchiv* so that anyone can have free online access to this wealth of different forms and can do research on the place and time of origin of these paper brands.

Watermarks remained a signature of European handmade papers into the nineteenth century. Originally mostly found in just one half of the sheet, they now became ever more elaborate. Single-piece watermarks were superseded by two-part ones and main marks were complemented by countermarks. Many papers featured reproductions of the coats of arms of imperial cities or territorial sovereignties, depending upon ownership and power relations. Increasingly, names of towns and papermakers

Paper mill in Fabriano, Italy, c. 1820.

Mold-making workshop, from Denis Diderot: *Encyclopédie ou dictionnaire raisonné des sciences, des arts et des métiers*, Paris, c. 1770.
In the thirteenth century, Italian papermakers achieved a decisive technological breakthrough. They not only revolutionized the paper-making process itself. The sheets of paper were now scooped from a vat filled with suspended fibers using molds with metal screen wires. Mold making became a highly specialized trade.

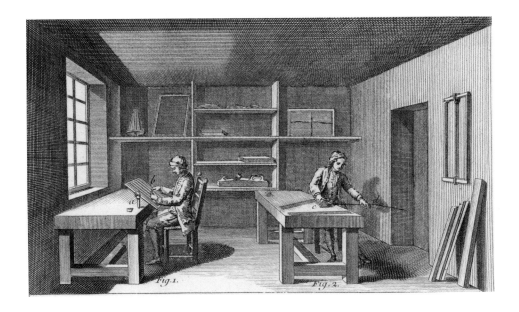

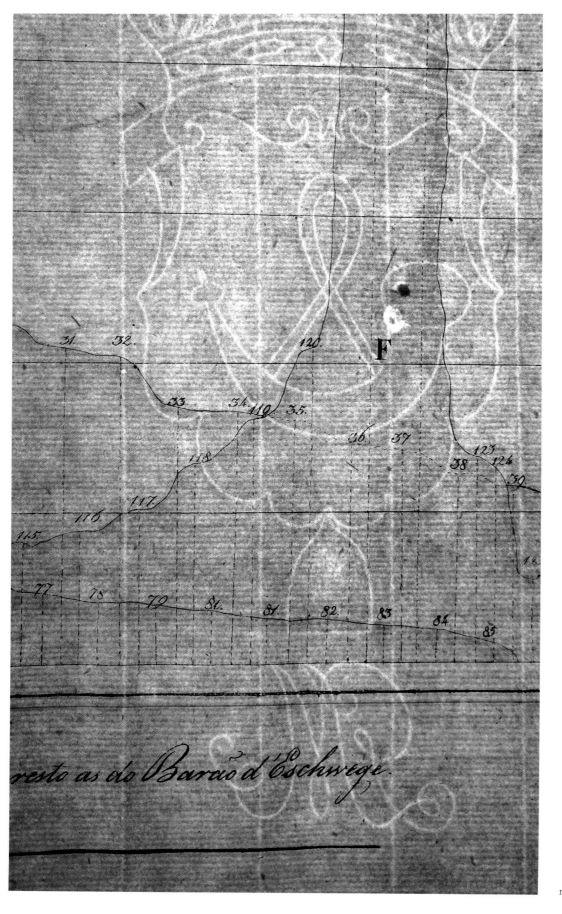

Detail of a historical map with watermark from the collection of Peter J. Roehrich.

Opposite: A selection of European watermarks from the collection of Gerhard Piccard, which comprises roughly 130,000 watermarks.

appeared in papers. In the seventeenth and eighteenth centuries the number of paper mills and papermakers increased sharply. Because dip molds are often worn out after just a few years of use, periods of rapidly growing paper consumption saw the emergence of a great variety of watermarks. Notably, the paper historian Karl Theodor Weiss (1872–1945) and his son, Wisso Weiss (1904–1991), have distinguished themselves by compiling an extensive collection of watermarks from this period. Today their collection, which from 1957 until 1964 existed as the German Paper Museum in the Thuringian town of Greiz, serves as the nucleus of the Collections of Historical Papers of the German Museum of Books and Documents at the Leipzig branch of the German National Library.

With industrialization in the early nineteenth century everything changed rapidly and radically. Towards the end of the previous century some papermakers had already worked with new dip molds featuring a woven wire metal cloth rather than ribbing wires. The resulting texture was now no longer ribbed but smooth and this new kind of paper was called vellum paper. Nicolas-Louis Robert (1761–1828) had equipped an experimental model of a paper machine with this type of metal cloth that was sewn together to form a continuous panel and received a French patent for it. In England, the English machine manufacturer Bryan Donkin (1768–1855) constructed the first long screen paper machines for industrial use on the same basis. Since these mesh cloths moved continuously around two rollers, it was not possible to attach rigid wire figures to the flexible metal cloth and so adding watermarks to the paper was no longer an option. New ways of doing this were developed only several decades later. Paper could also be produced with round screen paper machines that came in use around 1820. Their screen cylinders had a rigid shape, thus allowing for the familiar wire figures to be attached them. Screen rolls called *egoutteurs* or dandy rolls were developed for the long screen paper machines as well: these screens pressed into the still-wet paper web and displaced the already almost immovable paper fibers in such a way that watermarks could be created from the screen side as well as from the opposite felt side.

In the last third of the nineteenth century watermarks thus experienced a renaissance even in machine-made paper. Not just the production technology had fundamentally changed in the course of industrialization, but the whole raw material base of papermaking as well. In 1843, the Saxon inventor Friedrich Gottlob Keller (1816–1895) had succeeded in producing paper-ready fibers from wood in a wet grinding process. Yet these fibers contained not just cellulose but also the lignin that is contained in wood. When Heinrich Voelter (1871–1887) refined the wood-grinding process so that it could be applied on an industrial scale, it soon became evident that this lignin was a constant source of the yellowing and rapid aging of paper. For this reason, authorities regulated paper quality

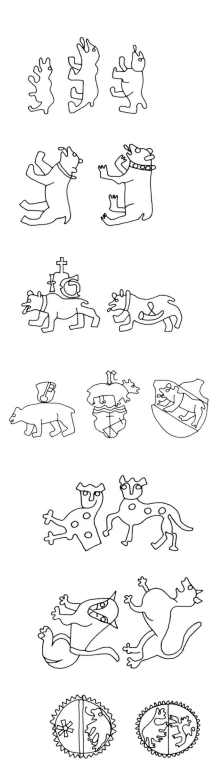

in various classes according to how well it aged and how easily it could be archived. Age-resistance was specified in several so-called 'normal paper' classes. The particular quality had to be identified in the paper itself by means of watermarks which had to include the name of the manufacturer. These regulations were in effect from the 1890s until the mid-twentieth century. Hence every fine paper manufacturer who wanted to supply government agencies with their products had to be able to deliver watermarkable paper. In the German Reich more than a hundred paper manufacturers were eventually listed as official paper suppliers.

Once these technological foundations had been created, it became common for commercial and industrial enterprises, as well as well-off private individuals, to use corporate or personal stationery with individually designed watermarks. Some highly specialized companies, such as Andreas Kufferath in Düren-Mariaweiler, North Rhine-Westphalia and the O. Seele metal cloth factory in Pausa, Saxony, translated the desired designs into corresponding watermark dandy rolls. In doing so, they had to bear in mind that, during drying, watermarks produced with those rolls did not simply retain their proportions as a copy of the dip hand mold. The processes were more complicated in paper production with a long screen paper machine: the paper was stretched in the rolling direction and shrunk again while running through the steam-heated drying cylinders. In order to produce a circular watermark, one had to solder an elliptical watermark figure onto the dandy roll.

Watermarks were very well suited for items that needed to be protected against counterfeiting. Stocks and bonds are cases in point. For German securities it was specified that only papers with all-over watermarks of one of the specific securities' printing companies could be used. This means that, as opposed to stationery watermarks, securities' watermarks consisted not of a single,

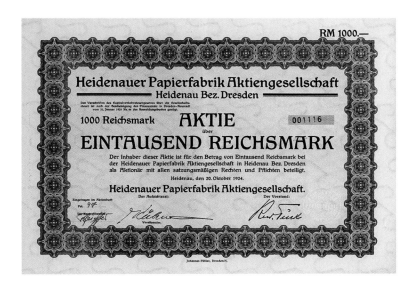

centered figure, but rather of an all-over pattern covering the entire surface of the sheet. This was also the case for all related coupons. Today, watermarked papers are used only in areas where they represent one security feature among others, as in banknotes. They no longer play a role in the production of stamps. Real watermarks are still found in the products of round screen paper machines or in papers produced by the few workshops that still make handmade paper, such as the Basel Paper Mill, the Homburg am Main Paper Mill and the Paper Workshop of Gangolf Ulbricht in Berlin.

— *Frieder Schmidt*

1000 Reichsmark share certificate dated October 20, 1924. The security watermarks become visible when the paper is held against light.

Treaties and Laws

Some contracts in our everyday life do not require legal form, even the important ones. Rental agreements for a car or for an apartment that is to be rented for no longer than one year, for example, can be settled orally in some countries, such as Germany. However, until the invention of digital text, paper was the bearer of legal acts, the decrees of secular rulers, the papal bull, and intergovernmental agreements. Long ago, stone served the same purpose; from Moses and the Ten Commandments to the Code of Hammurabi, the Babylonian King, who inscribed his laws on a basalt stele. It is sometimes said that 'paper is patient', essentially meaning that many things can be written on it. However, it is also said, if an agreement is not upheld, that it was 'not worth the paper it was written on.' Documents and treaties such as the United States Declaration of Independence on July 4, 1776, exude an almost sacred aura, even after all sorts of different printed versions have surfaced. This is also the case for the original version of the 1847–1848 *Communist Manifesto* published by Marx and Engels. All texts that form ways of thinking, briefs or rulings that directly affect the lives of the individual or the many, have this characteristic: the paper bearing the load may be fragile or transient, the text old-fashioned or even cruel, but the document persists as a symbol of social processes, historical agreements and declarations and its effect on man and mankind is historical and long-lived. Seen in this light, it can be considered as an irony of history that the thirteen former colonies renounced Britain with their written declaration, for Britain to this day has only individual laws, no written constitution. — *Philipp Hontschik*

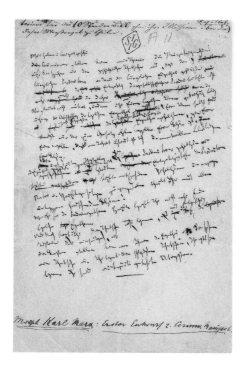

Left: Barely legible manuscript page of the manifesto of the Communist Party, signature of Karl Marx, 1847.

Opposite: The Declaration of Independence of the United States of North America, July 4, 1776. Depicted here is the official complete copy of the document which includes fifty-seven signatures that were added on August 2 and on later occasions.

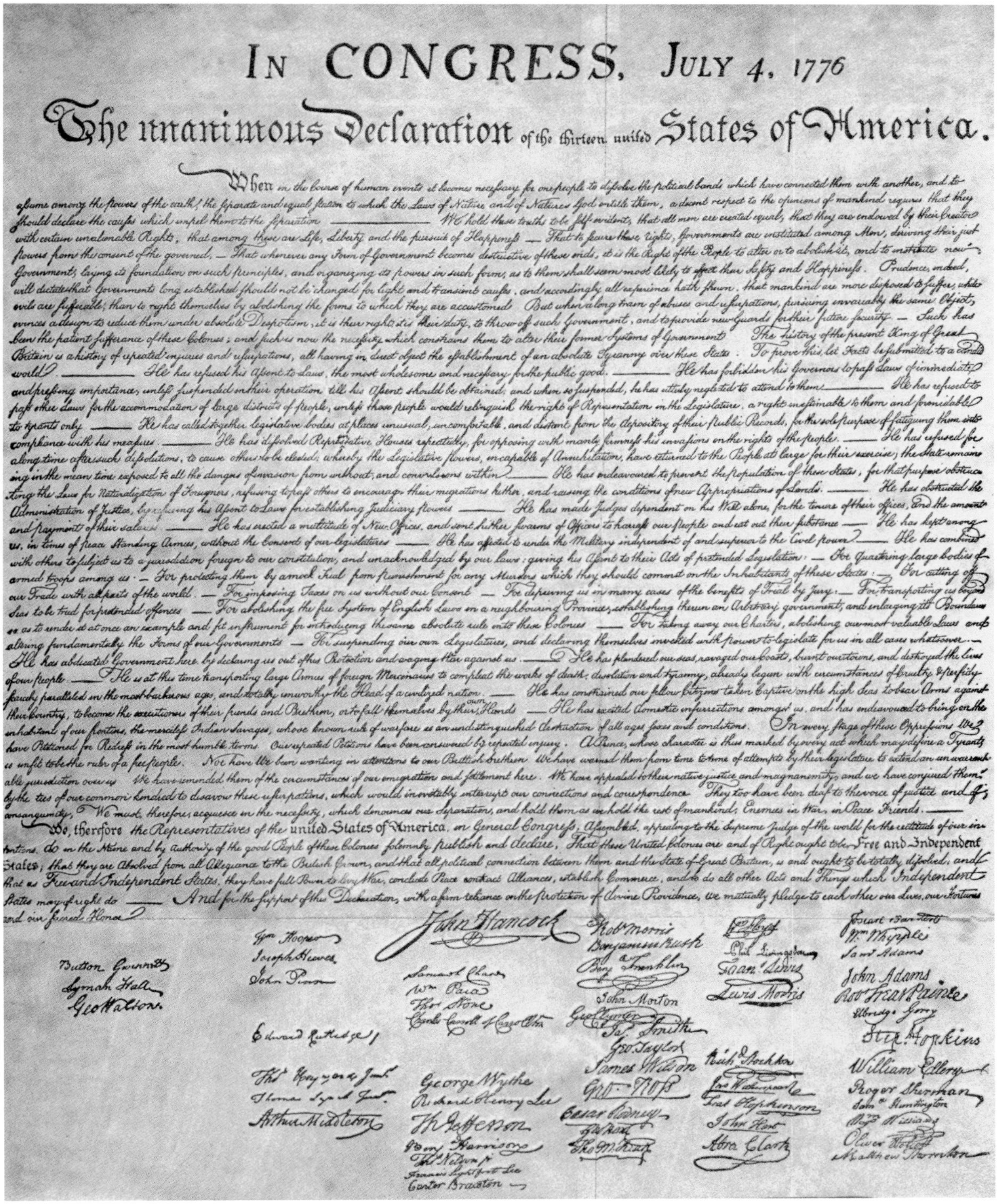

Paper Money

When the Bank of England began to distribute smaller, more manageable polymer-plastic five pound notes in 2016, there was a bit of an uproar among vegetarians, vegans and certain religious faiths that these 'fivers' contained animal fat. A petition to abolish the new banknote quickly gathered 85,000 signatures. The Bank of England argued, however, that it would be far too costly to remove the tiny amount of beef tallow from the notes and that recalling them would be both expensive and time consuming.

Thus the controversial 'fiver' shows not only an anxious, yet ultimately confident, Winston Churchill and, as tradition has it, the Queen on the reverse side, but also how central banks and their printers are increasingly turning to plastics. Alongside credit and debit cards, they represent the end of the very long lifespan of paper money.

A Chinese emperor of the Northern Song dynasty issued paper currency shortly after the year 1000 to finance a war. Because he had the notes issued at will, the world experienced its first case of inflation. Marco Polo (1254–1324) was the first European to come into contact with paper money during his travels in the Far East and he went on to tell of it on his return.

In Europe, the advent of paper money is linked to the *Reconquista*, the 'liberation' of Spain from the Moors, which was completed in 1492. The commander of one city there, which had been besieged by Arabs, is said to have issued promissory notes to its inhabitants in exchange for natural produce.

Indeed, it is striking how closely the history of paper money is linked to war. Nazi Germany also tried to capitalize on this when they forged sterling notes. With great efforts and on Hitler's personal order, inmates of the Sachsenhausen concentration camp were forced to mass-produce high-quality British pound notes. This went surprisingly well, although many of those working in the concentration camp's print shop attempted to sabotage the counterfeits. Although the Nazis were unable to bring the forged pound notes into full circulation, they did manage to buy foreign currency and carry out certain transactions with it abroad. Shortly before the end of the war, the Nazis then sank the counterfeit cash and printing plates from Sachsenhausen in Lake Toplitz in Austria. Divers were able to retrieve some amounts of the money and parts of the equipment in the 1950s.

The American statesman Benjamin Franklin, a trained printer, designed this $55 note.

Opposite, bottom: The first 5 Deutsche Mark bill introduced with the currency reform of 1948 under the sovereignty of the western allies in West Germany shows the image of Europa on the bull.

The new British £5 note (*below*), issued in the United Kingdom in 2016 to replace the old £5 (*left*), is crafted out of synthetic polymer, making it more resilient, damage-proof and water resistant. In addition, new security features were added, such as an integrated hologram.
Some of the new features have not even been made public.

Today, anti-forgery is critical when it comes to paper money. The techniques involved are becoming ever-more complicated and sophisticated, simply because the counterfeiters kit themselves out afresh every time there is a new digital image-making development. However, the new 50 Euro note, made out of cotton-fiber paper and introduced in April 2017, put the greatest test on the skills and techniques of the forgers. If you hold the note up to the light, a hologram strip becomes visible, showing the mythological figure of Europa, which can also be seen on the front and the back of the note as a watermark. The design was by the Berlin-based graphic artist, Reinhold Gerstetter, and it should outwit even the most talented of forgers.

There is a small irony attached to European integration here: The euro, as a currency, was meant to lead to European unity, but has possibly achieved quite the opposite and continues to provoke mistrust. When the new German five Deutschmark bill of 1948 was issued, it too showed Europa, but this time as she was being abducted. — *Philipp Hontschik*

The remote ancestors of
the computer: punched
cards as data carriers,
which were used both in
Jacquard looms (1805)
and, as Hollerith punch
cards (1890), to tabulate
census data.

Punch Cards

In the US presidential elections' run-in at the poll in Florida's Miami-Dade County in 2000, the two candidates, George W. Bush and Al Gore were running neck-and-neck. The electorate had voted by using polling machines and punch card ballot systems. Court decisions led to the polling station carrying out a recount. The issue was whether a punched ballot card should be interpreted as a vote for the nominee in question, or if they should be declared invalid because they had not been completely punched out. Election aides eventually rebelled and had to be forced to continue counting out the ballots. The goings-on in Miami-Dade during this time were a massive blot on the record of punch-card technology in the USA, a system that had previously taken a great burden off many of the bureaucrats running elections and censuses.

Herman Hollerith, born in 1860 in Buffalo, New York, to German immigrants, was the inventor of the punch card to process data. As his model, Hollerith used the designs of two Frenchmen, who were able to control looms using punch cards. In addition, Hollerith observed railway conductors, who punched tickets in different places. In this way, they marked certain characteristics of the individual passenger, such as gender and skin color in order to prevent or make it more difficult for the same ticket to be used by more than one person.

In the case of barrel organs, it is the punch card positioned above the bellows that determines the tune. According to the principle: the position of the punched paper equals the pitch, and the shape of the punching equals the length of the tone. Which in theory meant that Hollerith's punch card could also enable the ballot counter to gather at a glance basic data on U.S. voters. In essence, Hollerith's punch cards could be compared to today's so-called 'big data'. The binary principle of 1 and 0 apply here. In other words: 'hole' or 'paper or no hole' (on that part of the ballot paper) means 'yes' or 'no' or, in other words, equals a decision between '1' and '0'. The world of electronics and modern PCs has subsequently ensured that paper as the carrier of binary information has gradually made itself redundant. To be even clearer about it, we could say that punch cards were, in fact, the beginning of the end of paper, at least in data processing.

— *Philipp Hontschik*

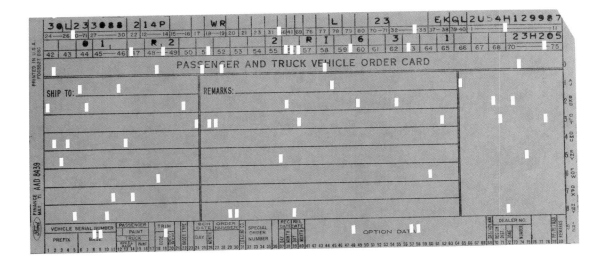

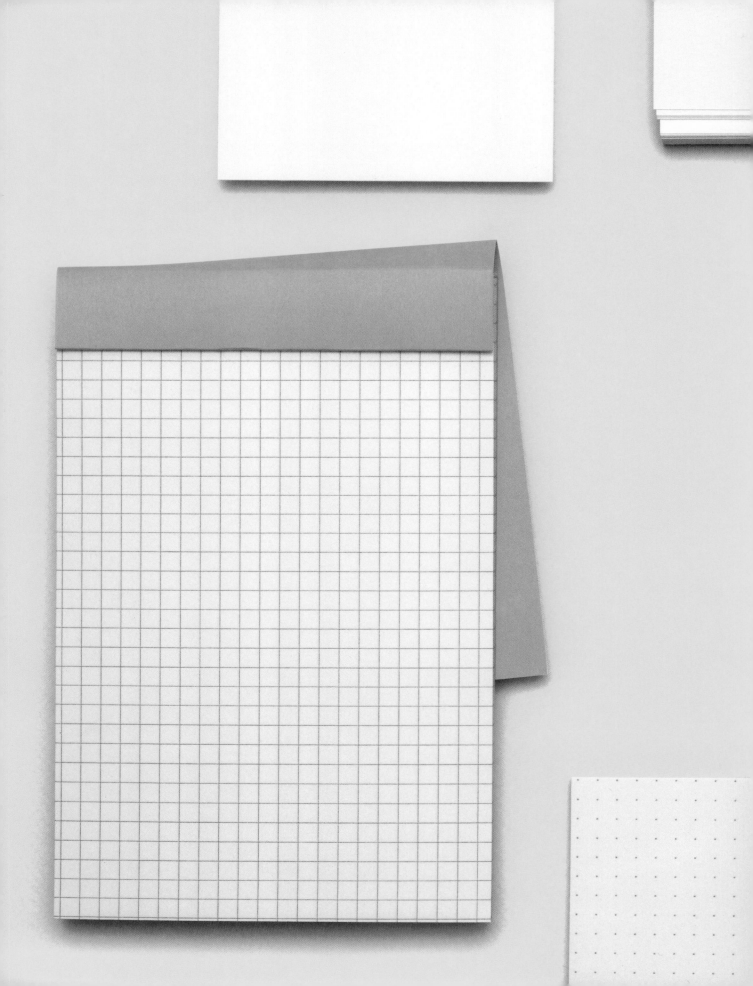

Paper
Surfaces

Paper as a Rectangular Surface

The plain, usually rectangular sheet of paper is, on the one hand, a springboard into the infinite possibilities of what unfolds on it – be it marks, drawing, writing, or any form of printing. Whatever happens on this surface is at the same time defined by the boundaries of the format. On the other hand, a blank sheet invariably also marks the touching delimitation of a surface on which very little or nothing has yet happened – that initially is empty, a white sheet of paper: a silent impetus to possible production or a defined surface of calm pause?

Lothar Müller opens his seminal book *White Magic: The Age of Paper* (first published in German in 2012, English edition 2014) with a reference to an outrageous thought experiment concerning a microbe that attacks and corrodes all paper. In 1932, Paul Valéry came up with this idea of the total destruction of all paper in 1932 to bring home the indispensability of paper in his day. At the end of the twentieth century, Jacques Derrida proposed considering the universality of paper in the context of its gradual retreat. Müller conflates these two approaches into three thematic layers in his book: he looks at the physical, material shape of paper and the technology of its production, then at the function of paper as a cultural technique or a medium of storage and circulation, and finally he pursues the question to what extent the age of paper described by him has "developed an awareness of itself." Alternating between these approaches and accurately referencing historical cultural sources, he tells his complex and fascinating history of the paper age.

But where is the place of the plain sheet of paper in this cultural historical synopsis? Müller addresses it once physically, as the sheet of paper, "the way in which it is scooped and which determines the shape of paper." Sheet sizes and formats can be derived historically from the size of the dip molds or the various manipulations at the pulp vat. But the sheet of paper might just as well signify all that can take place on a sheet, from the broadsheet and the newspaper to the deck of cards, the index card, and the many ephemera of everyday life. — *Nicola von Velsen*

Paper as as White Space

We come across paper as a surface, especially as a designed surface, every day in many, very different situations. It has a variety of disparate functions that have changed in everyday digital life. Some things, such as business cards or paper-covered globes, receive more (and more interesting) attention, while others, such as entry tickets, have vanished from daily life. Paper, as white space and in its physical structure, as material and as surface, plays an essential role in design and production. Highly specialized professions (including font foundries, typesetters, graphic designers, typographers, etc.) have always concerned themselves with exactly how printing ink actually marks the page. Typographers and graphic designers unite messages and information with paper. The form evolves from the requirements of content and function; starting with manuscripts, ideas and sketches, the designers develop a finished product, a printed substance. They fix something fleeting, translating content and message into a visual language with the objective of making it accessible and legible for third parties. As an artifact, as designed and printed matter – be they books, brochures or ephemera – they remain as they are for future generations.

Paper as a Playing Field

In essence, typography means designing within limited boundaries: in addition to type objects, twenty-six letters are used in the Latin alphabet, plus numbers 0–9, as well as punctuation and special characters. Ink was originally black, which when combined with white paper affords the highest possible contrast.

The designer arranges, composes, and structures these elements on a surface that is, effectively, his or her playing field. In the case of printed matter this playing field is almost always paper. Designing printed matter also means an enduring commitment, since both the ink and paper enter into an inseparable connection. Once something has been printed it cannot be undone. Design using fonts, images, lines and surfaces is commonly called typography. In addition to design themes of layout, white space and typesetting, the

The empty field surrounds the printed area, the type area. It becomes an empty space in the background. The white space has a practical function: it buffers the text, shielding it from distractions in the immediate setting.

typographer will also take into account the choice of paper, binding and packaging. At the micro level, typographical design focuses on font, character and line spacing; at the macro level design is concerned with the fine balance of graphic elements.

Typography could also be described as minimalist insofar as it is essentially characterized by the subtle interaction of form and counter-form. Take the shape of a letter, for example: the white inner spaces are part of the form. The unprinted surface is by no means 'undesigned' or undefined, but an integral part of the letter.

As with the micro, the relationship between white space and content is equally evident at the macro level. White space, together with questions of composition and form, has a very important purpose. With white space, content is shaped and structured, connections strengthened and other content kept apart. White space helps the reader orientate.

Paper as a Physical White Space

On both the macro and the micro level, an unprinted surface is a perceptible, uncovered white paper. Since printed and unprinted matter form a united whole, the texture and characteristics of the paper, especially the paper's tone and brightness, will always have an influence on the design process and affect the result. Paper is therefore an integral part of the design. It gives white space a physical dimension, allowing it to be experienced beyond the visual. In other words, it can be felt, touched, and even smelt and heard. With every design, it is the overall impression, resulting from the complex interplay of all these factors, which counts. Perhaps in this context one can also speak of an aura or sound that radiates from a truly well designed piece of printed matter (poster, invitation, booklet) or a book. The judicious choice of paper suitable to the specific task plays a big part.

The proportion of white space can vary greatly depending on the design medium. Hardly any white paper is visible in printed newspapers; the typeface is small and dense. Here white space is conserved for economic reasons, and lines between the columns offset the missing white. A printed letterhead, on the other hand, has a lot of white space: the paper surface here is a platform for an individual person or a business. Paper at work!

From Paper to Screen

With the development of digital media, typography increasingly takes place without paper. There many are new applications, and many products, which previously would have been printed, have been replaced by digital forms.

When designing for and on paper, the size of the paper limits the design's format and proportions, much like a painter's canvas. When designing for the screen, the rules are different. The space to be

Aa	Bb	Cc	Dd	Ee	Ff
Gg	Hh	Ii	Ji	Kk	Ll
Mm	Nn	Oo	Pp	Qq	Rr
Ss	Tt	Uu	Vv	Ww	Xx
Yy	Zz	Ää	Öö	Üü	

1	2	3	4	5	6
7	8	9	0		

.,	:;	– =	„"	– +	*
!?	()	/†	% §	$ £	&

A typographer's typical inventory principally consists of twenty-six letters.

politani etiam tractus extimantur. Niuibus per hyemem ferè totus mons ca-
net: cacumen neqz per aeftatem uiduatur.
B. P. Quid, quod hyemare tantum
eas meminit Strabo? B. F. A experien
tia ita te docet, ufqz ipfe auctor (quod qui
dem uenia illius dixerim) non deterior.
Quare illud mi pater etiã, atqz etiam uide;
ne quid te moueat, fi aliqua ex parte huius
noftri de Aetna fermonis cum uetuftis feri
ptoribus diffentimus: nihil enim impedit
fuiffe tum ea omnia, quae ipfi olim tradi
dere, quorum permãferint plurima in no
ftram diem; quaedam fe immutauerit; ali
qua etiam furrexerint noua: nam (ut cãete
ra omittam); quod cinerofa partim effe
fumma cacumina dictauere; eius rei nunc
ueftigium nullũ apparet: cinis enim, qui
queat confpici, toto mõte nullus eft: neqz
id tamen omnibus annis fuit: nam mul
torum teftimonio accepimus, qui uide
re, annos ab hinc quadraginta tan-

tos ex Aetna cineres euolaffe; ut per to-
tam eam infulae partem, quae uerfus Pe
lorum iacet, uniuerfam oleam abftule-
rint; eos etiam in Italiam uentis feren
tibus latos. Sed (ut ad niues illas redea
mus) addebat idem Vrbanus Kalen-
dis Iuniis afcendente fe fatis largiter, a-
bundèqz ninxiffe; tum iterum, qui fe-
ptimus fuerit poft eum diem, dum
ipfe Randatii moraretur, in uniuerfam
montanam plagam niues ferè in pedis al
titudinem defcendiffe: in quo ipfo licet
et Pindarum fufpicias fcite cognomento
ufum; qui Aetnam niuium nutricem ap
pellarit. Quo latere fubeft Catana, me
dia ferè inter ipfam, et cacumen regione
puriffimus, et perennis fons erumpit do
rico uocabulo Crana ab incolis appella
ta: caeterum toto monte fupra radices nul
lae aquae funt; nifi quae uel ex niuibus
emanant; cuius quidem rei etiã Theocri
tum tefte habemus; in quo dum Galateae

D iii

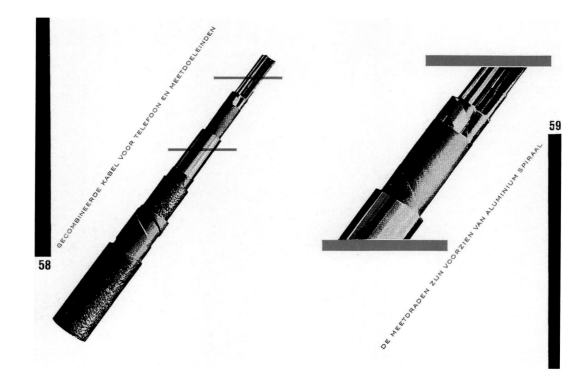

GECOMBINEERDE KABEL VOOR TELEFOON EN MEETDOELEINDEN

58

DE MEETDRADEN ZIJN VOORZIEN VAN ALUMINIUM SPIRAAL.

59

designed can be large or small, wide or narrow. With digital design, the designer's challenge is no longer to execute a design for a single given format. A visual concept needs to work equally well on any number of differently sized monitor or screen, where size and proportions can differ enormously from one device to the next (RWD or responsive web design).

It is still more enjoyable and less tiring to read large amounts of text on paper than reading from back-lit screens. A truth borne out by the displays developed for e-book readers, which try to replicate the reading experience of a printed book as faithfully as possible.

— *Neil Holt*

Opposite: A blank white surface frames the printed 'type area.' It becomes the empty space in the background. Unlike the Renaissance, Modernism elevated the unprinted areas to equal status as an element of design. Surface tension supersedes envelopment. In twentieth-century typography, here exemplified by an ad for the Delft Cable Factory by Piet Zwart, the unprinted is given the same creative importance as the printed. The dominating angle results in an intense white effect as inner counter-form.

For this 2012 poster design Felix Pfäffli exploits the impact of maximum contrast (between black and white). A poster doesn't have to be brightly colored to attract attention.

Type is 'imprinted' in a slightly depressed,
relief-like manner. In book printing, type
leaves a physical mark.

Type on Paper

With well-measured pressure, the letters are set down. They almost shimmer on the soft, dull and fibrous paper, standing out in relief, slightly recessed, 'impressed'. At the edge of the impression, a typical crushed border is visible. Letters leave a physical mark. Ink and paper are more than superficially connected at this point. This union of lead, printing ink, and paper, is inseparable.

Paper and Type

The relationship between paper and writing (as a printed typeface) has been influenced by technical and social developments, and vice-versa, since printing was invented.

Due to the way it was made, early paper had a coarse, rough surface, and was heavily fibrous. The creators of the first typeset works had to take this into account in their work. They needed to design letter type robust enough to achieve an acceptable, legible printed image given the paper quality. In the eighteenth century, the English printer, John Baskerville (1706–1775), and one of the most famous typographers of his generation, improved the quality of his printing paper and developed it into a smoother, firmer and less fibrous surface. These papers allowed the use of finer line widths on the cast letters, which consequently allowed for the development of higher-contrast type. It was only later that smoothed paper surfaces made it possible to print typeface with very fine lines.

The Italian typesetter and printer, Giambattista Bodoni (1740–1813), followed in Baskerville's design path, taking heightened contrast between broad strokes and thin lines to the extreme. His much-used, eponymous Bodoni font is the most famous example of this style. These kinds of fonts make the highest demands on paper and printers. Only very smooth paper allows the imprint of hair-fine serifs, otherwise the fine lines will break off during printing, leaving the text disfigured and hard to read. Paper tone also plays an essential role: too white a paper leads to a blurring, akin to over-exposure, of the fine lines, which can also distort the shape of the letters and inhibit readability.

Lead type or 'sorts' are rectangular forms, carrying a reverse relief of the character to be printed.

Advances and refinement in printing techniques have influenced the development of type design, producing darker and denser inks, meaning letters can be applied to paper using far less pressure. Printing onto paper is now only a slight touch on the surface of the material.

The invention of the Foudrinier machine around 1800 led to the mechanization of paper production, meaning larger and lower priced paper formats could be produced. This had an influence on the newspaper printing industry, which was emerging in the latter part of the 19th century: larger formats and much higher print-runs could be printed in a much shorter time. However, the cheaper paper was of poor quality and coarse surface texture. This, once again, had consequences for typefaces. The high-contrast, fine serif types widespread at this time were simply not suitable for printing under these conditions. Therefore, appropriate fonts were developed. These were often based on transitional typefaces, increasing the line weight and strengthening the serif. As a result, robust newspaper fonts appeared, such as the now famous Times New Roman (1930), which went on to become the standard font in a many writing programs.

The typesetter composes lead type by hand into words, lines, and then turns the lines into columns. The result is a printing form, onto which ink is applied.

Type as an Image

The introduction of phototypesetting (or photosetting) in the 1950s led to the 'dematerialization' of type. Until that time, typesetting materials had always been physically present as tangible lead objects. In the new compositing technique type became pure image. Letters now exist as film negative. Light passes through a photographic template, like a slide projection in letter-form, onto a film material. This meant that, for the first time, type as a material-bound string of letters was no longer static. Instead, it has become flexible and changeable. Letters can be distorted and enlarged. At the same time, offset printing was gradually replacing traditional book printing. In the case of offset printing – a process derived from lithography – ink is no longer transferred onto the paper directly, but by way of a rubber cylinder. Since the letters are applied indirectly and without putting pressure on the paper itself, the squeezed edges disappeared, and in addition, letters are rendered with more sharpness. When designing typefaces for this new printing process, these new physical and technical conditions need to be taken into consideration so that existing font designs can be adapted accordingly. The dematerialization of typeface moved further with digital typesetting: letters consist of pixels and vectors, which effectively means that character sets are based on a collection of coded characters.

With photosetting, light is projected through a template with negative character, and then through an optical system, onto film or photographic paper.

Paperless Fonts

For many centuries, paper was almost always the bearer of words and letters, (apart from inscriptions on gravestones or house and shop signs and plaques and so on). Today, written information and communication is increasingly taking place on mobile devices or computers. Letters behave differently on paper than on illuminated displays. The conditions for fonts are therefore different from when printing on paper. On one hand, screen resolutions are usually low so a sharp representation of all font details is not possible. On the other hand, the bright screen background can lead to readers becoming irritated. Serif fonts, especially those with very fine lines, are not as well suited for this purpose, which is why sans-serif types are often preferred. Some media that used to be printed in the past, such as directories and dictionaries, have been completely replaced by digital applications, newspapers have reduced their print runs and novels are often read on e-books. It is certain that other printed media will be replaced by digital applications in the future. However, if the decision falls in favor of a product or item being printed on paper, then that paper plays an important role and is chosen with great care. Increasingly, these will be uncoated papers, where the tactile materiality of paper makes its touch and feel special.

— *Neil Holt*

A present-day digital character set consists of a collection of glyphs. A glyph is a graphic representation of a single character.

Maps and Globes

Everything our ancestors saw and experienced outside the cave was recreated through wall paintings and petroglyphs inside the cave. The touching and remarkable early-human quantum leap was to situate the self in the image of the world they saw. The ability to define and express the notion of 'where on earth are we?' in a 'map' must have been meaningful for the group, to which each individual belonged.

In basic terms, the ability to comprehend three dimensions, such as understanding distances, contours, boundaries, had to be rendered in a two-dimensional reproduction. In prehistoric times, depicting a saber-toothed tiger was far less challenging than showing the accurate distance from the dwelling place to the nearest source of water.

The history of cartography goes back to an almost 12,000-year-old mammoth tooth and one of the oldest 'maps' ever carved. By the year 1666, when Sir Christopher Wren presented an urban planning proposal – never executed – for the rebuilding of London in the wake of the Great Fire, mapping had come a very long way.

A similar leap occurs from Wren to the modern GPS (Global Positioning System) or to the well-known German walking guides known as 'Falk' maps, which often left many struggling with folding and unfolding, especially in high winds. The first people would have struggled likewise.

During antiquity, natural philosophers led a countermovement, moving from a two-dimensional map to a three-dimensional globe. In 600 BCE, the Babylonians produced a map of the world, portraying the earth as a flat circle, with Babylon at the center surrounded by all the other countries. The idea of a spherical earth was already being upheld by Eratosthenes of Cyrene – head of the library at Alexandria – in the third century BCE, with his model globe whose circumference he attempted to calculate and upon which he based his maps. And so the representation of the Earth slowly returned to the notion of the three-dimensional: Ptolemy (c.160–100 BCE) regarded the Earth as round, but still placed it at the center of the universe; Copernicus (1473–1543) overturned everything when he put the sun at the center of all the planets. In 1492, when the New World was first encountered by Europeans, the Moors were expelled

Bellerby & Co. Globemakers in London are makers of fine handmade globes. Preparing the flat maps of the world and the stars and applying them onto the spherical globe presents a major technical challenge. For this purpose the cartographic data are transferred into a projection consisting of about twelve elliptical paper segments.

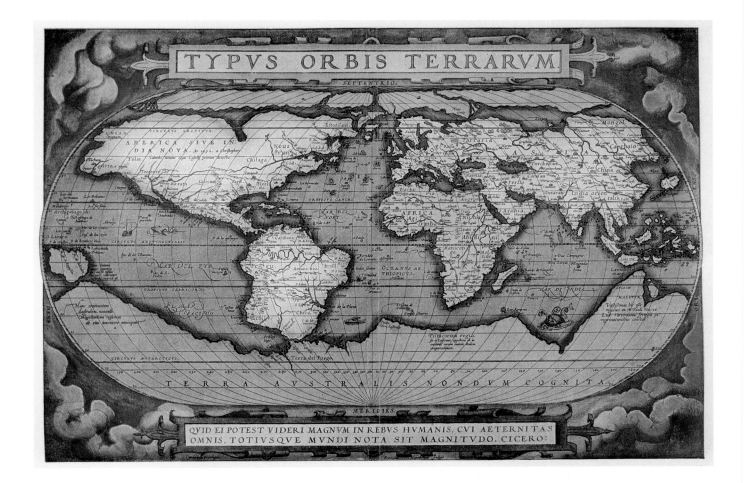

from Spain and the Renaissance prince Lorenzo de Medici (1449–1492) died, Martin Behaim created the 'Erdapfel' – literally 'earth apple' – the oldest extant terrestrial globe. Since then, people have continued to enjoy the miniature models of the planet they on which they live. To navigate the planet, all civilizations have used the night sky as their guide, not least, the coastal mariners, which probably explains the origin of celestial globes, depicting the constellations as they were then understood, revealing only ever a fleeting picture of the starry firmament as it is in perpetual motion. In most cases, terrestrial and celestial globes were produced at the same time and set up in pairs.

Today, cartography is all about the computer and its superhuman accuracy. However, the manual production of a globe is still a demanding craft, requiring the greatest concentration and care. Narrow elliptical strips of pre-printed map-paper are applied to the spherical shape and high-quality map paper then covers the two polar ice caps, which depict the Arctic and Antarctic, hiding the joins. Relief globes and their three-dimensional reproduction on the earth's crust, do have a wonderful a tactile appeal, but they are not to be trusted: Everest would be just 0.5 mm high according to the scale of a 60-cm-diameter relief globe. This would hardly be perceptible at all if the manufacturer were to deviate from scale in even the smallest way.
— *Philipp Hontschik*

Typus Orbis Terrarum is a 1570 world map from a collection of maps titled *Theatrum Orbis Terrarum*, the so-called 'Ortelius Atlas' published by Abraham Ortelius in Antwerp. This atlas represents the summary of sixteenth-century cartography and appeared in numerous editions in its time.

Playing Cards

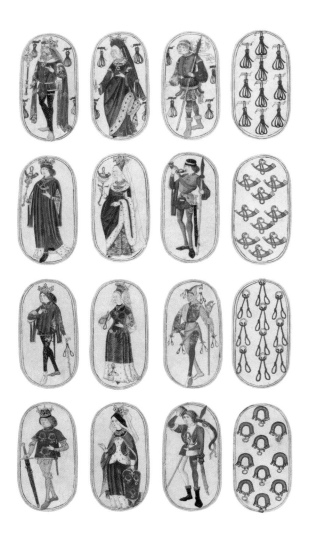

There is probably nothing more dull than a stack of dormant playing cards: they only become interesting when the game begins. This might be true today when image upon image is available to us, but what might the imagery and numerical values of the cards have meant to people in the image-poor centuries of times gone by?

Rectangular playing cards, printed on both sides, and based on the size of a human hand, spread rapidly in Europe from the fourteenth century, alongside the rapid expansion of paper production and printing technology. Popular with both the aristocracy and the people, they were easy to transport, handy, inexpensive and available everywhere – not unlike the smart phone you might say. Playing cards have been produced in factories in Europe since around 1500. Ironically, their triumphal march across Europe was, if anything, due to their prohibition – gambling being the devil's work – rather than to any one game.

Card games generally fall into shedding, accumulating, comparing, and fishing types. A special group are tarot cards, however, some extraordinary educational card games have also emerged since the late eighteenth century. Collectible card games such as 'Magic: The Gathering' are a more contemporary form of game.

A card player's sensual pleasure is varied: tapping the pack of cards on the table before shuffling, the shuffling itself, both skilled and casual, dealing the cards with a flick of the wrist, picking them up, sorting the hand. Then the cards, still slightly warm from the dealer's hands, are suddenly filled with life: queen, king and jack even seem to have facial expressions.

In the classic poker movie *Cincinnati Kid* (1965), as the eponymous 'Kid' reveals the all-important jack of diamonds, the camera flashes between the playing card and the eyes of the other actors in quick succession. But how do gamblers do it in reality? Do they focus on their opponents, or just the money? Even those playing scat or thirty-one with their friends for a few pennies feel the excitement when the game is going their way. At some point, the card night is over and the playing cards return back to that simple, slightly worn pile of paper. — *Philipp Hontschik*

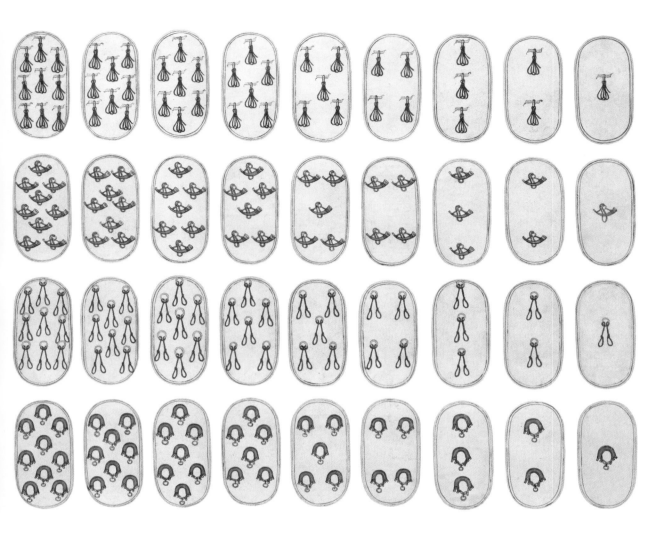

Playing cards from c. 1475–80, made in Burgundian territories. Pen and ink, opaque paint, glazes, applied silver and gold on paper (four layers of pasteboard), 5 ³⁄₁₆ × 2 ¾ in. (13.2 × 7 cm) each. Metropolitan Museum of Art, New York. This deck of cards from the fifteenth century is remarkable because it has survived complete and in good condition. King, queen, and jack are easy to identify and the numerical value of the playing cards is indicated by the number of symbols.

Ephemera

Motorists occasionally find a card stuffed into the rim of their side window, asking if they would be interested in selling their car. No, not interested, and the card-sized business offer ends up on their dashboard. Done and dusted for today. 'Ephemera' comes from ancient Greek and means 'just for one day.' Most commonly, English-speaking countries understand ephemera to be small, printed, disposable paper objects: the thin paper wrapper around an air-freighted orange, the place card from a wedding, never thrown away even though the divorce happened years ago – not something a new spouse would enjoy coming across. Cards received to congratulate the birth of the kids and cards sent to announce them.

What went into thinking how to make them attractive and original, rather than just the mundane run-of-the-mill? The tickets to that once-in-a-lifetime Rolling Stones concert; business cards on the office pinboard – those who present themselves professionally on such a small card deserve far better even if the first meeting, when the card was received, did not result in a follow-up one; postcards stuck to the fridge for a week or so by magnets, eventually get stored in a box and never seen again. Feng-shui is the natural enemy of paper ephemera, but oceans of memories are attached to it; suitcase labels from the hotel in Beijing, reminding one how spicy the food was there, and sky over the city, how blue!

Looking back, ephemera are collections of life stories. Some people even leave a small photographic portrait of themselves with an obituary

A selection of various ephemera from the past 150 years or so, ranging from the admission ticket, the wine label, and the birth announcement to stationery and the small calling card, here presented by a loyal dog.

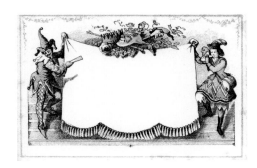

and a quote from the Bible as a last testimony of their life. A death image, ephemeral in relation to how well the deceased was known to the living. Ephemera have different lifespans. A secret message should be seen as briefly as possible, like a note with two or three numbers handed to the Chancellor by an aide before a speech at the Bundestag.

One of the most elaborate ephemera is certainly counterfeit money. 'Duds' go from the producer's side to the unwitting consumer and then manifest themselves as 'cash'. Theoretically, they can lie about their true value for years until they eventually get caught out. In contrast, psychological warfare leaflets usually fall victim to the enemy's fastest possible elimination. During World War II each side tried to wear down the enemy, dropping request after request for submission. It was forbidden for soldiers and civilians even to pick up the papers, let alone read or redistribute them – the same went for pamphlets. This was the case for the 'White Rose' resistance group, based at the University of Munich, which circulated pamphlets opposing the Nazi regime during 1942–1943 at certain risk of death. These leaflets should be classed as ephemera – designed to be read hastily and disposed of without a trace. Understandably given the danger, hardly any of them survived, those that did becoming the glories of resistance to Hitler. On the other hand, John F. Kennedy's crib note for his famous speech did survive – *"Ich bin ein Berliner."* This quote remains slightly crumpled in history's verbal coat pocket.
— *Philipp Hontschik*

The pamphlet of the White Rose resistance group in Nazi Germany as a representative example of all ephemera that have become historical documents. John F. Kennedy's handwritten note spelling out the famous words he spoke in Berlin in 1963 is not printed and therefore, strictly speaking, not an ephemera but, on the other hand, a casual piece of paper as a personal pledge of history.

Opposite: And even more freely put together ephemera. Here the poster joins a postcard, inflation-ravaged bank notes and box labels.

Paper: A Practical Guide

The qualities of varying types of paper are more often than not extremely subtle and only perceptible when studied by closer visual inspection or touch. Often, the exact differences between types and qualities of paper only become clear when making a direct comparison. It could be that this is one of the reasons for paper often being underestimated in terms of designing printed matter.

To differentiate between papers, there are, on the one hand, objective and measurable qualities that can be expressed in numerical form, such as grammage, volume and format. On the other, features such as shade of tone, feel, look and effect of the paper are of a more subjective nature.

Making the right choice of paper has a decisive influence on the outcome and appearance of printed products. The following pages explain the properties of paper most relevant to printing. As a designed and printed surface, paper comes to life in the subtle interplay between surface and area and the interaction of printed and unprinted surfaces. When it comes to choosing paper, concrete questions of what is actually technically possible in the given conditions are just as important as questions of design or visual effect. A designer should familiarize herself or himself with the basic characteristics and technical requirements of paper. Ultimately, choosing a paper that's right for a particular task will decide whether a printed matter 'feels right' overall.

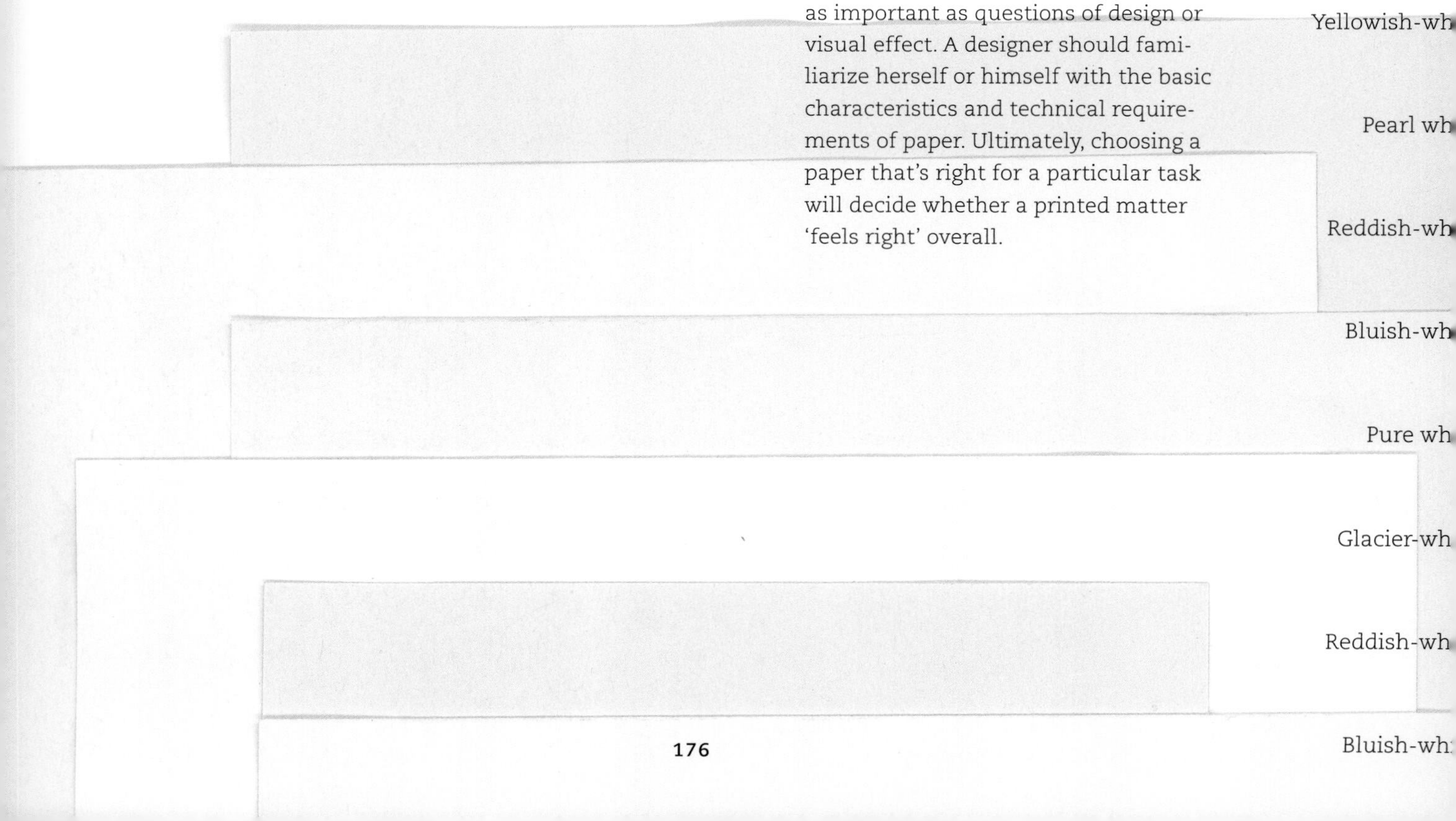

Cre

Cham

Yellowish-wh

Pearl wh

Reddish-wh

Bluish-wh

Pure wh

Glacier-wh

Reddish-wh

Bluish-wh

Paper Shades

Although a sheet of paper may at first be perceived as simply white, there is, on closer scrutiny, and compared against other 'white' papers, a variety of different intensities and shades of tone. Papers in certain tones will be seen as brighter than others.

The measure of whiteness determines how white undyed paper is. A sheet of paper can be bright white or less white, cold toned, such as bluish whites or, like yellowish and reddish white, warm in tone.

Paper is dyed at the production stage using bleaches, pigments and controlled additives. The shade and whiteness of paper influences everything that is printed on it. An image on cream-colored paper will differ greatly from one printed on high white. Pure white paper allows for color-neutral reproduction, with illustrations, for example. Large volumes of text, however, are easier to read when the contrast with the paper is not too strong. For most novels, for example, yellowish paper is preferred.

Fewer shades are available to the trade today, because paper shades can be simulated in color printing. This has become technically possible due to the creation of ever-more fine print screens. It is possible to make out the grid dots with the help of a line counter, and the true shade of the unprinted paper can be seen at the trimming edge, but a printed shade can hardly be differentiated from a true one with the naked eye.

Surfaces

Uncoated papers are manufactured using wood that has been processed into a chemical pulp that removes the lignin from the wood fibers – they consist only of fiber and additives. Since synthetic and subsequent surface treatment is not required, they are also referred to as 'natural' papers. Uncoated papers have a rough, porous surface and will therefore soak up a lot more of the ink. How strongly this effect occurs depends on how coarse, open, or fine is the surface of each paper. Uncoated paper is preferred for text prints because there is no reflection from the matte surface, which might disturb the reader's eye.

Reproducing images on fine surfaces, however, limits detailed reproduction. This lack of sharpness, however, if skillfully used, can also in itself create a particular mood.

Uncoated paper, often called factory-printing paper, is to be frequently found in the printing of large amounts of text material, such as paperback novels and non-fiction books.

Coated papers have a treated surface. After production, the length of paper is finished with a layer of special additives. This closes up the 'pores' of the paper, leaving it with a smooth and firm surface. Printing inks do not penetrate the paper so deeply and remain on its surface. This allows high level of detail and better print quality. Formerly known as 'picture printing paper,' these coated papers are preferred for printing images, in art books, cookery books and magazines, for example.

Coated paper comes in a variety of finishes, from chalky matte to high gloss. With the glossy type, it should be noted that depending on the amount of light, reflection can occur, which consequently affects reading.

Opacity

Opacity is the opposite of transparency or, in other words, the opacity of a paper describes how opaque or translucent it is.

If paper is too translucent, anything printed on it will appear on the paper's reverse side, which again makes for difficult reading. Complete opacity is not always achievable, especially with thin paper, and because there will almost always be a certain degree of translucency in paper, text needs to be printed exactly in line with the matter on the reverse. A degree of transparency is always welcome because the rhythm of the design and the sequence of a book are visually easier to follow.

A high opacity is achieved when more fillers are added to the fibers for certain paper grades. Opacity also depends on the color, strength and mass of the paper. There is a simple scale to measure the opacity of paper.

The lower the opacity of paper, the more strongly the back-to-front printed lines will appear on the reverse side, and vice versa. Provided that the lines are compatibly set and printed, the indentation of the printed lines will be less distorted and the printed matter is easier to read.

The greater the opacity of a paper, the less the inverted lines show through its reverse. When the lines are printed in line with the text on the other side, the show-through of type is less disturbing and more likely to improve legibility.

Paper Weight

Paper Volume

Paper weight, or grammage, is determined by weighing one square meter of a paper. This defines the grammage of the paper, given as grams per square meter (gsm or g/m²).

This provides a good point of reference. How paper is perceived from a subjective and tangible perspective, however, depends on the interaction between weight and volume.

Grammage is also the differentiating criterion when defining paper, card and cardboard, eventhough figures may vary.

Paper's volume is the ratio between its thickness to its weight in gsm. With normal paper of a standard smoothness, the definition of its volume is simple 1/1 volume. With equal grammage paper should be more resistant the bulkier it is.

Paper thickness is calculated from its volume and its weight. In the book printing industry, it is important that a paper's thickness is known in order to determine the width of the spine.

Paper
up to 170 g/m²

Semi-card
170–200 g/m²

Card
200–700 g/m²

Paperboard und Cardboard
300 to 2400 g/m²

Wallboard
400 to 2400 g/m²

So, for example:

At a weight of 100 gsm

x 1 volume
= 0.100 mm thickness

x 1.25 volume
= 0.125 mm thickness

x 1.5 volume
= 0.150 mm thickness

x 1.75 volume
= 0.175 mm thickness

x 2 volume
= 0.200 mm thickness

x 2.2 volume
= 0.220 mm thickness

Running Direction and Web Width

The running direction, also known as the machine direction, is the course in which paper passes through the paper-processing machine. All industrially manufactured papers have a running direction. It defines the grading of the fibers related to the width of the paper.

Paper's running direction plays a critical role in further processing because paper is more be easily folded and turned – and with thicker papers, laminated – with, rather than against, the running direction. With book and magazine production, the machine direction must always be parallel to the spine. If this is not adhered to, the pages are then difficult to turn or crimp.

With sheet-paper processing, a distinction is made after cutting the sheets from paper rolls between 'long grain' and 'short grain' papers, depending on whether the short or the long edge lies parallel to the paper's edge. The running direction still needs to be monitored for printed matter and tailored printing jobs so that the sheet can cut in the right direction or be further processed.

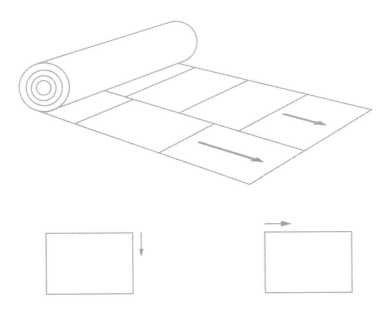

DIN / A-Formats

For centuries there were many different
sizes stemming from old paper formats
and from the size of the scoop used to
make the paper. A standard paper size
was not introduced until 1922 when the
German Institute for Standardization
(DIN) registered entry DIN 476 paper size.

The engineer Walter Porstmann, annoyed
that every letter, envelope and stapler
was a different size, invented a mathematical system that soon spread across
the world. The ratio between width and
height for all formats is 1:root 2 (or
1:1.4142). Folding the base format in half
produces the next format down the scale.
The aspect ratio is always the same.

The A-standard (also known as A series)
starts out with a sheet sized 1 m² and
with an aspect ratio from the page length
to the diagonal length of a square. The
basic format is thus, 841 mm × 1189 mm
and is referred to as DIN A0 or A0.

The A paper size series was supplemented
by the B and C series, which are used for
envelopes, postal packages and so on that
would be holding the A formats.

A0	841 × 1189 mm
A1	594 × 841 mm
A2	420 × 594 mm
A3	297 × 420 mm
A4	210 × 297 mm
A5	148 × 210 mm
A6	105 × 148 mm
A7	74 × 105 mm
A8	52 × 74 mm
A9	37 × 52 mm
A10	26 × 37 mm

Other Paper Formats

Almost all states in the world have adopted the DIN/A format. The major exceptions in the western world being the USA and Canada, where a large number of non-interrelated formats still exist to this day.

The most commonly used stationery format in the United States is the U.S. Letter format, which with the measurements of 8.5 × 11 inches (215.9 × 279.4 mm) is a bit wider and shorter than the A4 (8.3 × 11.7 inches) commonly used in Europe.

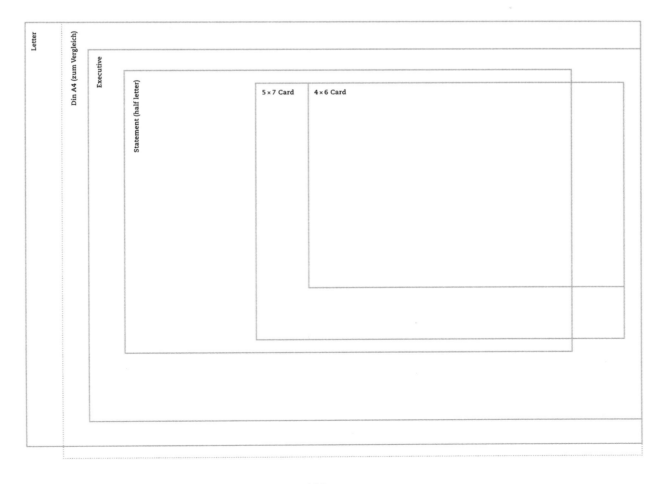

Historic Book Formats

Before paper production was mechanized, paper used to be handmade. The format of the scoop always determined the format of the finished sheet. The most common scoops (and therefore subsequent sheets sizes) were 20 × 30 and 30 × 40 cm.

Book formats derive from the number of pages a printer could create from a single sheet. The book was made by the book-binder through folding, trimming, joining the so-called quires (in each case double pages, front and back) and finally binding. The format was designated by the number of folds made to the sheet of paper.

The ratio between height to width varies according to the folding method. For 6, 12 and 24 degree formats, the width is narrower in relation to the height than with 2, 4, 8 and 16 degree formats, (2:3 to 3:4 respectively).

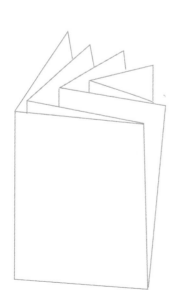

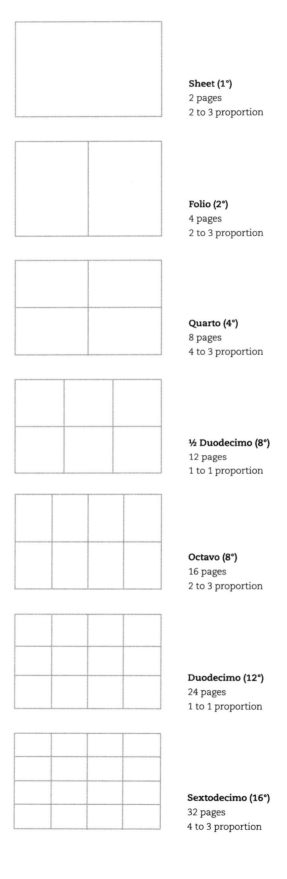

Sheet (1°)
2 pages
2 to 3 proportion

Folio (2°)
4 pages
2 to 3 proportion

Quarto (4°)
8 pages
4 to 3 proportion

½ Duodecimo (8°)
12 pages
1 to 1 proportion

Octavo (8°)
16 pages
2 to 3 proportion

Duodecimo (12°)
24 pages
1 to 1 proportion

Sextodecimo (16°)
32 pages
4 to 3 proportion

Letter and Envelope Paper Formats

All measures in centimeter

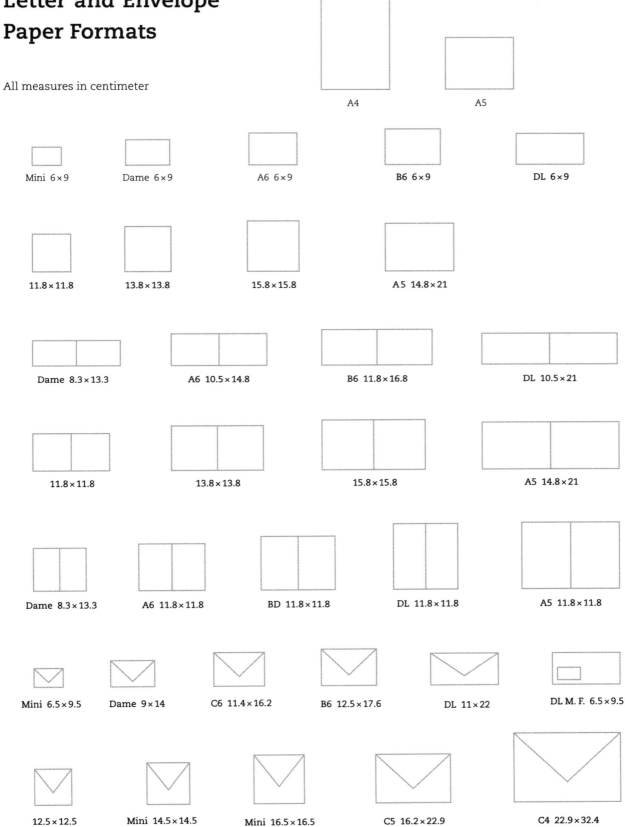

A4

A5

Mini 6×9

Dame 6×9

A6 6×9

B6 6×9

DL 6×9

11.8×11.8

13.8×13.8

15.8×15.8

A5 14.8×21

Dame 8.3×13.3

A6 10.5×14.8

B6 11.8×16.8

DL 10.5×21

11.8×11.8

13.8×13.8

15.8×15.8

A5 14.8×21

Dame 8.3×13.3

A6 11.8×11.8

BD 11.8×11.8

DL 11.8×11.8

A5 11.8×11.8

Mini 6.5×9.5

Dame 9×14

C6 11.4×16.2

B6 12.5×17.6

DL 11×22

DL M. F. 6.5×9.5

12.5×12.5

Mini 14.5×14.5

Mini 16.5×16.5

C5 16.2×22.9

C4 22.9×32.4

Printing Processes

All printing processes are about reproducing copies from a master-printing template. They differ in the way the ink is applied to the paper. Which method best suits a particular print job depends on the artwork and the desired end product.

Letterpress Printing
(Relief and Flexo-Printing)

Letterpress is the collective term used for a printing process in which the printing components of the printing plate are raised in relation to the non-printing parts. The raised parts are inked by rollers and then placed under pressure from the printing plate directly onto the paper. Print media ranges from letters and rubber, plastic or metal blocks, which have been cut or etched from a substrate. This high-pressure printing approach includes letterpress and flexographic printing. This is the oldest printing process of all, but due to its expense, it is rarely used industrially.

Planographic Printing (Offset Printing)

Offset printing is an indirect lithographic printing process that does not involve printing directly from the printing plate, but first onto a rubber-covered roller and then onto the paper from there. As the printing plate is spared, large runs can be printed and even rough paper can be easily used. The planographic printing process is based on the principle that water and fat cannot mix. The printing and non-printing surfaces are on the same level. With each rotation, the print head is initially wetted by dampening rollers and subsequently coated with ink by another roller. Where the pre-treated panels have taken on water, ink is repelled, while all the other areas are inked. Planographic printing is the most commonly used printing technique. The forerunner to offset printing was lithography, also known as stone printing.

Letterpress Printing
(Relief and Flexo-Printing)

Planographic Printing
(Offset Printing)

Gravure Printing

This is an indirect printing process, in which the printing plates can be either flat or cylindrical depending on the printing technique. The name gravure derives from the fact that the parts in the plate meant to take on the printing ink, are positioned lower and are scratched and etched into it. While dyeing the printing plate, the ink fluid flows into small wells and is then removed from the plate's surface by a blade or wiper. Due to the high contact pressure, the paper sucks the ink back out of the wells. This process is conventionally used on an industrial level in printing newspapers and packaging production, where long printing runs are prevalent. It is also used in fine art.

Screen Printing (Silk-screen Printing)

Also known as silk screen or serigraphy, screen printing is a stencil-based approach, in which the printing ink is pulled across a fine mesh textile or wired screen by a scraper and then placed on to the paper. In those places where ink is not wanted, a stencil is applied onto the screen and paper. Silk-screen printing is especially used where broad, two-dimensional graphics are desired and it can be carried out on many other flat or molded materials, as well as paper.

Risography

This is a brand of silk-screen printing. Developed by the Japanese Riso Kagaku Company in the 1980s, risography is a relatively ecologically sustainable and cost-effective printing method. Using a print template, the risograph creates a thin master copy made out of vegetable fibers, stretches it onto an ink drum and then uses this device to apply a soya-based pigment onto the uncoated paper without the aid of chemicals or heat.

Digital Printing

Digital printing is the newest of the printing methods listed here. It is a direct printing process that transfers information directly from the computer to the printer and then onto the paper, obviating the need for a print plate. The ink or pigment used in this process is dry toner for digital or xerographic printing, or liquid ink for inkjet printing. This method is less expensive for small print runs than offset printing. — *Anita Brockmann*

Gravure Printing

Screen Printing
(Silk-screen Printing)

Other Paper Processing Approaches

Printing alone does not make a product out of paper. This only occurs after further processing. There are many design options to choose from:

Slot-Pressing

Creating a groove is an actual weakening of the material. In this instance, a physical chip of thick paper, card or cardboard is removed to allow for the material to be bent or folded, and to prevent bursting or splitting. It is mostly used in the production of cardboard boxes.

Stamping or Embossing

This technique is done manually. A motif or type is embossed into the printing material using a specially produced stamp and high pressure. This technique is mainly used on book covers and printed packaging. It can be applied without pigment, known as blind embossing, or with pigment, known as embossed foil printing or hot foil embossing. In the latter case, the printing dye runs between the stamp and the substrate by means of a thin layer of color film that is transferred with heat and pressure onto the material being embossed.

Grooving

This is making linear depressions in card, paper, cardboard, etc. The displaced material is visible as a ridge. The application is performed in a creasing machine. Grooving prevents breakage, as well as pigment or dye from flaking when bent or compressed. This method is common in the production of folding boxes or cartons and when binding brochures.

Punching

This method can be used to make paper into individual formats. It is cut out of the material with a punch by a hammer using a press or stamp, which results in dotted perforations or slits.

Slot-Pressing

Stamping or Embossing

Folding

Folding is collapsing paper in order to create smaller formats. The sharp creases are usually produced mechanically, or in the case of smaller quantities, by using a bone folder. There are different types of folding, with the most common being wrapping, gatefold and concertina folds. This process is used for books, brochures, postcards, greeting cards and in packaging. For grammage less than 170 g/m², the paper needs to be creased before folding.

— *Anita Brockmann*

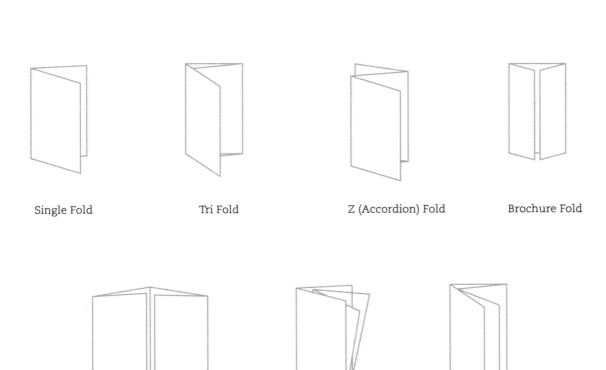

Single Fold   Tri Fold   Z (Accordion) Fold   Brochure Fold

Double Gate Fold   Quarter Fold (French Fold)   Inside Quarter Fold

The Anatomy of Type

Every letter has its own width, often called the *flesh*, which consists of the letter's actual image, as well as its pre- and post-width. This indicates the distance to the next letter and it is also called the character spacing. Some letters, such as '*f*' can extend beyond the next character space and should they actually contact the next letter then a ligature takes place. The

x-Height refers to the mean line. The anatomy and technical terms of the characters derive from typesetting with the use of lead to cast the letters. Whilst the type body, once a piece of lead, is no longer physically present in the digital age, it is nonetheless still present as a visual unit for determining the size of a letter.

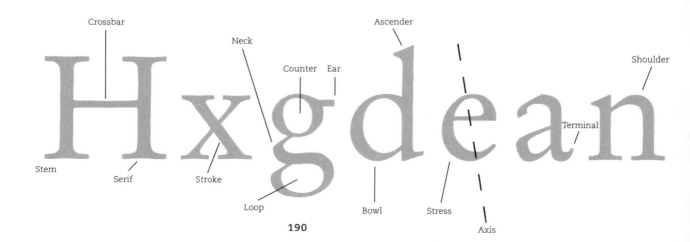

The Development of Type

An essential criterion for the evaluation of a typeface lies in the contrast of its stroke thickness. It defines the ratio between thin and thick strokes within the font. Depending on the font design, this can be more or less distinct. The contrast has, over the centuries, increased with time.

Emerging in the nineteenth century, the 'grotesque' or 'sans-serif' fonts (without serifs) have virtually no line-thickness contrast. Purely as an optical correction, the stroke thickness tapers off slightly, for example, where two lines meet in order to avoid a visual compression at these points.

Garamond

Baskerville

Bodoni

Helvetica

The Designed Space

The field of typography is divided into micro- and macro-typography. Whilst the former is about letters and their details, their sizes and character spacing, the latter deals with the composition of text and images on a surface or book page.

Systems of order in the form of type area and, in the case of more complex tasks, typographical grids, facilitate and system-ize the design, especially for multi-page printed matter. They denote the creative backbone and safeguard consistency throughout a design project. Depending on the task at hand, such ordering systems may be made more open or more rigid.

When designing pages, double-page spreads or whole publications, the white area is given structure by a typesetting area. This page shows the type area of this book and some of the possible design options of the pages. A defined type area also clarifies to what extent the interplay between the surface of the paper and the print area affects the design itself. Par-ticularly with illustrated books, it is not just about surfaces gray with writing, but also how illustrations are placed, not only on an individual page but also within the overall context of the book's design.

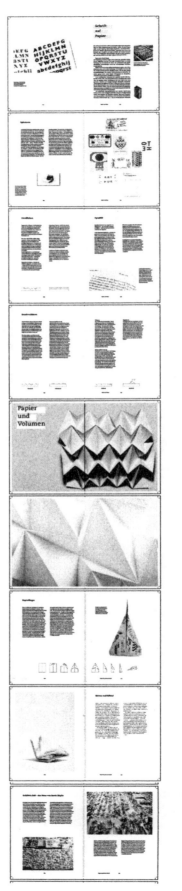

Image area 170 × 240 mm

Type area 150 × 220 mm

Paper
Spaces

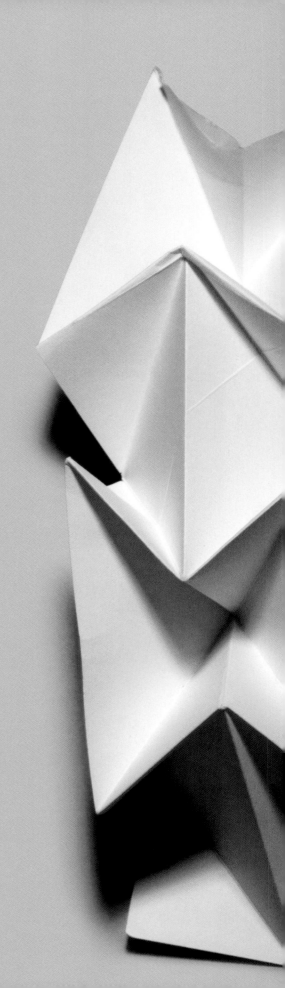

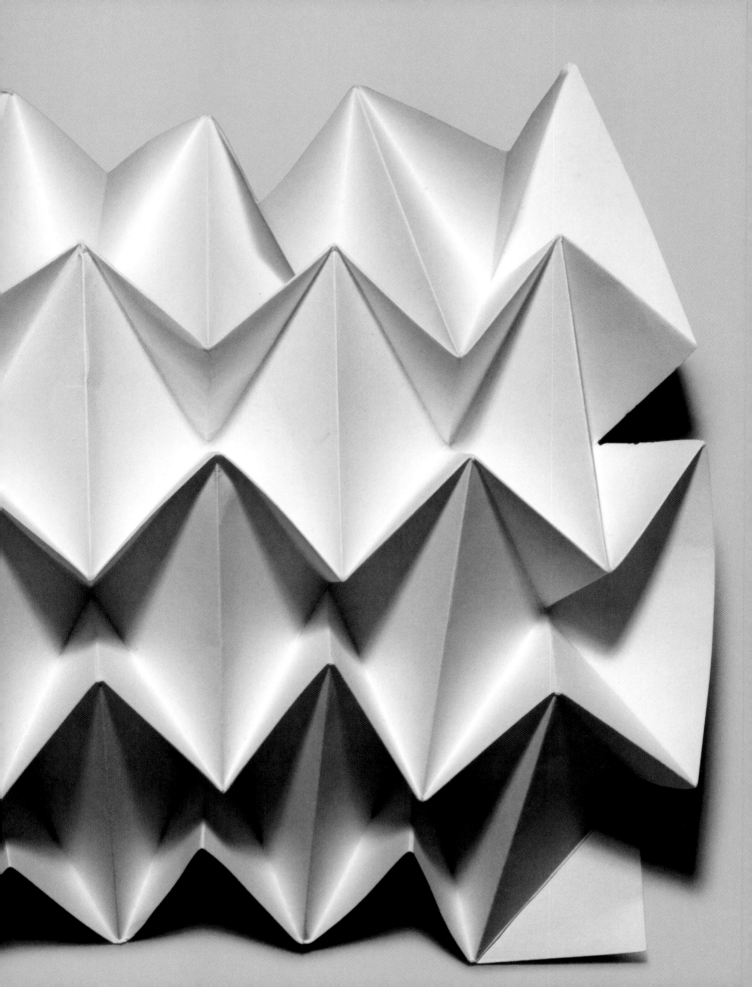

Folding

Paper

In the introduction to one of his reference works, *Complete Pleats: Pleating Techniques for Fashion, Architecture and Design* (Laurence King, 2015), Paul Jackson explains the origin of the word 'to fold' and discusses how many words include the Latin syllable 'pli', such as application, duplicate, explicit, compliment, complicated, simplify, etc. In the same vein, he also demonstrates to what extent the concepts of 'folding' and 'unfolding' have historically referred not only to the way paper is handled, but also to aspects of emotion, abstract feelings and actions.

Paul Jackson talks exactingly about 'pleating.' In practical terms, that includes – each according to country of origin – gathering, ruffling, draping, pleating, smocking, tousling, crinkling, crushing, crenellating, ribbing, and layering. Jackson's definition is as follows: 'A fold is created by bending a flat piece of material upwards and downwards. Or, as they say in origami: a 'mountain fold' and a 'valley fold.' Folds can be straight or curved, as a one-dimensional entity, stand-alone, or in an endless sequence.' There are flexible, purely decorative and functional folds, as well as folds that consist of a single part or material, and ones that are pulled together. Although it is simple to describe and define a fold, there is no limit to the diversity of creative opportunities they present. Each one depends on the materials being used and the ingenuity of the designer. Folding by hand is as low-tech as it possibly gets. It is an instantaneous handicraft and a piece of paper. No other tools or materials are required and that is perhaps the reason for origami becoming so popular among those who spend their mundane, 'digital' day in front of computer screens. Of course, every piece of paper can be folded, but not every type of paper is equally suitable for different projects.

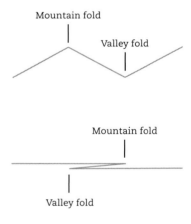

Mountain fold

Valley fold

Mountain fold

Valley fold

Paul Jackson prefers white paper at a weight of 90 gsm. In addition to standard tools such as a ruler, compass, pencil and a cutter, a major role in the development of elaborate folding techniques has also been transferred to computer programs. The dynamic between complex, analogous folding knowledge and digital calculation and reproduction on the PC has opened up a whole new world of opportunity when it comes to complicated folds and creative ideas, as well as to applications in the fields of architecture, design and engineering. — *Nicola von Velsen*

It is said that a piece of paper in any size can folded no more than 7 times. With 7 folds, the sheet of paper will then consist of 128 layers ($=2^7$) and would be 1.28 cm thick at a sheet thickness of 0.1 mm. Attempts using extremely thin paper have been made for the Guinness Book of Records and, indeed, more than 7 folds was achieved. This simple trial should clearly demonstrate how paper's volume comes about through layers and folds.

Folding
and
Thinking

When we fold our hands together, we abandon the busy, discerning and accessible world around us and gather them into a gesture of retreat, cessation and contemplation. When a person folds his hands together, he is no longer with that which is around him but with what is within him and, in the Christian understanding, in a special contact with God. Cultural and religious implications to one side, intertwining one's fingers represents an anthropological primal event, which the French philosopher, Michel Merleau-Ponty (1908–1961), called 'chiasma' (Gr.: χίασμα). The visual image of the Greek letter X clearly shows a crossing of hands, giving way to a spark of corporal energy. The individual's touch is not encountering an alien body, it is sensing itself. But the question is: which hand is truly sensing itself? And which is the one being felt? Either hand can swap roles. What makes me different is not the act of interlocking rather the occurrence of the action itself. As a person, I am a living self-perception that becomes aware of itself in its bodily conduct. Thinking, as put by the doubting Descartes (1596–1650), intellectualizes this theme. Even in this case, reflection equates to some kind of folding back into oneself – not only am I able to think, I am also able to think about myself as a thinker. In the backdrop of this chiasma, all things and thoughts encounter me.

What happens to a person when he folds his hands in reflection, is in some way akin to paper when it is being folded: it is bent back on itself. Folding creates an opening to the world and a closed edge, which holds the layers of paper together and expresses their original identity. The folded shape literally creates an *explicated* (from the Latin ex 'out' and plicare 'to fold') metaphor of our existence. Folds (Gr.: πλέκω) become the model of our understanding of the world. Diversity overwhelms the simple-minded. Our thoughts unfold. We contrast complexity with simplicity. We analyze the implications and fear complications. The folds of our existence reflect the diversity of the world in which we live. — *Matthias Burchardt*

Opposite: Foldings by
Erwin Hapke.

Giang Dinh, *Figures*, 2003.
The figures are folded from a
square, uncut sheet of watercolor paper. Born in Vietnam,
Giang Dinh is an architect
living in Virginia.

Origami

The origins of origami are uncertain. The when, where, what, and why are all unknown and are the subject of much debate among historians of origami. Given the perishable nature of paper, we may never know the answers to these questions. It does, however, seem likely that paper folding had separate origins in East Asia and in Europe.

The word 'origami' is Japanese ('ori' means 'to fold' and 'kami' means 'paper', which becomes 'gami' in combination with ori). However, the word is not used out of any regard for historical accuracy – there is no proof that paper folding began in Japan – but because it affirms Japan as the spiritual home of the art.

Development

We do know that the first true paper originated in China approximately two thousand years ago. However, we cannot assume that people in China, and later in Japan and elsewhere in East Asia, were folding paper in any meaningful way, until we meet the first incontrovertible evidence of paper folding found in a poem written in 1680 by the Japanese poet Ihara Saikaku (1642–1693), which describes folded paper butterflies being given as a wedding gift. Theories abound as to what may have been folded in those missing 1600 years, but there is no surviving evidence.

The first known origami book, the 'Senbazuru Orikata' was published in Japan in 1797, followed by a few others in the nineteenth century. The models in these books are notable for their liberal use of cutting and decoration. By the beginning of the twentieth century, it is estimated that a few dozen origami models (cut and uncut) were known in Japan.

Surprisingly, the first known occurrence of paper folding in Europe precedes that in East Asia by almost 250 years, in a Flemish Book of Hours dated to 1440, which shows in the margin steps for making a paper box. Strong traditions of paper folding are known to have existed across Europe, and especially in Spain and Germany, through to the modern era. The mid-nineteenth-century German educationalist, Friedrich Froebel (1782–1852), included sophisticated paper folding in his kindergarten program.

Masashi Tanaka, *Tanaka Butterfly*, 2004. Folded from a square sheet of paper. Masashi Tanaka lives in Gifu, Japan.

There is almost no overlap or duplication of traditional models in Japan and Europe, suggesting that the art developed synchronously in at least two different locations.

The Modern Era

The rise of origami as a creative artform can be attributed to Akira Yoshizawa (1911–2005). His expressive wet-folded 3-D animals and figures were far in advance of other origami creations and are still revered today. His International Origami Center was the first of many organized groups in Japan.

A visit to Japan in the mid 1960's by New York resident by Lilian Oppenheimer (1898–1992) exposed her to origami, which she began teaching when she returned home. Her Manhattan loft became the focal point for a growing number of creative designers, eventually leading to the creation of the Friends of the Origami Center of America (1958) and later, the British Origami Society (1967) and other Societies in Europe and eventually, worldwide.

The coming of the Internet led quickly to an exponential increase in the number of creators, designs and followers of origami. There are now perhaps 40,000 known designs in a bewildering diversity of styles, from the minimal to the super-complex.

Today, origami is considered both an art and a mathematical science. It is studied by academics in many branches of science and engineering, from protein folding to space technology, serves as a learning tool in many math classes, is used by designers, exhibited as fine art and contemporary craft and is a fulfilling hobby for untold numbers of children and adults.

Origami is that most rare of creative activities: something anyone can do anywhere, anytime, with no tools. All you need is a pair of hands and a sheet of paper. — *Paul Jackson*

Cover of Lilian Oppenheimer and Shari Lewis' 1962 book about folding paper puppets.

Akira Yoshizawa is considered the father of modern origami. Here he is seen in a TV broadcast in Rome, 1987.

David Brill, *Rotating Double Cube Series*, designed in 1993, folded in 2005. David Brill is the vice-president of the British Origami Society.

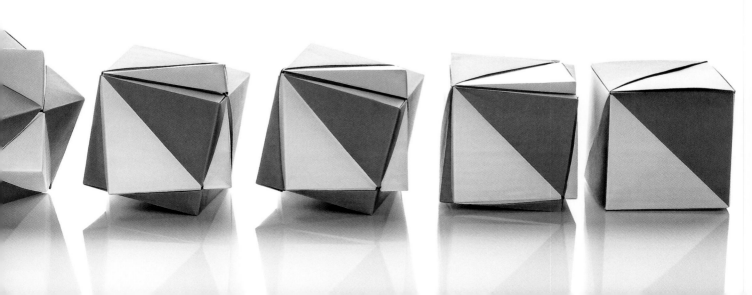

Paper Theater

Paper backdrops and stages in a theater that portrays our world on a small scale: this idea dates back to the early nineteenth century and was developed in England and Germany. The toy paper theater's forerunners were peep-boxes, 'Mandlbögen' and nativity scenes dedicated to representing folk traditions or dramatic events. Mandlbögen are sheets of paper cut out to show people or individual scenes and were very popular in bourgeois households at the time.

The actual paper theater was a small stage made of wood and paper, on which popular or classical plays and fairy tales were recreated. The creation of the stage could be in accordance with a publisher's kit or one's own imagination and creativity. Countless idiosyncratic theaters were created. Performances were for entertainment in a fun and informal family setting. It is also worth pointing out that, as a by-product, literary education was opened up to a wide audience of all age groups on these small stages.

Like its life-size counterpart, the paper theater has a proscenium or forestage, and a curtain. In the past, prosceniums were often

The paper theater for the play *Der Zauberschleier* (The Magic Veil) by the Austrian playwright Franz Xaver Told, which premiered in February 1842 and was a huge popular success. This replica of the original paper theater furnishings was produced by the Trentsensky publishing house in Vienna.

based on well-known theaters of the time. Furthermore, there are usually one or more stage sets, as well as several figures for each piece. The most common character rail comes in sideways. The figures are inserted individually or in small groups or taken out through the wings. They can also be moved from above and below.

Paper theater is still a vital art form, and numerous historical reproductions can be bought again today. At the same time, different toy theaters regularly open their stages for big and small theater-lovers. Many classics, as well as modern plays and themes are staged, including adaptions of novels such as Don Quixote, classic plays such as Romeo and Juliet, operas such as Carmen and even experimental performances.

— *Gordon Hoffmeyer*

At the Bauhaus

There was no other location where paper was so extolled as a material than in the preliminary course of Josef Albers (1888–1976) at the Bauhaus in Dessau. Walter Gropius (1883–1969) founded the art school in Weimar in 1919 and once referred to the preliminary course as "the artery of everyday Bauhaus work." From autumn 1920, the course became compulsory for every student. It was only after successfully participating in Alber's preliminary course that a student could apply for an apprenticeship in one of the various Bauhaus workshops, such as wall painting, metalworking or weaving. The preliminary course was geared to developing its students' creative abilities, freeing them from the conventions and ideas of previous movements and influences.

The course in Dessau focussed on the comprehensive investigation of materials such as glass, stone, metal, wood, paint, and, of course, paper, which could be drawing paper, corrugated paper, newspapers, as well as confetti and paper streamers. Albers recognized the chief driver for any future designer to be the exploratory and experimental aspects of the creative process. Neither the designer's own feelings, nor historical influences should determine form, rather it should be only function and the material itself, resulting in a contemporary, efficient form during a time of heightened economic awareness.

The biggest challenge facing the students during Albers preliminary course was probably substance applications, where the fundamental properties and potential of raw material – or its "internal energies," as Albers described it – were to be explored and demonstrated. This was not about imitating the familiar, but discovering the unknown and therefore new possibilities. According to Albers, this was an exercise in unravelling. Simulated maybe, but unravelling all the same. He explained his theory on paper in his programmatic essay of 1928 for the in-house magazine *Bauhaus* as follows: "it is mostly used horizontally (in craft and industry), flat and glued, one side of it loses its expression, the edge is almost never used. So this should give us cause to exploit paper vertically, unevenly, sculpturally, both sides and edges emphasized."

As an example: Albers brought a stack of drawing paper into the pre-course and challenged his students to explore its performance limitations and ultimately demonstrate the load bearing capacity of a sheet of paper. In the essay mentioned above, he explained how this might pan out: "drawing paper folded into equal ribbed strips of about 25 cm × 30 cm [×] 1 cm height holds two people." On another occasion and using folds and only a few cuts, the students were asked to present paper expansion in both a positive and negative light with a view to seeing what the strength and the design possibilities a sheet of paper were. In all things, Albers' key principle, which he ranked above all else, was labor and material economics – effectively finding simple solutions in the fewest steps. No single part of the paper could be left unused. This meant no waste and also only the use of as few tools as possible. The aim was for students to gradually develop constructive thinking and spatial perception.

In truth, Albers did not wish to teach anything. He did not wish to indoctrinate, rather his aim was for his students to have "experienced insight" through their own practices, responsibility and discipline – true learning through free and independent experimentation. The basic

The photograph taken by Otto Umbehr (Umbo) shows Josef Albers and his students during a group discussion about paper works at the Bauhaus in Dessau, c. 1928–29.

credo he frequently proclaimed was: "The proof of the pudding is in the eating." On another occasion, the Bauhaus master brought a stack of newspapers into the preliminary course and requested from his students a "respectful" exploration and "meaningful" use of the newspapers in the simplest way possible. Some time later, the results were spread out on the floor: boats, airplanes, masks and other experimental assemblies could be seen. Albers described the results as "kindergarten junk," but then pointed out and praised one piece of work. What one particular student had created was described by Hannes Beckmann, a fellow course member, in his book, *The Foundation Years*: "He had done nothing other than fold the newspaper lengthwise so that it could stand upright. Josef Albers then explained to us how well the material had been understood, how well it had been used and how natural the folding process had been which enabled such a soft material to become more rigid. He went on

to explain that a newspaper lying on the table only had one page visible, meaning the others could not be seen. Since the paper was now erect, it had become more visually active. The newspaper had therefore lost its boring exterior and its tired appearance."

The statements made by Albers – who continued to study paper in his courses at Black Mountain College in the USA – might have been important, but those of the students themselves were equally so, creating a virtuous circle that refined the vision of each participating individual. As Albers stated in his essay, *13 Years at the Bauhaus*: "Seeing is strength and indeed seeing in the English language sense means more looking at. For me, visual creative education seems to be one of the most important tasks of our times."
— *Boris Friedewald*

Folded Time

From 1981 until his death in spring 2016, Erwin Hapke lived, in a kind of self-imposed exile, a bleak life far removed from a comfortable bourgeois lifestyle – no internet, radio, television, no contact with the world outside and no income or health insurance. An eccentric and a crossover artist with a doctorate-level education in biology, Hapke was as stubborn as he was passionate in pursuing his artistic mission. A folded universe was cultivated by his hand at the old village school in the district of Unna, Germany. Hapke's universe was not unlike the windowless dream

world in 'Monadology', Leibniz's collection of metaphysical insights. The magic and diversity of this unique work cannot be reproduced by any single medium. With his paper folding skills, Hapke plays with every aspect of life: from formal, symbolic and abstract structures, through to insects and mammals. There are pieces showing scenes of mutual compassion or cultural objects. The range of his subject matter is far reaching: it could be a paper plow, or it could be a cathedral. Hapke's rigorous adherence to the principles of form leads to a truly endless variation of shape and color. He gives us a lesson in perception because his work demands leisure and lingering. Then, however, the delicate soul of the paper escapes the unimaginable depths of

time, which touches us and evokes an almost lost nostalgia for a reality that has long since disappeared in an age of digital information and flash imaging. "A soft white mark" is written on a strip of paper in the tiny handwriting of the deceased. Plato, convinced of the immortality of the soul, had complete distrust in handwriting – having to leave important thoughts on a transient carrier, paper – and even in the eyes of its restorer – Hapke's life's work is in danger. Nonetheless, his work has a poetic touch of eternity.

This is the soul of an artist's life, in all his labors and doubts, visions and passions, translated into fragile figures and over-expansive installations, which shows true intellectual conception and meticulous manual execution. The trace of symbols leads from life to paper and holds the secret of our existence there. — *Matthias Burchardt*

Folded paper forms in the home of Erwin Hapke in the Unna district near Dortmund, Germany, where he folded hundreds of thousands of figures over a period of thirty-five years.

Paper Planes

A place as sheer and vertical as Manhattan must always dream of flying. Certainly, some of the skyscrapers' peaks are nesting places for kestrels, many roofs have corners adorned by birds of prey, like gargoyles on Gothic cathedrals, and tourists fly around in helicopters 24/7. At one time a great transatlantic airship was even moored to the needle of the Empire State building, although the idea was given up after the first attempt as the passengers nearly came down on 5ᵗʰ Avenue. In short, what a setting for paper planes! To make them fly down from a great height, to follow their wind-blown course and to search for ever-cheaper, better, aerodynamic paper forms – an Aeolian pastime. For over twenty years, Harry Smith collected the paper planes that landed on the streets of New York. He would categorize them by location, date, and then keep them. Smith, who also pursued other rather eccentric pastimes, died in 1991. The papers that were used in the planes he collected show a tremendous variety of material: the yellow cover pages from phone books – doubtless used for their robust material – architectural drafting vellum containing drawings and plans, perhaps thrown by the architect in the perfect form to avoid crumpling the design, sticky Post-it notes transformed into umbrellas, or the menu of 'Max's Kansas City' nightclub. The paper planes that were saved by the hands of Harry Smith on New York's streets are now displayed at the National Aerospace Museum in Washington, D.C. One part, containing only 251 models of the once much larger collection, has been published in an illustrated book. Of those other planes that disappeared, it is said they had all crash landed in the Bermuda Triangle of paper pulp. — *Philipp Hontschik*

 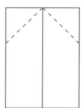 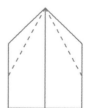 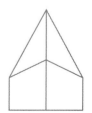

An example from Harry
Smith's extensive collection
of paper airplanes. In 2015
a *catalogue raisonné* of the
collection was published by
J&L Books with Anthology
Film Archives.

Paper Bags

Bags are transport containers made of various flexible materials and used for different purposes, they can carry different foods, small items or powdery materials and have very different shapes.

While the colorfully printed plastic bag made its triumphant progress with the economic miracle in West Germany, the former German Democratic Republic had its own aesthetic ideas of carefully produced and designed paper bags for consumers that beautifully embellished the joy and happiness of shopping. With the enormous ecological problems and environmental damage caused by plastic finally being recognized, paper bags are increasingly finding their way back into everyday life. Even in the larger sector of packaging and transport material, there has clearly been a significant re-evaluation of paper and the way it is processed.

Unfortunately, there is no certainty of when and where the first paper bags were produced by machines, but the following were pioneers in

Common paper bags are called wrapped and glued conical bags, flat bags, cross bottom bags, and block bottom bags. Commonly used materials are kraft paper single and double as well as bleached kraft papers or coated papers.

the industry: Francis Wolle (1817–1893) patented a machine for paper bags in 1852 and founded the Union Paper Bag Machine Company in Savannah, Georgia. It is believed that the first pointed paper bags were made in 1853 in Bad Sooden-Allendorf in Hesse, Germany. Finally in 1870, Margaret E. Knight (1838–1914) developed a machine to produce flat-bottomed brown paper bags, and in 1873 she founded the Eastern Paper Bag Company in Hartford, Connecticut. — *Nicola von Velsen*

"The Joy of Shopping" – paper bags printed by means of the flexographic printing process enjoyed great popularity in the former GDR. Because of their individual patterns and designs they are coveted collector's items today.

Boxes

This beautiful, individual, paper and cardboard packaging almost always makes you happy. They are usually printed with beautiful colors and there are frequently additional, inner papers sandwiched inside with fascinating folding techniques. And then they often contain fine delicacies, such as chocolates, wonderful perfumes or an exceptionally luxurious gadget. A good box brings back the childhood joy of a wrapped gift.

Boxes or cartons are extremely versatile and a good example of paper put to efficient use in both material and space. Collapsible boxes are often custom made and precisely measured in order for goods to remain as unharmed as possible on their receipt. Sometimes, goods must also be able to be stacked safely and easily in warehouses. The spectrum of carton type is remarkable. They can be mass produced, such as in the case of cigarette packets or the outer packaging of cereals, indeed, Kellogg's is said to have produced the first folding boxes for cereals. For luxury goods, different materials and curious designs are used to make elaborately produced boxes. The choice of material depends on the intended purpose of a box; quality cardboards such as solid or corrugated cardboard can be used. Today, these cartons are designed on computers, using a CAD program, whereby the first part of the process is to determine what goods are to be packaged in the box. For production, a white pattern is constructed which can then be used to find out how the box behaves and what alterations have to be made in the design. Folding boxes are made with punching tools that cut out the external shapes, before folding and gluing these shapes in different directions, depending on the shape of the box. Should the boxes need to be printed, the print work is carried before the punching process. — *Nicola von Velsen*

View of the production line of a box maker.

Opposite: Patterns for folding templates

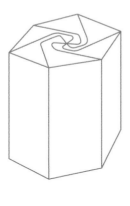

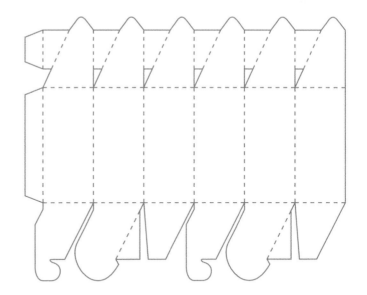

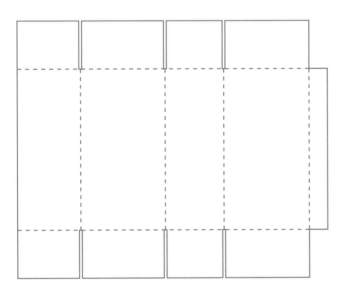

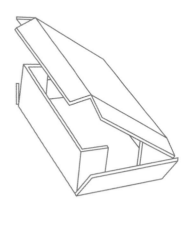

Pop-ups – Hingeless Paper

I know of no other material more suitable for creating pop-ups than paper or cardboard. On the one hand, the material needs to be very stable, but on the other its elements have to remain movable along certain axes. With other materials such as wood, metal, plastic, porcelain and so on, I would need to cut and attach separate hinges or adhesive tape to allow for such mobility. For paper and cardboard, one simply has to make a groove (for example with a bone folder) to change its properties. Paper or cardboard can then be folded along the creased line.

With good-enough quality material, this can be repeated as often as desired without the paper or card crumpling or breaking. In addition, paper and cardboard can be worked in many other ways: cut, folded, bent, torn, glued, lazered, punched, printed, refined, painted, embossed, perforated, crumpled and more. Depending on its type, light and airy filigree objects, as well as stable, static constructions can be produced from it. It is this diversity that inspires me. — *Peter Dahmen*

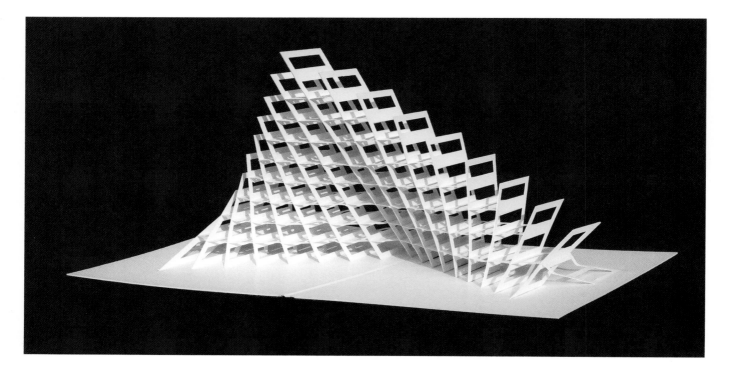

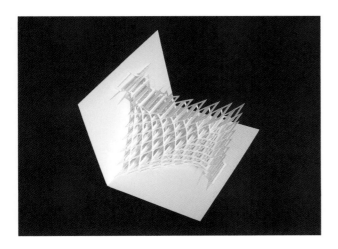

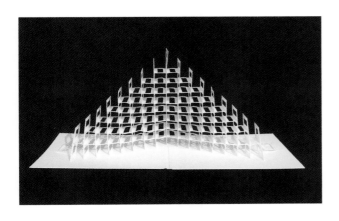

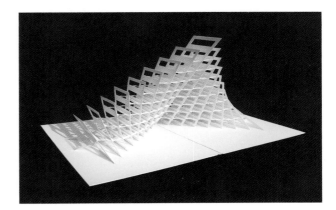

Peter Dahmen, *Ohne Titel 13*
(Untitled 13), 2012, dimensions
(opened): 60.6 × 42.1 × 27.5 mm,
paper: Fedrigoni Splendorgel
Extra White, 300 g/m².

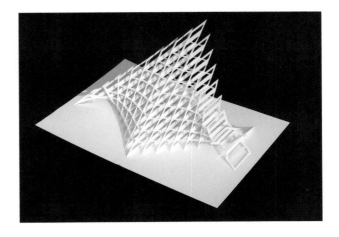

Paper Houses: Shigeru Ban

You might think that paper houses are small, unstable and fragile structures. However, that only reflects one aspect of the material. On the other hand, paper is also a tough, strong and supple material. The Japanese architect, Shigeru Ban (b. 1957), is fascinated by these different qualities of cellulose. For more than thirty years he has been developing – with great experimentation – temporary and permanent structures using paper, paper derivatives or fibers. Paper tubes, meant for the garbage, were the inspiration for his intensive examination of the material beginning in 1986. 'Why throw away something so light-weight, cheap and stable?' he wondered, going on to integrate the cardboard tubes in the exhibition design on which he was then working. Since then, the cylindrical, hollow support made of glued paper has been the fundamental building block of Shigeru Ban's architecture. He has optimized the technology of load-bearing cellulose, explored its capacity and improved its resistance. His concern with making the aesthetic soul of paper visible is shown early on by works as diverse as 'Miyake Design Studio Gallery' (1994) or 'Paper House' (1995), in which cardboard tubes hold the vertical load instead of walls. This gives the buildings unexpected openness and ease. Simple but elegant solutions like these are Ban's trademarks.

For the special tectonics of his paper tube constructions, the architect experiments with different materials and structures. This is particularly evident in his great hall and cathedral constructions such as the 35-meter-long, interlaced cardboard tubes made from waste paper that were used for the latticed ceiling structure of the Japanese EXPO pavilion in Hannover (2000), or in the 60-centimeter-thick and almost 20-meter-long card board tubes used in the supporting structure of the 'Cardboard Cathedral' (2013) in Christchurch, New Zealand. A step further is the 'Paper Log House,' emergency structures that Shigeru Ban developed after the devastating earthquake in Kobe, Japan, in 1995. They have since been used worldwide in disaster areas or as refugee shelters. Whether for private use, cultural and religious purposes, or emergency shelters, for Shigeru Ban the advantages of the cardboard tube are obvious: it can be prefabricated, it is lightweight, stable, widely available, easy to make water- and fireproof, readily assembled and re-usable. Once dismantled it can simply be composted. — *Anita Brockmann*

Opposite: Paper Log House,
realized in India in 2001.

Top: The Japanese pavilion
at the Expo 2000 in Hanover.

'softwall'

By experimenting with paper as a modelling medium, molo's founders Stephanie Forsythe and Todd MacAllen discovered the material's ability to retain strength across a range of scales. When structured with honeycomb geometry, paper can compress flat or flex open to create remarkably strong freestanding structures. By pairing this material discovery with a desire to reshape living and working environments for flexible use, the designers conceived *softwall* and the encompassing *soft collection*.

A compressed *softwall* resembles a tall book of less than 5 centimeters thick. When opened, the internal cell matrix stretches to form a wall that is 4.5 meters long. The partition then flexes, bends or connects to shape space. Magnetic end panels allow the final layers of paper to fold shut, giving stability. These same panels also connect to each other, turning *softwall* into a modular system that can build entire paper environments, from sculptural office installations to pop-up shops. Eschewing notions of rigid construction in favor of sustainable design that accommodates change over time and that encourages responsible material use, *softwall* should be considered a new building material. Praised for poetic beauty and innovative design, *softwall* and softseating were acquired by the Museum of Modern Art for its permanent collection. — *molo*

Magnetic end panels on *softwall*, closing them to add stability to the paper space partition.

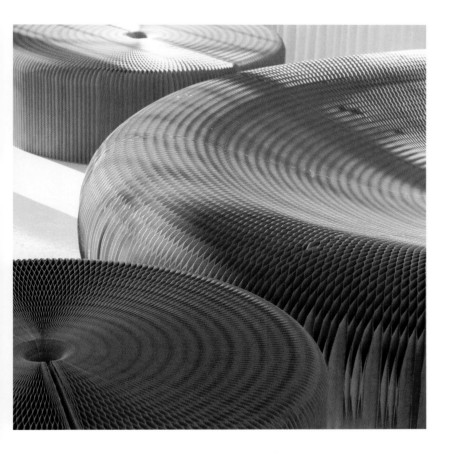

Inside molo's Vancouver workshop.

Paper softseating: a collection of flexible stools, benches and loungers.

Paper Installations

Why do you use cardboard and paper for the installations?

We started working with paper for different reasons. For Daniel, paper was the only material he could afford for his model buildings at university. Origami was Inti's hobby as a child. So everything happened a bit by accident, but the more we worked with paper, the more we enjoyed it. So we found a whole universe of undiscovered possibilities. It is a great pleasure for us to transform this everyday material into something so special. For each project, we unearth new techniques and wonderful craftsmanship, which gives us a variety of design possibilities for the paper. It is smart, light, eco- friendly, ecological and elegant. What's not to love about this material?

What are the challenges?

We were never taught anything about paper. From the beginning we took a sort of 'trial and error' approach to it. Even our own techniques are named by us. We have learned to deal with

fire, with water and sun. Despite all of this, our biggest challenge is always dealing with a customer who does not know what he wants.

What characteristics do you look for in the papers and boxes you use?

Every project is different. At the moment we are working with four major paper manufacturers: Gmund from Germany, Fedrigoni from Italy, Takeo from Japan and Arjowiggins from France. So we have a variety of paper offerings that overwhelm us a bit sometimes, but we love it so we can handle it.

Do you use any specific papers or special techniques?

We use all the papers that work for us and although our designs are 100 per cent handmade, in large-scale productions we do rely on new technologies to make our work possible. And we also use LED systems to light the installations.

The Wanda Barcelona studio was founded in Barcelona in 2006. Inti Velez Botero and Daniel Mancini, both from Columbia, discovered their shared passion for paper. Later they were joined by the Catalan artist Iris Joval who completes the triad of space, object, and fascination. Using new materials and techniques, Wanda Barcelona creates magical atmospheres in which perspective is constantly challenged.

Objects Made of Pulp

I am inspired by everyday objects and the materials around us, and I push the boundaries of materials to create new possibilities for objects like furniture and interior products. Much of my work is made from upcycled materials. After experimenting with paper pulp in my graduation project (2009) I discovered that paper is very versatile. I love the feeling and texture of paper pulp: soft and multi-purpose. I wanted to create my own building material, which I could use to design my own products like furniture and vases. I love the challenge of working with low-tech materials, without using a kiln for example. I got addicted to the material, and I still am :-). The material challenges me to discover the material and to find out what possibilities it offers to create interior objects. I have special interest in working with old paper. — *Debbie Wijskamp*

Debbie Wijskamp, various
objects made of recycled paper, pulp,
up to 70 cm high, *c.* 2016.

Made of Paper

I find paper is a wonderful material: it's easily accessible and does not weigh much. And it takes no more than a sheet of paper, a scalpel, and cutting pad to create both images and paper worlds.

Paper unlocks joy and creativity. It also suits me because it contains several different elements, from setting up an idea, to a sketch, either by hand or in Illustrator. Then I have to figure out exactly how to construct the buildings, and then I start working with my hands and build the worlds. Storytelling becomes possible, reminding me of the feeling of playing when I was little.

This is a good state of mind and a positive contrast to our digital, stressful world. Hopefully, many more people will take the time to sit down and create something. — *Fideli Sundqvist*

Poppy step by step

1 Draw the petals on sandwich paper.
2 Place the drawings on a red silk paper and trace them.
3 Because the paper is so thin and delicate, it is best to cut out the petals with scissors. Creased edges are not a problem.
4 Gently roll the petals between the palms of the hand and unfold them again.
5 On half of the sheet of black paper attach a narrow strip of double-sided tape (c. 8–10 mm). Cut a strip along the edge of the tape. Cut multiple strips.
6 Loosen the protective plastic from the tape about 10 cm, then cut it off.
7 Glue the pointed part of the petal to the edge of the black strip. Continue until approximately 6 to 7 petals are attached. The petals should overlap a little, keep rolling them up.
8 Push a thin piece of metal about 5 mm from below into the middle of the black sleeve. The stick is stuck quite well using the double-sided tape on the black strip. If it feels loose, add glue with a glue gun.
9 Wrap the flower band around the wire stem and the underside of the poppy flower.

Paper
and
Book

PLACE CARDS
Place cards are used to establish a specific seating plan. Is it possible to ignore that plan?
I have known people to simply change it. Sadly, it happens. But even if you had been looking forward to spending the evening next to Ms. Smith and then find yourself sitting next to Ms. Jones, you should never swap cards. Incidentally, I think place cards should have writing on both sides so that people can find their seats more easily and also know who they are sitting opposite.

LABELS AND ETIQUETTE
The connection between the words label (in German: *Etikett*) and etiquette (German: *Etikette*; as a term for ways of behaving) is revealing. How did that happen?
The origin is said to be as follows. The gardener of Louis XIV used to get annoyed about the distinguished gentlemen walking or galloping over his beautiful floral borders in Versailles. So he put up signs, the *Etiketten*. And those gentlemen obviously couldn't care less about what the gardener had done. So he went to the king and declared: "The etiquette must be observed!" Which led to the creation of court etiquette.
Bottle labels are hugely important, especially in the context of a ball. I recently went to the presentation of the Life Ball wine for 2016. The labels had been designed by students from the New Design University in St. Pölten, Austria. The Life Ball wine will be served at lots of events, though the ball itself is not being held this year.

DANCE CARD
The sequence of the dances used to be printed in small booklets in which the ladies made a note of which gentleman they had promised to spend each dance with. I imagine nothing along those lines exists now, does it?
People keep trying to revive it at various balls, but to only moderate success—because the gentlemen. In fact, it would be better to reverse the tradition, so that the ladies could reserve dances with the gentlemen. As far as the dances themselves are concerned, much has changed. Those we have in our program now are almost all more or less African American/Caribbean. One really good idea was the world dance program at the beginning of the 1960s, which included set rules and steps for particular dances. Previously it was the case that a student from the Elmayer dance school had difficulties dancing a waltz with a student from the Fränzl dance school, because they'd been taught different versions. Now practically everyone around the world can dance with each other.

LADIES' GIFT
The dance card evolved into the ladies' gift, which was at times very elaborate. Today it's usually a promotional gift. Very often, yes. I have an aversion to these ladies' gifts in principle.

Thomas Schäfer-Elmayer, CEO, Willy Elmayer-Vestenbrugg Dance School, Vienna (Excerpt from a conversation in April 2016)

/ 231

Books,
Libraries,
and Paper

Books continue to be a necessary part of our notion of reading and of literature. But why? What does a book have that a blog, for instance, doesn't? Books contain real worlds and spaces for us – on the page, in the page, and between the pages. They are, in effect, a hollow form and yet the epitome of the whole and the full. They are a place of cherry-picked passages and grand forms, of novels and encyclopedias. They materialize and dematerialize at the same time. They have the gift to transform what is inside them into spirit and feeling. We fill and empty books, devour and lose them, steal and disobey them, love and hate them. Unlike the blog, books are objects and can be furnishings, wallpaper, strangers or companions, housemates, loved ones. They raise us up and set us down; they are (heavy) children of the tree and (light) siblings of the air.

The history of the take-it-anywhere, movable book, be it in analog or digital form, shows that it is ineradicable. Its story is one of change, not doom. From the moment in the first century BCE when the scroll was superseded by wooden and wax tablets or parchment leaves bound together, and further entrenched when letterpress printing was invented in the fifteenth century, there could be no going back to, nor indeed beyond, what there had been before. Not even with e-books, which replace the book with surrogates of its form. The (often) audible acts of opening a book, turning a page, and closing the book; the idea of the white page that is clearly defined at top and bottom, left and right; the illusion of a space one first creates, then passes through and even finally erases; the concept that a text has a clear, physical mass and a particular volume, that it is a world between two covers; the possibility of leafing back and forth, or even placing several books side by side to read their pages in parallel, crosswise, and in their depth, in their before, during, and after, and to let them become transparent – all these are qualities of the analog book which are then simulated, or become even more literally and obviously possible in the digital book.

Interior view of the Upper Lusatian Library of Sciences in Görlitz, Germany. Comprising 140,000 volumes, it was established in 1951 as successor of the library of the former Upper Lusatian Society of Sciences and the Milich'sche Library, which had moved to Görlitz in 1727.

Every book is always a part and proxy of both a real and an imaginary library in which fixed locations promise to make them easy to find and remember, and yet in most cases cause a permanent gravitational shift: in the orbit of excerpting and referencing, incorporating, rearranging, and eliminating, pulling out, opening, leafing though, reading, and putting back, remembering, and forgetting – the books revolve around the various points of attraction. They are robust and strong, outwardly bounded but potentially open forms, even if, in a magical-religious attempt to boil down the world to a single essence, only a single text were to be printed again and again. With each repetition the same thing is a little different, and the spaces that are hidden in a book, that unfold as you read and are set out with the book as form, are each distinctively disposed. They smell different, feel different, are individually decorated, and carry the marks of time, location, and their readers through use or disregard.

In 2004, Christian Kracht (b. 1966) and Eckhart Nickel (b. 1966) built their 'Kathmandu Library' in Nepal with books left behind by travelers, exhibiting it at the Marbach Literature Archive in 2015: "Paper is the heaviest thing you can carry with you in your suitcase or backpack. What books you pack should not be left to chance or to a whim. However, if you go on a journey while relying on batteries and screens for your reading experience, you will never leave the outlet zone. You can reach the ends of the world only with proper books made of paper. Besides, a book is obviously more than a text. It is about the cover, the paper, page turning, marking paragraphs, and using a pencil to make personal comments. As you travel, boarding passes, checks, and dried flowers gather between the pages."
— *Heike Gfrereis*

The Sir Duncan Rice Library of the University of Aberdeen houses several historic collections on a floor space of 15,500 square meters (167,000 square feet), including a quarter million antiquarian books collected over the five centuries since the library was founded. The building was designed by the Danish firm of Schmidt Hammer Lassen Architects and opened in 2011.

Leafing Through

Books undoubtedly are among the most amazing things made of paper. Ever since the codex (or bound book) prevailed over the scroll in late antiquity, books have consisted of pages. Since that time, people have turned pages when they want to read something. In a culture that for centuries has drawn on this type of book as data carrier and storage medium for texts, page turning has become a cultural technique of appropriating written records whose importance can hardly be overestimated: wherever the book is a leading medium, cultural history inevitably also proves to be a culture and a history of page turning.

Books are not receptacles that are filled with texts as if through a funnel. Rather, they are what the French poet Paul Valéry (1871–1945) in his 1927 essay "The Two Virtues of a Book" (*Les deux vertus d'un livre*) pointedly called "reading machines". They are apparatuses operated through the turning of pages – which has consequences that are as obvious as they are remarkable and momentous.

It is not just that you *can* leaf through the pages of a book: you actually *have to* flip its pages, in order for it to reveal what it hides when closed. At the same time, one of the peculiarities of the codex is that it invariably shows just a section of what it contains: always just a spread at a time. The pages divide the contents into physical units which readers can appropriate only consecutively. The codex *spatializes* its contents and turns them into a multi-layered, tangible object.

Rather than just letting a text sit quietly in a book, leafing sets it in motion. It moderates between text and book: whenever you leaf through a book, you also leaf through the text contained in it. This dissolves the static entity of the book block, converting it into a process of acquiring its contents. Hence the turning of pages makes the text not just readable, but also physically palpable and intellectually vulnerable. Leafing allows the reader to very literally and tangibly *intervene* in the text.

Accordingly, the anatomy of a book at a very fundamental level calls into question the autonomy of its contents.

In literature, especially in novels, books take on a *hinge function* at the interface between the reality of the reader and the literary fiction, as it mediates between those two worlds. In the book, the autonomy of the work meets the *willfulness* of the readers, as the codex allows them to deal with the texts as they may see fit. The aspect of *manipulation*, in terms of a potentially distorting intervention, has earned leafing or browsing a bad reputation as an arbitrary act, especially in literary contexts – at least when referring to the impetuous skimming, or unfocused skipping, of pages which disrupts the continuity of content, rather than to the disciplined turning of one page after another.

Following the sequence of the narrative and the development of the protagonists within the narration is fundamentally important for the reading of many stories. In turning the pages, readers embrace this structure of the text, haptically tracing, as it were, the construction of the narrative and complying with the text's implicit demands. In this sense, linear narrative texts, in particular, seek to discipline the readers and reduce leafing to the habitual turning

Thorsten Kern, *Blättern* (Leafing), 2017.

over of pages as a necessity, in order to be able to continue reading. The book, one could say, is *tamed* by the text. In this, the successive turning of pages serves a very practical purpose as well: it prevents unwanted recurrences of passages. What the readers have read is on the left page and what is still ahead is on the right one.

Considering the fact that frantic browsing may become a problem – especially for literature's aesthetics of autonomy, in which the notion of a complete, whole work conceived by an author becomes particularly relevant – many eighteenth-century didactic approaches cautioned against chaotic skim-reading, because it threatened to confuse the mind. Yet at the same time people recognized the constructive potential of browsing, which allows for the knowledge scattered in different parts of a book to be interlinked with the contents of other books. And people also realized that first gaining an overall impression through browsing, before applying oneself to the whole in intensive reading, could indeed be conducive to a better understanding.

Alongside the theoretical reflections on page turning, curious practices of leafing have developed, as have books that are intended to be leafed through rather than read. In the Middle Ages opening books to a random page was widespread as a popular practice of divination. Randomly opened text passages were interpreted with a view to the future of the person seeking advice. In François Rabelais' (1494–1553) *Gargantua et Pantagruel* (published in five volumes between *c.*1532–*c.*1564), one of the major novels of the early modern period, several chapters revolve around the divinatory leafing through texts of the Roman poet Virgil. In fact, catering to this bibliomancy, a special type of book developed in the form of books of fate and oracle books, which enjoyed great popularity until well into the eighteenth century. In works by Hans Jakob Christoffel von Grimmelshausen (1622–76) we also learn of 'blow books' which were used by fair carnies to entertain their audiences: one of the bystanders was asked to blow on the book, whereupon its pages would show something related to that person. Due to clever variations in the way the book's pages were cut, weapons, coins, drinking vessels, or hearts would then seemingly magically appear depending on the position of the thumb while riffling, thus pointing to some guilty pleasure in which the flabbergasted volunteer was jocularly accused of indulging. During this period, the bookbinding trade also produced artful book objects made up of multiple book blocks bound together, which could be opened and leafed through in different directions.

Unlike many modern novels, their baroque precursors were still designed for a partial reading of select passages and often included annotated tables of contents, sometimes featuring entire summaries of the chapters, and extensive indexes. With their help, readers could filter out what was of interest to them, without having to read the entire text. A striking example of a work of literature that incorporates the book and its structure and artfully choreographs the turning of pages is Laurence Sterne's (1713–1768) novel *The Life and Opinions of Tristram Shandy, Gentleman* (1759–67). In attempting to commit his biography to paper, the narrator keeps sending readers crisscross through the book and asks them not only to leaf forward and backward, but also to consult other books to verify his assertions.

In avant-gardist literature of the second half of the twentieth century, the approach to page turning fundamentally changes. Experimental writing techniques and radical text conceptions challenge the reader to engage in unconventional ways of reading. For works not conceived in linear fashion, traditional models of reading, and hence also the obedient turning of pages, sometimes even prove counterproductive, because they are not commensurate with the compositional structure – the (dis)organization of the texts. William Burroughs' (1914–1997) *Naked Lunch* (1959) was one of the first novels to explicitly invite its readers to not read the book from beginning to end but, rather, browse through it and create their own versions in the process.

While the relationship between book and text usually is a competitive one, particularly in the case of novels and stories, reference works such as dictionaries and encyclopedias use the sequential structure of the codex for their own purposes: in such works the pages make it possible to access alphabetically organized texts in a targeted manner, with index tab cuts sometimes even facilitating the search for particular keywords. One of the main reasons why the bound book managed to prevail over the scroll was that, as a reading and page-turning machine, it allowed a wholly new approach to texts. — *Christoph Benjamin Schulz*

Pop-Up Books

In 1836, the book *Colorful Scenes from the Life of Man* (*Bunte Scenerien aus dem Menschenleben*), by the renowned Austrian illustrator Leopold Chimani (1774–1844), was published in Vienna. It included several cut-out illustrations, which could be raised by hand to create three-dimensional scenes before the viewer's eyes.

Considered the first pop-up book, Chimani's book should be seen in the context of the history and development of movable and toy picture books, which became fashionable during the nineteenth century. This development led to the production of books featuring illustrations with figures that could be mechanically moved like puppets through hinges by pulling a tab; books with pictures painted on vertical slats which, when turned, caused one image to transform into another, achieving an effect similar to the crossfade in film; picture books whose pages had slits into which small paper figures could be inserted; books with flaps that needed to be lifted to see the (visual) content underneath;

stand-up books and fanfolds, and these are just the most important types. Nineteenth-century book culture was varied and complex, hybrid and multimedia-based. Among the most renowned 'paper engineers' (today's term for the craft) of the time were Lothar Meggendorfer (1847–1925), Raphael Tuck (1821–1900), and Ernest Nister (1842–1909).

Sometimes the designers of these playful, interactive books used phenomena, elements, and effects that had been long known. For example, '*volvelles*,' or wheel-charts, which were attached to pages and usually served to visualize scientific knowledge, can be found in thirteenth-century manuscripts, and representations of human bodies consisting of multiple layers of paper were familiar from anatomical drawings. Geometrical solids found in sixteenth-century mathematical textbooks are also considered an early form of pop-up. Their bases were glued to the pages and their sides could be erected to complete the forms. In the mid-eighteenth century, 'harlequinades' came into fashion in England. These were folded montages that could be unfolded like fanfolds and featured additional movable panels at the upper and lower edges.

Pop-up books with figures that stand up when opened and fold together again when closed, while the norm today, are a comparatively recent invention. As late as 1929, the Englishman S. Louis Giraud took out patents in England and Germany for a technique of self-erecting pop-ups, which he called "pictures that spring up". The term 'pop-up' gained acceptance in the early 1930s in connection with the publications of the Blue Ribbon Press; appearing in the press release and on the cover of Harold B. Lentz's *Jack the Giant Killer* (New York, 1932), it established itself as the technical term and generic name, and is still commonly used today.

This technique is particularly interesting with regard to the use of the codex as the particular book form for pop-ups, because it cleverly transfers the energy and dynamics generated by turning pages to the structures folded between them, thereby setting off motion in the book. An understanding of the sequential structure of the codex is shown in the harnessing of page turning to the mechanics of lift and pull.

Until the 1930s, many movable books included attributes such as 'movable' or even 'animated' in their titles, as evidenced by two early examples: August Köhler's movable pop-up book *Permanent Transfer: An Animated Picture Book for All Ages* (*Die Immerwährende Versetzung: Ein Lebendiges Bilderbuch für Groß und Klein* [Berlin, 1865]) and the pull-out picture book *The Animated Picture Book* (*Das Lebendige Bilderbuch* [Augsburg, 1870]). Literary fantasies of books whose illustrations come to life are known from times even before the invention of pop-up books: E. T. A. Hoffmann's story *Little Zaches, Called Cinnabar* (*Der Kleine Zaches, Genannt Zinnober*, 1819) and two fairytales by Hans Christian Andersen are among the best-known examples.

Walter Benjamin (1892–1940), the philosopher and cultural critic, owned a large collection of toy picture books and occasionally reflected on the phenomenon in his essays, especially in *A Glimpse into the World of Children's Books* (1926).
— *Christoph Benjamin Schulz*

Opposite: Leopold Chimani, *Bunte Scenerien aus dem Menschenleben* (Colorful Scenes from the Life of Man), Vienna, 1836.

Geometrical solids as three-dimensional pop-up images in *Mathematical Preface*, the preface to an English edition of Euclid by John Dee, England 1570.

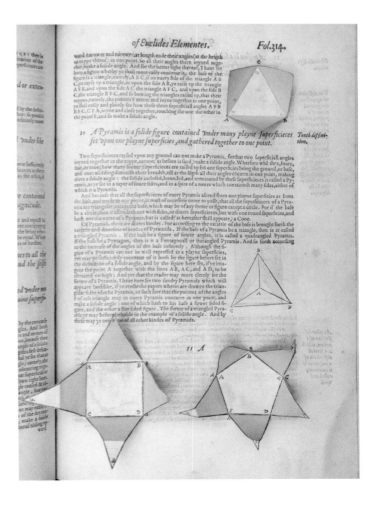

The Flip Book

In 1868 the English printer John Barnes Linnett filed a patent for a type of book which he called 'Kineograph' (or moving picture) and which to this day is known as the flicker, flick or flip book. The book's small pages featured series of pictures with motion sequences which, when activated by rapidly turning the pages, produced an effect of cinematic animation. As 'paper film,' the flip book reveals a structural affinity between the medium of the book and that of film, as both consist of series of individual and independent surfaces.

By 1868 it was already quite well known that the flip book worked. As a by-product of nineteenth-century laboratory experiments to study human optics, numerous versions of test assemblies were put out on the mainstream market and enjoyed great popularity as 'film before film.'

Among the many animation techniques of the nineteenth century, the flip book was the simplest one in technical terms. It required neither a mechanical apparatus nor a technical contraption, as it made use of the form of the book. This was a consequence of the need to link the individual image sequences and create a kind of a 'page-turning machine.' The images were set to paper and bound.

Even if the flip book by itself didn't represent a major innovation in the technological trajectory of pre-cinematic animation techniques, it did develop into a popular philosophical toy. It was not just about curiosity and taking delight in the amazing effect; what mattered even more was that this effect was *transparent* and comprehensible. It was about gaining knowledge. The viewers lead the mysterious process of the animation of static images. They are their own seducers and decide for themselves how rapidly

Max Skladanowsky at the presentation of his *daumenkino,* or 'thumb cinema,' in Berlin, *c.* 1900.

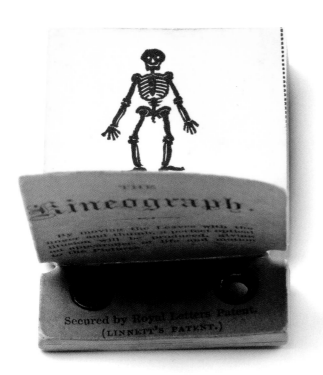

to turn the pages: whether they just want to enjoy the illusion or, take an analytic look behind the scenes of cinema and subject the nature of the illusion, which became inscrutable in the projection of film, to closer scrutiny.

By exploiting the inertia of the retina and tricking the eye, the flip book shows how easily this organ, which historically was associated in particular with gaining knowledge, is deceived. While other optical toys, such as the praxinoscope, the zoetrope and the mutoscope, fell more and more into disuse with the establishment of film as a mass medium, the flip book has lost none of its fascination and indeed has again gained in importance in view of the even greater immateriality of moving images brought about by digitalization. — *Christoph Benjamin Schulz*

Illustration from the 'kineograph' patent of John Barnes Linnett (1868).

The Book as an Object: Irma Boom

The Dutch book artist and typographer Irma Boom (b. 1960) is one of the world's most famous designers. Called the 'Queen of Books,' she has made more than 300 of them, opening up completely new design paths in the medium of books as well as in the use of paper. Her very individual approach to work and thought has changed traditional design methods and, in a way, created a whole new radical ideal and attitude. It re-invents, one might say, the body of the book and at the same time lends its medium a highly contemporary relevance. For Boom, books are a form of architecture and she sees each one as a unique carrier of information. Only after carefully reviewing its content, theme and subject matter, does she develop a book's shape. On the one hand, she wants to support the reader's understanding, on the other, she wants to create a beautiful object with its own qualities and an intense presence. Like an architect, Irma Boom takes the entire landscape into account, from its corners, edges, and gaps up to its structural tectonics, which also includes its binding and

its entire assembly. She always builds three-dimensional maquettes of her books, mostly in miniature, which means every detail of the design and product manufacturing are precisely taken into account and follow an underlying logic. Designed by Irma Boom in 2006, *Weaving the Metaphor on the Textile Works of Sheila Hicks* has been voted the most beautiful book in the world. It very clearly illustrates how her designs begin with a concept, but above all how totally ingeniously Irma Boom is able to picture a theme in her head and invent a new shape from the classic elements of a book, which has something to do with its subject matter. In this book, the cut edges have been designed to make the paper look like a textile surface. The individual layers of the many pages of the book suddenly become a haptically altered surface, which breaks the light and transforms the book form into an almost textile-like body. — *Nicola von Velsen*

Irma Boom's artist book *Biography in Books* (2010) has a format of merely 3.8 × 5 cm and yet consists of 704 pages. The book was published by the Special Collections of the University of Amsterdam in cooperation with the Grafische Cultuurstichting. Conceived as an exhibition catalog, it contains Irma Boom's works from the years 1985 to 2010.

Opposite: Irma Boom, Sheila Hicks: *Weaving as Metaphor*, 2006, Yale University Press

SHEILA HICKS

Binding Books

"You cannot have a book without the bookbinder and those have been around much longer as there have been paper and books." This is my rather blunt statement with regard to books and people involved with paper. I run my workshop – established in 1919 – in the center of Cologne and it is now on its fourth generation of owners. As a bookbinder, I work far less for the Catholic Church and the university libraries than my predecessors did. Even the training of this craft has changed a lot. Compared to forty years ago we have approximately a quarter of the apprentices we once would have had.

The bookbinder's tasks have grown and changed, however. This craft has been attracting more attention in recent years, with the regular customers concentrating on the few remaining master craftsmen. Handicraft is much in demand: from individually embossed bindings for successively produced calendars or notebooks, to the binding of private volumes, the restoration of beloved recipe books or inherited bibles, the construction of cases and boxes, right through to binding photo albums in linen with inscriptions. The list of personalized projects could go on and on.

Traditionally, it was the bookbinder that bound the individual paper sheets, the pages for folders and periodicals, and then later into books with a cover. The bookbinder can provide precious bibles or valuable editions with additional inserts. He can create luxury book covers, attach loose spines and replace torn threads with sturdy linen ones.

The main steps in the binder's work include collating and folding printed sheets in line with their pagination, stitching the sheets with yarn, and then gluing and inserting the body of the book into a prepared book cover. The bookbindery also produces colored paper to decorate end sheets and covers. Coloring and gilding of a book section occurs in the workshop, too.

Traditional bookbinding is essentially manual work, with the industrial approach splitting off in the middle of the nineteenth century. In the arts and crafts, only a few stages have been

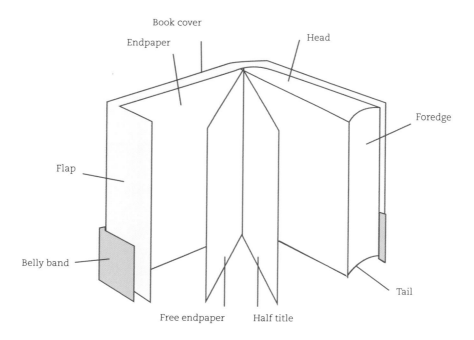

mechanized along the way: we have cutting and stapling machines and, as the latest development, digital book-title stamping machines. Ultimately, this very book about paper will end up being bound in two covers. Everything ends up with the bookbinder.

The creative design idea to have books with an open spine so that the book's pages can be seen, is something of which the bookbinder heartily disapproves. He regards this as a 'trendy gimmick' that is likely to have a negative impact on the book's durability. When it comes to durability, the craftsman probably has a point, but because this book is about paper it is aimed to appeal to all the senses and to illustrate both its inside and outside, we will concede there is a lot going for this kind of design finish.

— *Dirk Jachimsky*

Simon Goode and Ira Yonemura with a collaborator at the work shop of the London Centre for Book Art, which was founded in 2012.

Appendix

Contributors and Other Paper Lovers

Anita Brockmann (b. 1962) is an author, editor, and translator. She lives and works in Bochum and Cologne. Her passion for paper deepened in the Himalayas and Japan.

Matthias Burchardt (b. 1966) studied German philology, philosophy, and pedagogy in Cologne and earned a doctorate with a thesis on philosophical anthropology. He is the founder and director of the *Gesellschaft für Bildung und Wissen* (Organization for Education and Knowledge) and has published extensively on topics related to art, philosophy, and politics.

Peter Dahmen (b. 1967) lives and works in Dortmund where he studied communication design at the University of Applied Sciences. After graduating, he turned to designing three-dimensional pop-up objects made of paper and cardboard. A short film on YouTube from 2010 has, to date, had more than 4.5 million hits. (www.peterdahmen.de)

Boris Friedewald (b. 1969) studied art history, pedagogy, and theater arts in Bochum and Berlin. His publications focus on modern art and the Bauhaus.

John Gerard (b. 1955) born in Michigan, USA, he founded a workshop for hand-made paper in Berlin in 1985, which, since 1992, he has run in Rheinbach near Bonn. He occasionally teaches and also participates in Paperart-Festivals.

Heike Gfrereis (b. 1968) is a literary scholar and curator. Since 2001, she has headed the Museum Department of the Germany Literature Archive in Marbach and in 2013 she was awarded an honorary professorship at the University of Stuttgart.

Siegfried Gohr (b. 1949) ist an art historian, curator und freelance publicist. He lives in Cologne and Berlin.

Erwin Hapke (1937–2016) was born in East Prussia from where he fled with his family, ultimately settling in the Unna district in North Rhine-Westphalia. After apprenticing as a mechanic and further education at night school, he studied, and earned a doctorate in, biology. After working at the Max Planck Institute in Wilhelmshaven until 1981, he lived a reclusive life at his family home in the Unna district where he folded hundreds of thousands of figures out of paper and metal.

Viola Hildebrand-Schat studied literature, philosophy and psychology. She works as a freelance art historian with specialization in artists' books, in Frankfurt/Main.

Gordon Hoffmeyer (b. 1973) is a German philologist and media scholar who worked for various Düsseldorf advertising agencies. Since 2006 he has been working as an independent writer. (www.gordonhoffmeyer.de)

Neil Holt (b. 1973) studied design with a focus on typography and book art in Cologne and Düsseldorf. He works as a book designer and typographer in Cologne and teaches at the Ruhrakademie in Schwerte. (www.neilholt.de)

Philipp Hontschik (b. 1968) grew up near Regensburg and studied literature and communication in Munich. After sojourns in Great Britain and Italy he is now working as an independent author for various newspapers, magazines, and book projects.

Dirk Jachimsky (b. 1968) started his apprenticeship in the early 1990s in Frankfurt and works in Cologne since 1991. He became a master bookbinder in 2006 and has owned the bookbindery since 2008.

Paul Jackson (b. 1956) is a paper artist. Born in England, he became involved with origami and started creating folded paper on a professional basis in 1982. To date, he has authored more than thirty books on paper art and folding techniques and taught at numerous art and design schools. He has lived in in Tel Aviv, Israel, since 2000. (www.origami-artist.com)

Dr. Stephanie Jacobs (b. 1963) studied literature, philosophy and psychology. She has been the director of the German Museum of Books and Writing (*Deutschen Buch- und Schriftmuseums der Deutschen Nationalbibliothek*), in Leipzig since 2007.

Thorsten Kern (b. 1968) received his training from 1993 until 1997 and has since been working as an independent photographer and artist in Cologne, realizing exhibition and book projects in Germany and abroad. (www.kern-fotografie.de)

Ulrich Knaack (b. 1964) was born in Darmstadt and studied architecture at RWTH Aachen University, earning a doctorate in 1998. Since 2005 he has been Professor of Design and Construction at Delft University of Technology and, since 2014, also Professor of Façade Technology at Darmstadt University of Technology where he is involved in the BAMP, or Building with Paper, research project.

Esther Krop (b. 1974) studied at the Gerrit Rietveld Academy and De Ateliers in Amsterdam and has been working as an independent graphic artist and designer since 2002. In 2009 she founded *Alauda Publications* and in 2013 *De Monsterkamer*. (www.monsterkamer.nl)

Dirk Lange (b. 1973) was born in Sangerhausen, Saxony-Anhalt, and has been a professional paper marbler since 2008. His works are shown internationally and included in numerous collections. (www.handmarmorpapier.de)

Makkiko
photographs artists going about their creative work. Her photographs document the specific sensitivities and sensibilities of artists at work. (www.makkiko.com)

Nanne Meyer (b. 1953)
was born in Hamburg and today lives in Berlin. She attended the University of Fine Arts in Hamburg and was Professor of Drawing at the Berlin Weissensee School of Art from 1994 until 2015. (www.nannemeyer.de)

molo
is a design and production studio founded in the 1990s by Stephanie Forsythe and Todd MacAllen and based in Vancouver. Combining art, design and architecture, molo's projects are grounded in space making and range in scale from tea set to museum. (www.molodesign.com)

Raoul Mörchen (b. 1967)
grew up in Arnsberg in the Sauerland and studied musicology, philosophy, and art history in Münster and Cologne where, today, he works as an independent cultural journalist, music critic, and radio broadcaster.

Felix Renker (b. 1961)
grew up in Zerkall in the district of Düren on the western border of Germany and attended Darmstadt University of Technology, graduating with a degree in industrial engineering. After working for several years in the paper industry, 1994 he took over the family business, the Zerkall Paper Factory, as the fourth generation. (www.zerkall.com)

Julia Rinck (b. 1970)
is from Dohna, Saxony, and studied German philology, art history, and musicology at the University of Leipzig. As an expert in historic colored paper techniques and modern paper finishings she has worked at museums and academic institutions. She also initiated the website www.buntpapier.org.

Frieder Schmidt
attended the University of Stuttgart from 1976 until 1983 and earned a doctorate with a thesis on the history of paper. For twenty-five years he served as Head of the Collection of Historical Papers at the German Museum of Books and Writing in Leipzig until his retirement in November 2017.

Christoph Benjamin Schulz
is a literary scholar and art historian and works as a research associate at the Research Center for Visual Poetry of the University of Wuppertal as part of the German Research Foundation (DFG) project "The Artist's Book As an Aesthetic Experiment." His exhibition projects include *Daumenkino – The Flip-book Show* (2005), and *Alice in Wonderland – Through the Visual Arts* (2011/12) for Tate Liverpool and the Hamburger Kunsthalle.

Heinrich Spies
is managing partner of MAY+SPIES GmbH in Düren, a family business since 1920. (www.mayspies.com)

Fideli Sundqvist (b. 1987)
was born in Uppsala, Sweden, and studied graphic design and illustration at Konstfack, the Swedish academy of arts, crafts, and design. Today she lives and works as a paper artist in Stockholm. (www.fidelisundqvist.com)

Nicola von Velsen (b. 1960)
works as an editor and develops illustrated books on subjects related to art, culture, and cookery. Since 2013 she has run a paper shop called *Pop up Papier* in Cologne, dealing in products on, and made of, paper. (www.pop-up-papier.de)

Wanda Barcelona
is the architectural, design, and art studio of Inti Velez Boetro, Daniel Mancini, and Iris Joval who, since 2007, have been creating installations made entirely of paper. Their clients include Hermès, DIOR, Karl Lagerfeld, and the Guggenheim Museum.

Therese Weber
grew up in Röschenz, Switzerland, and is Professor of Aesthetic Education at the University of Applied Sciences of Northwest Switzerland in Liestal, Canton of Basel. Her artistic explorations took her to the U.S. in the pioneering days of paper art in the early 1980s. After several working visits to studios in Japan she undertook research trips to China and other places in the Far East. In addition to exhibitions in Germany and abroad, she published *Die Sprache des Papiers. Eine 2000-jährige Geschichte* in 2004.

Thomas Wessel
is an art historian specializing in Venetian Rococo and contemporary art as well as their preservation and value development. He has worked as an art insurance manager and nowadays lives in Markgräflerland south of Freiburg.

George Whitman (1913–2011)
after extensive travels, he opened the English-language bookshop, *Le Mistral*, in Paris, in 1951. His shop became a meeting point for the Beat Generation, just as Silvia Beach's *Shakespeare and Company* had once been for the authors of the Lost Generation until 1946. In 1964, two years after Silvia Beach's death, Whitman renamed his shop *Shakespeare and Company*.

Debbie Wijskamp
studied product design at the University of the Arts in Arnhem, the Netherlands. Since 2009 she has been working as an independent artist, developing her own collection of handmade interior products. (www.debbiewijskamp.com)

Selected Literature

The literature on paper includes extensive contributions on the history of paper as well as knowledgeable discussions of the history of papermaking in the context of cultural history. In addition, there are numerous books on specialized fields ranging from paper production and various media-related topics (such as printmaking, colored paper, and paper restoration) to paper applications such as paper engineering works, paper design, and folding techniques. The number of titles in the field of craft and origami books is also growing rapidly.

Below is a selected bibliography listing works that were of special importance to the authors and editors of this book.

A comprehensive bibliography can be found through the library catalogs of the German National Library (http://www.dnb.de/EN/Home/home_node.html) and the Dutch National Library (https://www.kb.nl/en).

Asunción, Josep. 2002. *Papermaking: Traditional Techniques and Methods of Production*, London: Batsford.

Bardt, Juliane. 2016. (First published 2006). *Kunst aus Papier. Zur Ikonographie eines plastischen Werkmaterials der zeitgenössischen Kunst*. Hildesheim, Zürich, New York: Olms.

Bayerl, Günter. 1987. *Die Papiermühle. Vorindustrielle Papiermacherei auf dem Gebiet des alten deutschen Reiches. Technologie, Arbeitsverhältnisse, Umwelt*, Published in two volumes. Frankfurt am Main, Bern, New York, Paris: Lang.

Bierma, Wigger, 2015. *Walter Nikkels Depicted. Abgebildet. Afgebeeld.* Amsterdam: Tropen.

Blana, Hubert. 1993. *Die Herstellung: Ein Handbuch für Gestaltung, Technik und Kalkulation von Buch, Zeitschrift und Zeitung*. München, New Providence, London, Paris: Saur.

Blechschmidt, Jürgen, ed. 2010. *Taschenbuch der Papiertechnik*. München: Hanser.

Bolofo, Koto. 2014. *Paper Making*. Göttingen: Steidl.

Bose, Günter Karl. 2013. "Das Ende einer Last: Die Befreiung von den Büchern," in *Ästhetik des Buches* 2. Göttingen: Wallstein.

Bosshard, Hans Rudolf. 1980. *Technische Grundlagen zur Satzherstellung*, Vol. I. Verlag des Bildungsverbandes Schweizerischer Typografen BST (Publishing house of the Education Association of Swiss Typographers): Bern.

Bohnenkamp, Anne and Wiethölter, Waltraud, eds. 2008. *Der Brief: Ereignis und Objekt*, (Ausst.-Kat., Freies Deutsches Hochstift – Frankfurter Goethe-Museum, Goethe-Universität Frankfurt und Deutsches Literaturarchiv Marbach), Frankfurt am Main, Basel: Stroemfeld.

Buisson, Dominique. 1991. *The Art of Japanese Paper: Masks, Lanterns, Kites, Dolls, Origami*. Paris: Terrail.

Burke, Peter. 2000. *A Social History of Knowledge: From Gutenberg to Diderot*, Volume I. Cambridge: Polity Press.

Craig, James. 1990. *Production for the Graphic Designer*. New York: Watson-Guptill Publications.

Eimert, Dorothea, ed. "PaperArt: Geschichte der Papierkunst." in *History of Paper Art*, 1994. (Fifth International Biennale of PaperArt, Leopold-Hoesch-Museum und Papiermuseum Düren). Köln: Wienand.

Giersch, Ulrich, ed. 2015. *Freude am Einkauf: Papiertüten in der DDR*. Berlin: Bien & Giersch.

Gottschalk, Elke. 1996. *Papierantiquitäten. Luxuspapiere von 1820 bis 1920*. Augsburg: Battenberg.

Göttsching, Lothar, ed. 1990. *Papier in unserer Welt: Ein Handbuch*. Düsseldorf, Vienna. New York: Econ.

Hara, Kenya. 2009, 2015. *White*. Zurich: Lars Müller Publishers.

Hoyer, Fritz. 1929. *Papiersorten-Lexikon: Ein Nachschlagewerk für die tägliche Praxis*. Stuttgart: Franckh.

Hunter, Dard. 1974. (First published 1943). *Papermaking: The History and Technique of an Ancient Craft*. New York: Dover Books.

Jackson, Paul. 2011. *Folding Techniques for Designers: From Sheet to Form*. London: Laurence King Publishers.

2012. *Structural Packaging: Design Your Own Boxes and 3D Forms*, London: Laurence King Publishers.

Jury, David. 2002. *About Face: Reviving the Rules of Typography*. Mies, Hove: Roto-Vision.

Klacsmann, John and Lampert, Andrew, eds. 2015. *Paper Airplanes: The Collections of Harry Smith*. Catalogue Raisonné, Volume I. Atlanta, New York: J&L Books and Anthology Film Archives.

Klanten, Robert. 2011. *Papercraft: Design and Art with Paper*. Berlin: Gestalten.

Kurlansky, Mark. 2016. *Paper: Paging through History*. New York, London: W.W. Norton & Company.

Lorentz, Frank. 2013 *Zerkall: Die unzeitgemäße Geschichte der Eifeler Büttenpapierfabrik Zerkall Renker & Söhne.*

Frechen: Römerturm und Cologne: V8 Verlag.

Marks, P. J. M. 2015. *An Anthology of Decorated Papers: A Sourcebook for Designers*. London: Thames & Hudson.

McArthur, Meher. 2017. *New Expressions in Origami Art: Masterworks from 25 Leading Paper Artists*. Vermont: Tuttle Publishing.

Miyake, Riichi, Luna, Ian, and Gold, Lauren A. eds. 2009. *Shigeru Ban: Paper in Architecture*, New York: Rizzoli.

Monro, Alexander. 2015. *The Paper Trail: An Unexpected History of a Revolutionary Invention*. Penguin: London.

Morlok, Franziska, and Waszelewski, Miriam. 2016. *Vom Blatt zum Blättern: Falzen, Heften, Binden für Gestalter*. Mainz: Hermann Schmidt.

Müller, Lothar. 2014. *White Magic: The Age of Paper*. Cambridge, Malden, Massachusetts: Polity Press.

von Oettingen, Dirik. 2007. *Verhüllt um zu verführen: Die Welt auf der Orange*. Potsdam: Vacat.

Orsenna, Érik. 2014. *Auf der Spur des Papiers: Eine Liebeserklärung*. München: C. H. Beck.

Pias, Claus. 2016. "Das bewegte Buch: Ein Katalog der gelesenen Bücher" *Marbacher Magazin*. Issued in conjunction with exhibition catalog, Literaturmuseum der Moderne, Marbach am Neckar: Deutsche Schillergesellschaft. pp.150–152.

Renker, Armin. 1934. *Das Buch vom Papier: Die Kulturgeschichte des Papiers*. Leipzig: Insel.

Ruder, Emil. 2001. (First published 1967). *Typografie: Ein Gestaltungslehrbuch*. Sulgen, Zürich: Niggli.

Schmidt, Frieder. 2011. "Ders. Maschinenpapierwasserzeichen in den Sammlungen des Deutschen Buch- und Schriftmuseums." In: *Dialog mit Bibliotheken 1/2011*, S: pp. 62–66 (Online-Edition: https://d-nb. info/1016073941/34).

"Die Welt der Papierfabrikation als künstlerisches Sujet." In *Dialog mit Bibliotheken 2/2012*: pp. 38–46. (Online-Edition: https://d-nb. info/1038601851/34).

2016. "Bahnriss?! Papier | Kultur." In *Dialog mit Bibliotheken 1/2016*. [Dialogue with Libraries] Vol. 1: pp. 42–46. (Online-Edition: https://d-nb. info/108253787X/34).

Schmidt-Bachem, Heinz. 2011. *Aus Papier: Eine Kultur- und Wirtschafts- geschichte der Papier verarbeitenden Industrie in Deutschland*. Berlin, Boston: De Gruyter.

Schulz, Christoph Benjamin. 2015. *Poetiken des Blätterns*. Hildesheim, Zürich, NewYork: Olms.

Schwieger, Heinz G. 1992. (6th edition). *Papier-Praktikum: Herstellung, Beurteilung, Verarbeitung. Textbuch*. Wiesbaden: PR-Verlag Schwieger.

Schwieger, Heinz. 1939. *Kleine Papierfibel*, Potsdam: Rütten & Loening. (Includes paper samples).

Seipel, Peter and Wagner, Stefan, eds. 2005. *Masters of Origami at Hangar 7: The Art of Paperfolding*. [Die Vielfalt der Faltkunst] (exh. cat. Hangar 7, Salzburg), Ostfildern-Ruit: Hatje Cantz.

Thun-Hohenstein, Christoph and Pokorny-Nagel, Kathrin, eds. 2017. *Ephemera: The Graphic Design of the MAK Libarary and Works on Paper Collection*. [Die Gebrauchsgrafik der MAK-Biblio- thek und Kunstblättersammlung]. Exhibition catalog in conjunction with MAK –Museum of Applied Arts, Vienna. Vienna: Verlag für Moderne Kunst.

Tschudin, Peter F. 2012. (2nd edition). *Grundzüge der Papiergeschichte*. Stuttgart: Hiersemann.

Turner, Silvie. 1994. (First published 1991). *Which Paper? A Guide to Choosing and Using Fine Papers for Artists, Crafts- people and Designers*. New York: Lyons.

1998. *The Book of Fine Paper: A World- wide Guide to Contemporary Papers for Art*. London: Design & Decoration.

Valéry, Paul. 1937. *The Politics of the Spirit*. [Die Politik des Geistes] *Lecture, held November 16, 1932*. Vienna: Bermann- Fischer.

Walenski, Wolfgang. 1994. *Wörterbuch Druck + Papier*, Frankfurt am Main: Klostermann.

Weber, Therese. 2004. *Die Sprache des Papiers: Eine 2000-jährige Geschichte*. Bern/Stuttgart/Wien: Haupt.

Williams, Nancy. 2004 [1993] *Paperwork: The Potential of Paper in Graphic Design*, London: Phaidon Press.

Zender, Joachim Elias. 2008. *Lexikon Buch, Druck, Papier*, Bern/Stuttgart/ Wien: Haupt.

Films

Duregger, Katja, dir. *Das sinnliche Buch* (The sensual book). 2016. (52 minutes).

Lund, Christian, interviewer. *Irma Boom. The Architecture of the Book*. Louisiana Museum of Modern Art. 2015. https:// vimeo.com/144725089 Link active February 2018. (14 minutes).

Vives, François-Xavier, dir. *Der Origami- Code: Forscher entdecken das Falten*. 2015 (45 minutes).

Paper Museums and Places of Special Paper Interest

This list gathers together places with a special focus on paper, its artisane processing and its function as material and medium.

The list starts with Great Britain and the US and then continues in an alphabetical order by countries.

Further information

AEPM – Association of European Printing Museums
www.aepm.eu/museum-finder

Europe Guide Schwarze Kunst
www.arbeitskreis-druckgeschichte.de/europeguide

IPH – International Association of Paper Historians
www.paperhistory.org/Museums/

GREAT BRITAIN

Museums, Collections and Paper Mills

Bodleian Libraries
Broad Street
Oxford
OX1 3BG
bodleian.ox.ac.uk

Frogmore Paper Mill
Fourdrinier Way
Apsley, Hemel Hempstead
Herfordshire
HP3 9RL
thepapertrail.co.uk

Museum of Papermaking
Heron Corn Mill
Mill Lane, Beetham
Milnthorpe, Cumbria
LA7 7PQ
www.heronmill.org

Pitt Mill
Two Rivers Paper Company
Mineral Line
Roadwater, Watchet
TA23 0QS
www.tworiverspaper.com/the-papermill

St Bride Foundation
14 Bride Lane
London
EC4Y 8EQ
sbf.org.uk

Wookey Hole Paper Mill
Wells
Somerset
BA5 1BB
wookey.co.uk/hand-made-paper-mill

Workshops, Organizations

British Association of Paper Historians
baph.org.uk

PaperShift
www.papershift.net

USA

Museums, Collections and Paper Mills

Archives and Manuscripts
Austin History Center
810 Guadalupe Street
Austin TX, 78701
library.austintexas.gov/ahc/about-us

Crane Museum of Papermaking
Off West Housatonic Street
Dalton, MA 01226
www.crane.com

Dard Hunter Studios
125 West Water Street
Chillicothe, OH 45601
www.dardhunter.com

Historic Rittenhouse Town
208 Lincoln Drive
Philadelphia, PA 19144
www.rittenhousetown.org

International Paper Museum
Research Institute of Paper
History & Technology
Carriage House
8 Evans Road
Brookline, MA 02445
www.papermakinghistory.org

Maine's Paper & Heritage Museum
22 Church Street
Livermore Falls, ME 04254
www.papermuseumofmaine.org

Paper Discovery Center
425 W. Water Street
Appleton, WI 54911
www.paperdiscoverycenter.org

Robert C. Williams Museum
of Papermaking
Renewable Bioproducts Institute
Georgia Tech
Atlanta, GA 30332
paper.gatech.edu

The Getty Research Institute
1200 Getty Center Drive
Suite 1100
Los Angeles, CA 90049–1688
www.getty.edu/research/

Wisconsin River Papermaking Museum
730 First Avenue South
Wisconsin Rapids, WI 54495

Workshops, Organizations

Carriage House Paper
www.carriagehousepaper.com

Catherine Nash's Resources for
Papermaking
www.papermakingresources.com

Dieu Donné
www.dieudonne.org

Magnolia Editions
www.magnoliaeditions.com

Paperslurry
www.paperslurry.com

Pondside Pulp and Paper
pondsidepulpandpaper.blogspot.de

Primrose Park Paper Arts Inc.
primrosepaperarts.wordpress.com

Pyramid Atlantic Art Center
www.pyramidatlanticartcenter.org/
papermaking

Seastone Papers
www.seastonepapers.com

Summer Art Institute,
Women's Studio Workshop
www.wsworkshop.org/summer-
art-institute

The Mobile Mill
themobilemill.tumblr.com

Twinrocker
www.twinrocker.com

AUSTRIA

Museums and Papermills

Österreichisches Papiermachermuseum
In der "Alten Fabrik"
Museumsplatz 1
A-4662 Laakirchen
www.papierwelten.co.at

Waldviertler Papiermühle Mörzinger
Bad Großpertholz 76
A-3972 Bad Großpertholz
www.papiermuehle.at

Workshops, Organizations

Kinderbuchhaus im Schneiderhäusl
www.kinderbuchhaus.at

Papieratelier
www.papieratelier.at

PapierWespe
www.papierwespe.at

AUSTRALIA

Workshops, Organizations

Papermakers of Victoria Inc.
papermakers.org.au

The Papermaker's Guild
of Western Australia
members.tripod.com/
papermakers_guild

BELGIUM

Museums and Paper Mills

Papiermolen Herisem
Fabriekstraat 20
B-1652 Alsemberg
www.herisem.be

Papieratelier
Malmundarium
Place du Châlet, 10
B-4960 Malmedy
www.malmundarium.be

Musée de l'Imprimerie
Bibliothèque Royale de Belgique
4, Boulevard de l'Empereur
B-1000 Brüssel
www.kbr.be

Musée National du Papier
Rou de Amours, 10
B-7100 La Louvière
www.centredelagravure.be

Musée Plantin-Moretus
Vrijdagmarkt 22
B-2000 Antwerpen
www.plantin-moretus.be

CANADA

Museums and Paper Mills

Histoire de l'Industrie Papetière
Boréalis Musée à Trois-Rivières
200, Avenue des Draveurs
Trois-Rivières, Quebec
G9A 5H3
www.borealis3r.ca

Workshops, Organizations

Joseph Wu Origami
www.origami.as

CHINA

Museums

Cailun Paper Culture Museum
Near the Cailun Tomb
Longting Town
Yang County 723300

Chinese Paper Cutting Museum
Dongguan Street
Guangling District
Yangzhou 225001

Museum of Handcraft Paper
Xinzhuang Village
Jietou Town
Tengchong County
Yunnan Province

CZECH REPUBLIC

Museums and Paper Mills

Handmade Paper Mill Velké Losiny
Paper Museum
Ručni Papírna
78815 Velké Losiny
Sumperk
www.rucnipapirna.cz

DENMARK

Museums and Paper Mills

Bruunshaab Gl. Papfabrik
Vinkelvej 97
8800 Viborg
www.papfabrik.dk

Papirmuseet
Museum Silkeborg
Bøttebygningen
Papirfabrikken 78
8600 Silkeborg
www.museumsilkeborg.dk

FINLAND

Museums and Paper Mills

Verla Paper Mill Museum
Verlantie 295
47850 Verla Kouvola
www.verla.fi

FRANCE

Museums and Paper Mills

Centre Culturel Papetier
Marius A. Peraudeau
63600 Ambert en Livraidois

Moulin à Papier, Brousses et Villaret
11390 Brousses et Villaret
www.moulinapapier.com

Moulin à Papier de la Tourne
173 Chemin de la Tourne
Lachat – St. André
73800 Les Marches
www.moulin-a-papier.com

Moulin à Papier du Liveau
En Vallée de Clisson
17 Le Liveau
44190 Gorges
lemoulinapapierduliveau.fr

Moulin à Papier Pen-Mur
Site de Pen-Mur
56190 Muzillac

Moulin à Papier Richard de Bas
63600 Ambert
www.richarddebas.fr

Moulin à Papier Vallis Clausa
Chemin de la Fontaine
84800 Fontaine de Vaucluse
www.moulin-vallisclausa.com

Moulin de la Rouzique
Écono-musée du papier de Couze
Route de Varennes
24150 Couze
www.moulin-rouzique.com

Moulin du Got
Le Pénitent
87400 St. Léonhard-de-Noblat
www.moulindugot.com

Moulin du Verger
16400 Puymoyen
www.moulinduverger.co

Musée Départemental du Cartonnage
et de l'Imprimerie
3 Avenue Maréchal Foch
84600 Valréas

Musée des Papeteries
Canson et Mongolfier
Rue de Vidalon
07430 Davézieux
www. musee-papeteries-
canson-montgolfier.fr

Musée du Papier d'Angoulême
134 Rue de Bordeaux
16000 Angoulême
www.musee-du-papier.fr

Papeterie de Vaux
Vaux
24270 Payzac
www.ecomuseesdelauvezere.fr/

Workshops, Organizations

Ateliers et mémoire du papier
www.ateliersetmemoiredupapier.fr

Art Paperwork – Contemporary
Art on Paper
www.artpaperwork.com/fr/

GERMANY

Deutsches Buch- und Schriftmuseum
Deutsche Nationalbibliothek
Deutscher Platz 1
04103 Leipzig
www.dnb.de/DE/DBSM/dbsm_node.html

Papiermühle Alte Dombach
LVR-Industriemuseum
Bergisch Gladbach
Alte Dombach 1
51465 Bergisch Gladbach
www.papiermuseum.de

Papiermuseum Düren
at Leopold-Hoesch-Museum
Wallstr. 2–8
52349 Düren
www.leopoldhoeschmuseum.de/
deutsch/papiermuseum/papiermuse-
um-dueren/

Deutsches Literaturarchiv Marbach
Deutsche Schillergesellschaft e.V.
Schillerhöhe 8–10
71672 Marbach am Neckar
www.dla-marbach.de

Museums, Collections and Paper Mills

Technisches Museum Neumannmühle
Kirnitzschtalstr. 5
01855 Sebnitz (OT Ottendorf)
www.neumann-muehle.de

Heimat- und Papiermuseum Fockendorf
Fabrikstr. 10
04617 Fockendorf
www.papiermuseum.net

Museum Papiermühle Weddersleben
Quedlinburger Str. 2
06502 Weddensleben
www.lebenshilfe-hz-qlb.de/papiermu-
seum.html

Papiermühle St. Peter
Mühlenstr. 1
08371 Glauchau

Sammlung für Papier- und Druck-
geschichte Johannes Roßberg
Druckereimuseum Roßberg
Markt 8
09669 Frankenberg

Dauerausstellung Papiertechnik
Deutsches Technikmuseum Berlin
Trebbiner Str. 9
10963 Berlin
www.sdtb.de/technikmuseum/
ausstellungen/82/

Papiermanufaktur und -museum
Wolfswinkel-Spechthausen
Eberswalder Straße 27–29
16227 Eberswalde

Papiermühle Plöger
Kulturdenkmal und Technik-Museum
Im Niesetal 11
32816 Schieder-Schwalenberg
(OT Schieder)
www.papiermuehle-ploeger.de

Deutsches Tapetenmuseum
Museumslandschaft Hessen Kassel
Schloss Wilhelmshöhe
Schlosspark 1
34131 Kassel
tapeten.museum-kassel.de

Deutsches Plakat Museum
Museum Folkwang
Museumsplatz 1
45128 Essen
www.museum-folkwang.de

Internationales
Zeitungsmuseum Aachen
Pontstr. 13
52063 Aachen
www.izm.de

Papierabteilung
Gutenberg-Museum
Liebfrauenplatz 5
55116 Mainz
www.gutenberg-museum.de

Klingspor Museum
Museum für internationale Buch-
und Schriftkunst des 20. Jahrhunderts
Büsingpalais
Herrnstraße 80
63065 Offenbach am Main
www.klingspor-museum.de

Deutsches Verpackungs-Museum
Hauptstraße 22
69117 Heidelberg
www.verpackungsmuseum.de

Deutsches Spielkartenmuseum
Schönbuchstraße 32
70771 Leinfelden-Echterdingen
www.spielkartenmuseum.de

Papiermuseum Gleisweiler
im Kurpfälzischen Zehnthof
Zum Sonnenberg 1
76835 Gleisweiler
www.papiermuseum-gleisweiler.de

Abteilung Papiertechnik und Papierg-
eschichtliche Sammlungen
Deutsches Museum
Museumsinsel 1
80538 München
www.deutsches-museum.de

MD-Papiermuseum
Ostenstr. 5
85221 Dachau

Papiermühle und Klostermühlenmu-
seum Thierhaupten
Franzengasse 21
86672 Thierhaupten
www.klostermuehlenmuseum.de
Museum Papiermühle Homburg
Gartenstr. 11
97855 Homburg/Main
www.papiermuehle-homburg.de

Workshops, Organizations

Büttenpapierfabrik Gmund
www.gmund.de

Deutscher Arbeitskreis Papiergeschichte
www.ak-papiergeschichte.de

Eifeltor Mühle
www.eifeltor-muehle.de

Gangolf Ulbricht – Werkstatt für Papier
www.papiergangolfulbricht.de

Hamburger Buntpapier
www.hamburgerbuntpapier.de

Homburger Papiermanufaktur
www.homburger-papiermanufaktur.de

IADM – Internationaler Arbeitskreis für
Druck- und Mediengeschichte
www.arbeitskreis-druckgeschichte.de

Origami Deutschland – Verein zur
Förderung des Papierfaltens
www.papierfalten.de

Peace of Paper Workshop
www.peaceofpaper-workshop.de

Papiermanufaktur Klaus Wengenmayr
www.papiermanufaktur-wengenmayr.de

Papiermanufaktur Wrangelsburg
papier-druck.beepworld.de

Papierwerkstatt Oberschmitten
www.papierwerkstatt-oberschmitten.de

Peter's Bastelfix
www.peters-bastelfix.de

Verband Deutscher Papierfabriken
www.vdp-online.de

HUNGARY

Museums and Paper Mills

Diósgyőri Papírgyár Zrt
Museum of DIPA – Diósgyőr Paper
Factory Zrt
Miskolc
Hegyalja u. 203/1
www.dipa.hu/en/museum

Magyar Papírmúzeum
2400 Dunaújváros
Papírgyári út 42-46
magyarpapirmuzeum.webnode.hu

INDIA

Workshops, Organizations

Nirupama Academy of Handmade Paper
www.nirupama.org

IRELAND

Museums and Paper Mills

National Print Museum
of Ireland Beggars Bush Barracks
Haddington Road
Dublin 4
D04 E0C9
www.nationalprintmuseum.ie

ITALY

Museums and Paper Mills

Museo Bodoniano
Biblioteca Palatina
Strada alla Pilotta, 3
43100 Parma PR
museobodoni.beniculturali.it

Museo della Carta, Amalfi
Via delle Cartiere, 23
84011 Amalfi SA
www.museodellacarta.it

Museo della Carta di Mele
Via Acquasanta, 251
16010 Acquasanta GE
www.museocartamele.it

Museo della Carta Pescia
Strada Comunale Medicina Pietrabuona, 1
51017 Medicina PT
www.museodellacarta.org

Museo della Carta, Toscolano Maderno
Via Valle delle Cartiere
25088 Toscolano Maderno BS
www.valledellecartiere.it

Museo della Carta e della Filigrana,
Fabriano
Largo Fratelli Spacca, 2
60044 Fabriano AN
www.museodellacarta.com

Museo della Carta e della
Filigrana, Pioraco
Largo Giacomo Matteotti, 1
62025 Pioraco MC

Museo della Carta della Stampa, Rom
Via Salaria, 971
00128 Rom RM

Museo della Cartiera Papale
Via delle Cartiere, 1
63011 Ascoli Piceno AP

Museo Patologia del Libro
Via Milano, 76
00184 Rom RM

Workshops, Organizations

Lynn Sures
www.lynnsures.com

JAPAN

Museums and Paper Mills

Echizen Washi Paper &
Culture Museum
11–12 Shinzaike-cho
Echizen City, Fukui
915-0232
www.echizenwashi.jp

Ino-cho Paper Museum
110–1 Saiwai-cho
Agawa-gun Ino-cho, Kochi
781-2103
kamihaku.com

Mino-Washi Museum
1851–3 Warabi
Mino-shi
Gifu

Paper Museum, Tokio
1– 1–3, Oji, Kita-ku
Tokio
114-0002
www.papermuseum.jp

Workshops, Organizations

Keijusha
keijusha.com

LUXEMBURG

Museum

Luxemburgisches Druckereimuseum
Spielkartenmuseum Jean Dieudonné
Maacher Kulturhuef
54, Route de Trèves
L-6793 Grevenmacher
www.kulturhuef.lu

NEPAL

Workshops, Organizations

Paperworld Nepal
www.paperworldnepal.com

NETHERLANDS

Museums, Collections and
Paper Mills

Papiermolen De Schoolmeester
Museumspark Zaansche Mühlen
Guispad 3
1551 SX Westzaan
www.zaanschemolen.nl/molen/
de-schoolmeester

Papierhistorische Sammlung
Koninklijke Bibliotheek
Prins Willem-Alexanderhof 5
Postbus 90407
2509 LK Den Haag
www.kb.nl

Museum Papierfabriek
De Middelste Molen
Kanaal Zuid 497
7371 GL Loenen
www.demiddelstemolen.nl

Museum van het Boek
Museum Meermanno-Westreenianum
Prinsessegracht 30
2514 AP Den Haag
www.meermanno.nl

Stichting Papiergeschiedenis
De Ongekende Mogelijkheden
van Papier
CODA Archief & Museum
Vosselmanstraat 299
7311 CL Apeldoorn
www.coda-apeldoorn.nl

Veluwse Papiermolen
Nederlands Openluchtmuseum
Schelmseweg 89
6816 SJ Arnhem
www.openluchtmuseum.nl

Zaans Museum
Schansend 7
1509 AW Zaandam
www.zaansmuseum.nl

Workshops, Organizations

De Papierderij
Atelier für handgemachtes Papier
www.papierderij.nl

NORWAY

Museums and Paper Mills

Klevfos Industrimuseum
Klevbakken 45
2345 Ådalsbruk
www.klevfos.no

Pulp Mill
Kistefos-Museet
Samsmovein 41
Jevnaker
kistefos.museum.no

POLAND

Museums

Muzeum Papiernictwa
ul. Kłdzka 42
57–340 Duszniki Zdrój
www.muzeumpapiernictwa.pl/de

PORTUGAL

Museum

Museu do Papel Terras de Santa Maria
Rua de Riomaior, 338
4535–309 Pacos de Brandao
www.museudopapel.org

SWEDEN

Museum

Tumba Bruksmuseum
Sven Palmes väg 2
Tumba
www.tumbabruksmuseum.se

Workshops, Organizations

Kvarnbyns Handpappersbruk
www.kvarnbynshandpapper.org

SPAIN

Museums and Paper Mills

Museu Molí Paperer de Capellades
Pau Casals 10
ES-08786 Capellades
www.mmp-capellades.net

Museu Valencià del Paper
Municipal Park of Villa Rosario
03450 Banyeres de Mariola
www.museuvalenciadelpaper.com

SOUTH KOREA

Museums

Jeonju Hanji Museum
Pan-Asia Paper Museum
59, Palbok-ro, Deokjin-gu,
Jeonju-si, Jeollabuk-do
hanjimuseum.co.kr

SWITZERLAND

Museums and Paper Mills

Basler Papiermühle
Schweizerisches Museum für Papier,
Schrift und Druck
St. Alban-Tal 37
CH-4042 Basel
www.papiermuseum.ch

Gutenberg Museum
Schweizerisches Museum der
graphischen Industrie
Liebfrauenplatz 168–169
CH-1701 Fribourg
www.gutenbergmuseum.ch

Historische Papiermaschine PM1
Fabrikstr. 26
CH-9220 Bischofszell
www.pm1.org

Museum Stamparia Strada
CH-7558 Strada
stamparia.ch

Workshops, Organizations

Papierschoepfen.ch
www.papierschoepfen.ch

Schweizer Papierhistoriker
www.papierhistoriker.ch

TAIWAN

Museums

Suho Memorial Paper Museum
No. 68, Section 2, Chang'an East Road
Zhongshan District, Taipei City
Taiwan 10491
suhopaper.org.tw

TURKEY

Museums and Paper Mills

Ege Üniversitesi Kağıt ve Kitap
Sanatları Müzesi
Gençlik Caddesi No: 4
35100 Bornova, İzmir

İbrahim Müteferrika Kağıt Müzesi
Kazım Karabekir Mah. Şehit Ömer
Faydalı Bulv. No: 203
Yalova Merkez, Yalova

SEKA Mehmet Ali Kağıtçı Paper Museum
Kozluk Mahallesi, Mehmet Ali Kağıtçı
Sokak, No: 77
İzmit, KOCAELİ
sekakagitmuzesi.com

International Organisations

AEPM – Association of European
Printing Museums
www.aepm.eu

Friends of Dard Hunter, Inc.
www.friendsofdardhunter.org

Hand Papermaking, Inc.
www.handpapermaking.org

IAPMA – International Association of
Hand Papermakers and Paper Artists
www.iapma.info

IPH – International Association
of Paper Historians
www.paperhistory.org

Nordisk Pappersistorik Förening
www.nph.nu

Paper Online
www.paperonline.org

All links active Febrary 2018.

Index of Names

Picture and Text Credits

Page 2
Photo: Bildreich Martina Issler
Pages 4–5
Inside view of the pulping vat;
Photo: Papierfabrik Zerkall Renker &
Söhne GmbH & Co. KG, Hürtgenwald-
Zerkall
Pages 6–7
Photo: Shutterstock
Pages 8–11
Photos: Thorsten Kern
Pages 16–7
Photo: Thorsten Kern
Pages 18–9
'Fabrication du Papier,' copperplate print
from 1802, illustrating the five steps of
papermaking: rag-sorting, pulping vats,
paper mill, sheet making, and sizing;
Photo: akg-images
Pages 20–1
Illustrations courtesy of Awagami
Factory
Page 21
Top right: Matthias Koop's historical
account of the invention of paper,
Deutsches Buch- und Schriftmuseum
der Deutschen Nationalbibliothek,
Leipzig.
Page 22
Wooden model of a historical paper
mill, Deutsches Buch- und
Schriftmuseum der Deutschen
Nationalbibliothek, Leipzig;
Photo: Stephan Jockel.
Page 24
Photo: Papierfabrik Zerkall Renker &
Söhne GmbH & Co. KG, Hürtgenwald-
Zerkall, Deutschland, 2002. All rights
reserved.
Page 25
Wikimedia Commons
Page 26
Photo courtesy of Büttenfabrik Gmund
Page 27
Photo: Marco Tribastone.
Page 28
Photos (top): Shutterstock; (bottom):
Association of the Swiss Pulp, Paper
and Board Industry (Verband der
Schweizerischen Zellstoff-, Papier- und
Kartonindustrie).

Page 30
Photos (top): Deutsches Buch- und
Schriftmuseum der Deutschen
Nationalbibliothek, Leipzig; (center):
Association of German Paper Mills
(Verband deutscher Papierfabriken, VDP),
Bonn; (bottom): Shutterstock.
Page 31
Photos: Association of German Paper
Mills (Verband deutscher Papier-
fabriken, VDP), Bonn.
Pages 32–3
Rag room in front of a paper mill,
illustration from, "Encyclopédie ou
Dictionnaire raisonné des sciences, des arts
et des métiers," Denis Diderot, c. 1750.
Pages 34–5
Photo: MAKKIKO
Pages 36–7
Photo: Maxi Uellendahl, from the
'Zerkall' series.
Page 38
Photo courtesy of Awagami Factory
Page 39
Photo: Bildreich Martina Issler
Page 40
Photos (top and center): Therese Weber;
(bottom) Awagami Factory.
Page 41
Photo: Kyoko Ibe
Pages 42–3
Photos: © James Cropper Paper
Page 44
Sample materials; Photo: Ulrich Knaack
Page 47
All numbers are taken from the annual
report of the German Paper Industry
Association: Courtesy of Verband der
Papierindustrie VDP, Bonn, Germany,
2017.
Pages 46–64
Text courtesy of the Association of
German Paper Mills, (Verbands der Papier-
industrie), Bonn, Germany © VDP, Bonn.
Pages 48–9, 56, 60, 63
Photos: Thorsten Kern
Page 52
Photo: Shutterstock

Page 55
Photo: Shutterstock
Pages 64–5
Photo: Dirk Uhlenbrock
Pages 66–7
Taken from a sample book of endpapers
c. 1920, Deutsches Buch- und Schrift-
museum der Deutschen
Nationalbibliothek, Leipzig
Page 68
Colored etching, in Martin Engelbrecht:
Künstler, Handwerker und Professionen,
c. 1730, Library of Art History, Berlin
State Museums; Photo: bpk/ Kunst-
bibliothek, SMB/ Knud Petersen
Page 69
Photo: Deutsches Buch- und
Schriftmuseum der Deutschen
Nationalbibliothek, Leipzig
Page 70
Photo: © Julia Rinck, buntpapier.org
Pages 71–5
Photos: Deutsches Buch- und Schrift-
museum der Deutschen
Nationalbibliothek, Leipzig
Pages 76–7
Spines of different volumes of the
Insel Library, Leipzig; Photo: Bildreich
Martina Issler
Page 78
Photo: © Insel, courtesy of Insel Verlag,
Deutsches Buch- und Schriftmuseum
der Deutschen Nationalbibliothek,
Leipzig; (bottom right): Editor's archive.
Page 79
Book covers with colored papers by
Gisela Reschke, © Gisela Reschke;
Photo courtesy of Insel Verlag.
Pages 80–1
Photos: Julia Rinck © buntpapier.org
Photos: © Herzog August Library,
Wolfenbüttel, Germany.
Pages 84–5
Photos: De Monsterkamer, Justina
Nekrašaitė
Page 86
Photo: Nicola von Velsen
Page 87
Photos (top and center): Nanne Meyer;
(bottom) Dr Ewald Judt.

Pages 88–9
Photo: Thorsten Kern

Pages 91–9
This text is an edited version of "Papierplätze. Materielle Formen der Inspiration" ("Paper places: material forms of inspiration") published in *Die Raumzeitlichkeit der Muße*, ed. by Günter Figal, Hans W. Hubert, and Thomas Klinkert (Tübingen: Mohr Siebeck, 2016), pp. 309–37, courtesy of the author.

Page 90
Walter Benjamin: Hamburger Stiftung zur Förderung von Wissenschaft und Kultur / Akademie der Künste, Berlin, Walter Benjamin archive.

Page 95
Gottfried Benn, "Ein Wort," in idem, *Statische Gedichte*, © 1948, 2006 Arche Literatur Verlag AG, Zürich-Hamburg.

Page 99
Photo courtesy of Suhrkamp Verlag

Pages 100–1
Photos: Nekes Collection, Uschi Richert-Nekes

Pages 102–3
Photos from the author's archive

Pages 104–5
Photos: © The Emily Dickinson Collection, Amherst College Archives & Special Collections
Photo: Martin Url; © Arno Schmidt Stiftung, Bargfeld.

Pages 108–9
Text: © George Whitman and his heirs. Cited from Shaun Usher, *Letters of Note*: http://www.lettersofnote.com/2017/01/we-all-wish-for-peace.html (last accessed on February 2, 2018);
Photo: Anne Frank Foundation, Basel/ Getty Images

Page 110
Photo: ullstein bild – Granger, NYC.

Page 111
Photo (top): ullstein bild – AKG: (bottom) by Menahem Kahana/ AFP/ Getty Images

Page 112
Photo (bottom): BWV 232 Mass in B minor, first page of the *Credo*, Berlin State Library, Wikimedia Commons

Page 114
Photo: ullstein bild – Granger, NYC

Page 115
(Top left): Oil on canvas, 84 × 70.5 cm, Tiroler Landesmuseum Ferdinandeum, Innsbruck, Photo: akg-images / Erich Lessing; (top right): Joseph Karl Stieler, *Beethoven with the manuscript of the Missasolemnis*, 1820, Oil on canvas, 62 × 50 cm, Beethoven-Haus, Bonn; Photo: akg-images / Beethoven-Haus, Bonn.

Page 116
Photo: ullstein bild – Phillip A. Harrington

Page 117
Photo courtesy of C.F. Peters Musikverlag, Leipzig – London – New York

Page 118
Pietro Pellini © VG Bild-Kunst, Bonn 2018

Page 119
Fondazione Bonotto, Molvena © Estate Ben Patterson; Photo: Oscar van Arpken

Page 120
Pencil and ink on paper: *Album de dessins et croquis, c.* 1230, Bibliothèque Nationale de France, Paris; Photo: bpk/ BnF, Dist. RMN-GP.
(Left) Silver pen, charcoal, brush, watercolor, 12.9 × 8.8 cm, Staatliches Kupferstichkabinett, Dresden; Photo: akg-images. (Right): chalk on paper, 30 × 23 cm, Berggruen Collection; Photos: akg-images.

Page 122
(Left): Collage, watercolor, pencil, 50 × 65 cm, Sprengel Museum, Hanover, Georges Braque © VG Bild-Kunst, Bonn 2018; Photo: bpk/ Sprengel Museum Hanover/ Michael Herling/ Aline Gwose. (Right): Collage, ink, charcoal, paper on newspaper, 62.5 × 44 cm, Musée Picasso, Paris
Pablo Picasso © Succession Picasso/ VG Bild-Kunst, Bonn 2018; Photo: bpk/ RMN - Grand Palais/ Hervé Lewandowski.

Page 123
Collage, paint, paper on cardboard, 43.4 × 38.2 cm, Sprengel Museum, Hanover, Kurt Schwitters © VG Bild-Kunst, Bonn 2018; Photo: bpk/ Sprengel Museum Hanover/ Michael Herling/ Aline Gwose.

Page 124
Assemblage (silkscreen, cardboard, nails, pins) on resin, 151 × 96.2 × 8 cm, Sprengel Museum, Hanover, Robert Rauschenberg © Robert Rauschenberg Foundation/ VG Bild-Kunst, Bonn 2018; Photo: bpk/ Sprengel Museum Hanover/ Michael Herling/ Aline Gwose.

Page 125
Color print, 66.7 × 50.5 cm, Matthew Marks Gallery, New York, Thomas Demand © VG Bild-Kunst, Bonn 2018; Photo courtesy of Matthew Marks Gallery, New York.

Page 126
Watermark and pulp drawing on paper, 50 × 60 cm, published by Dieu Donné Papermill Inc. New York und David Krut Fine Art, New York, William Kentridge © the Artist, Dieu Donné Press, and David Krut, New York / courtesy of the Goodman Gallery Cape Town; Photo: David Krut Fine Art, New York.

Page 128
(Left): Drawing with handmade Washi-Paper and mulberry fibers, 285 × 185 cm, private collection © Monika Grzymala, photo by Monika Grzymala. (Right): Installation, dOCUMENTA (13), Kassel, 2012; Photo © Therese Weber.

Page 129
(Top): Watermark, abaca and cotton paper with charcoal pigments, 29.8 × 23.5 cm, edition of 5, Dieu Donné Press and Dieu Donné Papermill, Chuck Close © courtesy of the artist and Pace Gallery. (Bottom): Handmade paper, 142.2 × 111.8 cm, Pace Gallery, New York, Chuck Close © Courtesy of the artist and Pace Gallery;
Photo: Maggie L. Kundtz.

Page 130
Mulberry-Kozo, colored by hand, nagashizuki / Japanese technique, pulp, oil chalk, 50×65 cm, Basel, Therese Weber © VG Bild-Kunst, Bonn 2018.

Page 131
(Bottom left): Papier mâché, iron, washing machine, 495×1300×900 cm, installation view *Amoy/ Xiamen*, Musée d'art contemporain de Lyon, Yong Ping Huang © VG Bild-Kunst, Bonn 2018; Photo: Kamel Mennour. (Bottom right): handmade paper casts, 34 parts, approx.150×800×300 cm, Installation measures variable, Bayerische Staatsgemäldesammlungen – Sammlung Moderne Kunst in der Pinakothek der Moderne, Munich Andreas von Weizsäcker © VG Bild-Kunst, Bonn 2018; Photo: Bayerische Staatsgemäldesammlungen, Munich/ Sabrina Hohmann.

Page 133
White paper cut on blue, 18.2×11.5 cm, Hamburger Kunsthalle, Hamburg; Photo: bpk/ Hamburger Kunsthalle/ Christoph Irrgang.
Nanne Meyer, 2003, pencil, collage on paper, 29,7×42 cm; Photo: Farbanalyse, Cologne, © Nanne Meyer, 2017.
Wall installation of toilet paper, 375×650×10 cm, Galerie Peripherie, Tübingen, Şakir Göçebağ © VG Bild-Kunst, Bonn 2018; photo: Şakir Göçebağ.

Pages 138–9
Photo: Thorsten Kern

Pages 141–2
Deutsches Buch- und Schriftmuseum der Deutschen Nationalbibliothek, Leipzig; Photo: Stephan Jockel

Page 143
Photo (top): Fabriano Paper Mills; (bottom): Deutsches Buch- und Schriftmuseum der Deutschen Nationalbibliothek, Leipzig.

Page 144
Photo: Peter J. Roehrich

Pages 145–7
Watermarks from the Landesarchiv Baden-Württemberg/Hauptstaatsarchiv Stuttgart

Page 147
Photo: Deutsches Buch- und Schriftmuseum der Deutschen Nationalbibliothek, Leipzig.

Page 148
Photo: Wikipedia Commons

Page 149
Photo: akg-images

Pages 150–2
Photos from the editor's archive

Page 153–5
Photos: Thorsten Kern

Page 160
(Bottom): Pieter Zwart © VG Bild-Kunst, Bonn 2018.

Page 161
© Studio Feixen. Felix Pfäffli.

Page 162
Photo: Thorsten Kern

Page 163
Photo (top): © Ralf Roletschek

Page 164
Photo (bottom): courtesy of Typografie. info.

Page 165
Typographic samples from the author's archive.

Pages 166–7
Photo: Thorsten Kern

Page 168
Photo: © Andrew Meredith / Bellerby & Co Globemakers, London.

Page 169
Photo: akg-images

Pages 170–2
Photo: akg-images

Pages 172–4
Photo: akg-images
All ephemera are originals from the editors' archives.

Page 173
© Neil Holt

Page 174
(Center): Coffee-Festival-Poster © Daniel Wiesmann, Berlin

Page 175
Photos: Wikipedia Commons

Pages 176–7
Different papers scanned from the original samples.

Page 179
Photo by Thorsten Kern

Page 185
Illustration courtesy of Carta Pura, Munich.

Pages 194–5
Folding by Sabrina Ginter; Photo: Thorsten Kern.

Page 196
Photo: Thorsten Kern

Page 199
© Erwin Hapke; Photo: Matthias Burchardt.

Pages 200–1
Photos: www.staudinger-franke.com

Pages 202–3
Photo (bottom): www.staudinger-franke.com

Pages 204–5
Folding by Sabrina Ginter; Photo: Thorsten Kern.
KHM-Museumsverband, photo: © Kamilla and Gert Strauss, Vienna, Austria.

Page 209
Photo: Otto Umbehr, courtesy of the Josef and Anni Albers Foundation; Otto Umbehr © Phyllis Umbehr/Galerie Kicken Berlin/VG Bild-Kunst, Bonn 2018.

Pages 210–1
© Erwin Hapke; photo: Matthias Burchardt.

Page 212
Photo: *Paper Airplanes: The Collections of Harry Smith, Catalogue Raisonné*, vol. I, edited by John Klacsmann and Andrew Lampert, © Anthology Film Archives and J&L Books.

Page 216
Photo courtesy of Schmidt Kartonagen, Norken.

Pages 218–9
Photos: Peter Dahmen.

Page 220
Shigeru Ban © Shigeru Ban Architects Europe; Photo: © Kartikeya Shodhan.

Page 221
Shigeru Ban © Shigeru Ban Architects Europe; Photo: © Hiroyuki Hirai

Pages 222–3
Photo: © molo
Pages 224–5
Photos: Wanda Barcelona –
all rights reserved.
Page 227
Photo: Debbie Wijskamp
Pages 228–9
Photo: Fideli Sundqvist/ Magnus Cramer
Pages 230–1
The book depicted is Christoph
Thun-Hohensteil (ed.): *Ephemera. Die
Gebrauchsgrafik der MAK-Bibliothek und
Kunstblättersammlung*, exh. cat., Vienna,
2017; Photo: Thorsten Kern.
Page 232
Oberlausitzische Bibliothek der Wissen-
schaften, Görlitz; Photo: Thomas Meyer/
OSTKREUZ
Pages 233–4
This text is based on Heike Gfrereis: *Das
bewegte Buch* (= Marbacher Magazin),
2016, translated by Bram Opstelten.
Page 235
Photo: Getty Images/Adam Mork/
ArcaidImages
Page 239
Photo: Thorsten Kern
Pages 240–1
Photo: Thorsten Kern
Page 242
Photo: Christoph Benjamin Schulz
Page 243
Photo: Sammlung Nekes
Page 244
Bags from the editor's archive
Page 245
Photo: Kodak Collection/ National
Science & Media Museum/ SSPL
Page 246–7
Irma Boom © VG Bild-Kunst, Bonn 2018;
Photos: Thorsten Kern.
Page 249
Simon Goode and Ira Yonemura. *Making
Books* (2017). Reproduced with kind
permission of Pavilion Books Company
Limited.
Pages 250–1
Photo: Thorsten Kern

Translations
Pages 12–5: Bram Opstelten
Pages 21–7: Bram Opstelten
Pages 29–31: Paul Kelly/Liam Tarr
Pages 34–7: Paul Kelly/Liam Tarr
Pages 38–41: Bram Opstelten
Pages 42–6: Paul Kelly/Liam Tarr
Pages 68–75: Bram Opstelten
Pages 78–9: Bram Opstelten
Pages 82–3: Bram Opstelten
Page 86: Paul Kelly/Liam Tarr
Pages 91–9: Bram Opstelten
Pages 100–3: Bram Opstelten
Page 105: Paul Kelly/Liam Tarr
Pages 106–7: Paul Kelly/Liam Tarr
Page 110: Paul Kelly/Liam Tarr
Pages 112–5: Bram Opstelten
Page 116: Bram Opstelten
Pages 118–9: Bram Opstelten
Pages 121–4: Bram Opstelten
Pages 127–31: Bram Opstelten
Page 132: Paul Kelly/Liam Tarr
Page 134: Paul Kelly/Liam Tarr
Pages 136–7: Paul Kelly/Liam Tarr
Pages 140–7: Bram Opstelten
Page 148: Paul Kelly/Liam Tarr
Pages 150–3: Paul Kelly/Liam Tarr
Page 156: Bram Opstelten
Pages 158–65: Paul Kelly/Liam Tarr
Page 168–9: Paul Kelly/Liam Tarr
Pages 170–1: Paul Kelly/Liam Tarr
Pages 172–5: Paul Kelly/Liam Tarr
Pages 176–93: Paul Kelly/Liam Tarr,
   Neil Holt, Hannah Young
Page 196–8: Paul Kelly/Liam Tarr
Pages 206–7: Paul Kelly/Liam Tarr
Pages 208–9: Paul Kelly/Liam Tarr
Pages 210–1: Paul Kelly/Liam Tarr
Page 212: Paul Kelly/Liam Tarr
Pages 214–5: Paul Kelly/Liam Tarr
Page 216: Paul Kelly/Liam Tarr
Pages 218–9: Paul Kelly/Liam Tarr
Page 220: Paul Kelly/Liam Tarr
Pages 233–4: Bram Opstelten
Pages 236–9: Bram Opstelten
Pages 242–3: Bram Opstelten
Pages 244–5: Bram Opstelten
Pages 246–9: Paul Kelly/Liam Tarr
Back cover and all captions:
Bram Opstelten

The editors and the publisher have
made every effort to obtain proper
credit information and permission
to reproduced images. Should any
copyright holder accidently not have
been credited accordingly, this will be
corrected in subsequent editions and
compensated within the usual terms
of agreements.

Acknowledgements

Many people have helped and supported us
tirelessly during this project. The authors and
the whole team who worked on this book – and
whose names are mentioned in the table of
contents and in the colophon – were immensely
committed. We would like to thank them all
from the heart for their endurance and their
expertise.

Beyond that we would like to thank a further
number of people for having supported us and
who shared their knowledge in such a personal
and generous manner, or simply, because they
put their trust in us and showed their vivid
interest in our topic and our work.

Aya Fujimori von Awagami Factory

Siegfried Gohr

Gordon Hoffmeyer

Ursula Holt-ter Veer und John Holt

Ian Holt

Paul Jackson

Nikoline Kästner

Nanne Meyer

Lothar Müller

Jonathan Osthoff von Carta Pura

Tanja Pöpping mit Arthur und Theo Holt

Felix Renker

Tanja Reinhold vom VDP

Christian Rieker

Frieder Schmidt

Christoph Benjamin Schulz

Angelika Thill

Maren Thomsen

Claudia und Gerd von Velsen

Stefanie Wieprecht-Roth

Hannah Young

Colophon

© Prestel Verlag, Munich · London · New York, 2018
A member of Verlagsgruppe Random House GmbH
Neumarkter Strasse 28 · 81673 München

www.prestel.de

Editors
Neil Holt, Stephanie Jacobs and Nicola von Velsen
Managing Editor
Nicola von Velsen
Layout, typography
Neil Holt
Museum Cooperation
Stephanie Jacobs
Translation
Paul Kelly and Liam Tarr (texts page: 29ff., 34f., 42, 86,
105, 106f., 110, 132, 134, 135, 148, 150f., 153, 158ff., 168f.,
170f., 172ff., 176ff., 198, 206–220, 236ff., 246, 248f.)
Bram Opstelten (Texts pp.: Back of cover, 12ff., 20ff., 38ff.,
68ff., 78, 82, 91ff., 100ff., 112ff., 116, 118, 121ff., 127ff.,
140ff., 233ff., 236ff., 244f.)
Picture Editors
Adeline Henzschel, Judith Klein, Angelika Thill
Research
Angelika Thill, Julia Vaje
Illustrations
David Hartgenbusch, Neil Holt
Copy Editor
Hannah Young
Typesetting
Hilde Knauer
Production management
Ingrid Reiter
Reprographics
Reproline Mediateam
Printing and Binding
TBB a.s. Banská Bystrica
Paper: Condat matt Perigord and
Munken Premium Cream
Type Face: PMN Caecilia
Verlagsgruppe Random House FSC N00 1967

Printed in Slovakia
ISBN 978-3-7913-8306-4

All rights reserved

In respect to links in the book, Verlagsgruppe
Random House expressly notes that no illegal
content was discernible on the linked sites at
the time the links were created. The Publisher
has no influence at all over the current and
future design, content or authorship of the
linked sites. For this reason Verlagsgruppe
Random House expressly disassociates itself
from all content on linked sites that has been
altered since the link was created and assumes
no liability for such content.

Copyrights
© 2018 all art works reproduced are with
the artists, their heirs or legal representatives.
© VG Bild-Kunst, Bonn 2018:
Irma Boom, Georges Braque, Thomas Demand,
Şakir Göçebağ, Yong Ping Huang, Pietro Pellini,
Kurt Schwitters, Andreas von Weizsäcker,
Therese Weber, Pieter Zwart
Shigeru Ban © Shigeru Ban Architects Europe
Chuck Close © Courtesy the artist and Pace
Gallery
William Kentridge © the Artist, Dieu Donné
Press, and David Krut, New York/ courtesy
the Goodman Gallery Cape Town
Ben Patterson © Estate Ben Patterson
Felix Pfäffli © Studio Feixen. Felix Pfäffli
Pablo Picasso © Succession Picasso/
VG Bild-Kunst, Bonn 2018
Robert Rauschenberg © Robert Rauschenberg
Foundation/ VG Bild-Kunst, Bonn 2018
Otto Umbehr © Phyllis Umbehr/ Galerie Kicken
Berlin/ VG Bild-Kunst, Bonn 2018

For all other image and text credits
see page: 266

This book was realized in cooperation with
Deutsches Buch- und Schriftmuseum der
Deutschen Nationalbibliothek, Leipzig

papesbook
papierfreunde